SICILY AND THE
UNIFICATION OF ITALY

Sicily and the Unification of Italy

Liberal Policy and Local Power
1859–1866

LUCY RIALL

CLARENDON PRESS · OXFORD
1998

Oxford University Press, Great Clarendon Street, Oxford OX2 6DP
Oxford New York
Athens Auckland Bangkok Bogota Bombay
Buenos Aires Calcutta Cape Town Dar es Salaam
Delhi Florence Hong Kong Istanbul Karachi
Kuala Lumpur Madras Madrid Melbourne
Mexico City Nairobi Paris Singapore
Taipei Tokyo Toronto Warsaw
and associated companies in
Berlin Ibadan

Oxford is a trade mark of Oxford University Press

Published in the United States
by Oxford University Press Inc., New York

British Library Cataloguing in Publication Data
Data available

Library of Congress Cataloging-in-Publication Data
Riall, Lucy, 1962–
Sicily and the Unification of Italy / Lucy Riall.
p. cm.
Includes bibliographical references.
1. Sicily (Italy)—Politics and government—1815–1870.   2. Italy
—Politics and government—1849–1870.   3. Liberalism—Italy
—History—19th century.   4. Decentralization in government—Italy
—History—19th century.   I. Title.
DG868.44.R53   1997
945'.808–dc21   97–18125
ISBN 0-19-820680-1

1 3 5 7 9 10 8 6 4 2

Typeset by J&L Composition Ltd, Filey, North Yorkshire
Printed in Great Britain on acid-free paper by
Biddles Ltd., Guildford & Kings Lynn

To my Parents

Acknowledgements

A great many people have helped me in writing this book. Above all I would like to thank Paul Ginsborg, who supervised the doctoral thesis on which this book is based, and who has been an unfailing source of support ever since. I am greatly indebted to John Davis, Denis Mack Smith, Jonathan Steinberg, and Diego Gambetta, all of whom read the thesis and made important suggestions on how to improve it, and to Richard Evans, Silvana Patriarca, and David Laven for their helpful comments on earlier drafts and sections of the book. In Sicily, I should like to thank Igor Mineo and Eliza Romano for their kindness and hospitality during my visits to Palermo. Clive Emsley and Charles Cooper involved me in a BBC Open University programme on Sicily, obliged me to address basic questions which had hitherto not occurred to me, and accompanied me on more than one memorable trip into the Sicilian interior. Jeremy Krikler gave me practical advice on writing the introduction. To the tolerance of all my friends this book owes a great deal, but a few people deserve a special mention. I am grateful to my mother for reviving my flagging energies on more than one occasion; to George and Fernanda Herford for their company while I was finishing the book; and to Robert Demers, whose humour and intelligence hugely enlivened an otherwise dreary period in Cambridge. Finally, my special thanks go to Fabian Russell-Cobb for helping me to enjoy both hard work and time off.

I also wish to thank the librarians of the national libraries in Palermo, Rome, and Florence and of the British Library in London, and the staff of the state archives in Palermo, Agrigento, and Rome, of the Istituto per la Storia del Risorgimento in Palermo, Rome, and Milan, and of the Public Record Office in Kew. My thanks also to the following people for allowing me access to particular archives: Clarice Mordini, for letting me consult her family's papers from the Archivio Mordini in Barga; Maria Pia Baroncelli of the Comune di Barga, for her help in arranging my visit to Barga; and Generale Licci and Maresciallo Cusimano of the Museo Storico dell'Arma dei Carabinieri in Rome, for giving me permission to consult *carabinieri* reports from the 1866 revolt in Palermo. The Economic and Social Research Council and the British Academy provided the main sources of financial support for my research in Britain and in Italy, while additional grants were given by Newnham College, Cambridge, the University of Essex, Birkbeck College, London, and the British School at Rome. Chapters 5 and 8 are modified versions of articles which were first published in *The Historical Journal*, 35, 2 (1992), 345–68 and *Meridiana*, 24 (1995), 65–94, respectively.

This book seeks to reassess a crucial period of Sicilian and Italian history which has often been studied but, it seems, little understood. The work of revisionist historians can take us some way towards such a reassessment, but it also leaves many new questions unanswered. On a more personal note, my aim in this book is to encourage historians to take a a second look at modern Sicily. Unlike Italy's liberal leaders in 1860, whose initial enthusiasm for and enjoyment of Sicilian life I describe below, my first experiences could scarcely have been worse or my impressions of the island more unfavourable. Yet while the liberal enthusiasm for Sicily soon faded into disillusionment, my rewards for scholarly persistence have been the gradual discovery of a much happier and altogether more compelling Sicily than the place which first presented itself to me in the mid-1980s. In this book I have therefore tried to demonstrate that there is in Sicily's political experiences something of greater interest than merely a history of violence, political deviance, and corruption. The story of Sicily is not just a series of tales about the *mafiosi* and their martyrs, perhaps the most common misconception about an island described in the fifteenth century as *un mondo lieto*: 'a happy place'.

L. R.
London, 1996

Contents

List of Maps

List of Abbreviations

ACSR Archivio Centrale dello Stato, Rome
ASAg Archivio dello Stato, Agrigento
ASP   Archivio dello Stato, Palermo
AMB   Archivio Mordini, Barga
BNF   Biblioteca Nazionale di Firenze
ISR   Istituto per la Storia del Risorgimento, Rome
ISRM Istituto per la Storia del Risorgimento, Milan
MSAC Museo Storico dell'Arma dei Carabinieri, Rome
PRO   Public Record Office, London

Introduction

I

Why was Sicily difficult to govern during the nineteenth century? More precisely, why did Sicily acquire a reputation among Italian liberals as a graveyard for political ambition, a region of riot and revolution where constitutional government could not work and efforts at reform were doomed to failure?[1] The dominant image of Sicily which emerges from the government, military, and police records during the period after Italian unification is one of a violent and impenetrable society, resistant to the efforts made by both bureaucrats and soldiers to impose law and order and organize a regular administration. What was it that set Sicily apart from Piedmont, where the same liberal policies had met with conspicuous success?

Part of the problem was that the unification of Italy happened suddenly and in a quite unexpected fashion. When Giuseppe Garibaldi and his 'Thousand' volunteers set sail for Sicily on 6 May 1860, few on board could have fully anticipated the momentous consequences of their actions. Yet the extraordinary success of Garibaldi's expedition in overthrowing the Bourbon government drastically altered the political structure of the entire Italian peninsula. By September 1860, after only four months, Garibaldi controlled the whole of Southern Italy and was preparing an army to take Rome from the Pope and make it the capital of a united Italy.

The success of the expedition also allowed Garibaldi, and with him the democratic movement, to seize the political initiative from their main rivals, the moderate liberals, who were based in the Northern kingdom of Piedmont and were led by the Prime Minister, Camillo Cavour. Largely in order to outmanœuvre Garibaldi, and specifically in order to prevent him from marching on Rome, Cavour ordered the Piedmontese army into the Papal States and south towards Naples to

---

[1] For a discussion of the contrasting images and 'myths of Sicily', see G. Giarrizzo, 'Per una storia della Sicilia', in *Mezzogiorno senza meridionalismo: la Sicilia, lo sviluppo, il potere* (Venice, 1992).

meet Garibaldi. The Piedmontese army and Garibaldi's volunteers met at Teano, to the north-east of Naples, in October. In the same month, plebiscites were held throughout Southern Italy which resulted in an overwhelming vote for Italian unification under Piedmontese leadership. By this means the Bourbon kingdom in the South was united with Northern Italy. And it is in this respect that the unification of Italy in 1860, often celebrated as the culmination of the Italian nation's 'risorgimento', can also be seen as a cynical exercise in damage limitation.[2]

As outsiders, many *garibaldini* and moderate liberals failed at first to perceive the scale of the political crisis caused by the revolution in the southern half of the peninsula. There is little evidence that anyone within ministerial circles in Turin seriously doubted the government's capacity to control what were considered to be largely local or administrative problems. Most Piedmontese liberals believed in what Salvadori calls 'the myth of the Mezzogiorno as a rich land but with the misfortune of corrupt government'.[3] They attributed the prevailing chaos in the South either to the political legacy of the corrupt and reactionary Bourbon government, or to the administrative disruption caused by Garibaldi (which concerned them much more).

Such confidence seemed quite justifiable. During the previous decade, under a liberal government, Piedmont had transformed itself economically and politically. Moderate liberals in Piedmont had established themselves as the leading political force in the Italian peninsula, able to dictate a new liberal and nationalist agenda to both conservatives and revolutionaries. Piedmont alone had avoided the twin threats of reaction and revolution which had beset the other Italian states after the disasters of 1848–9, while the collapse in rapid succession of all Italy's conservative monarchies during 1859–60 seemed to offer conclusive proof that a liberal-constitutional system was the only viable one for Italy. The crisis of Italian conservatism in 1859–60 offered, in other words, a striking and satisfying contrast to the successes of liberal Piedmont. If Northern moderate liberals (or the *Destra Storica*, the 'Historic Right', as they came to be known after unification) knew little about conditions in Southern Italy, they had no reason to doubt, after the achievements of the previous decade, that a liberal form of government would work there too.

---

[2] The classic account of these events is D. Mack Smith, *Cavour and Garibaldi 1860: A Study in Political Conflict* (Cambridge, 1954; 2nd edn., 1985).

[3] M. Salvadori, *Il mito del buongoverno: la questione meridionale da Cavour a Gramsci* (Turin, 1960), 30.

On his deathbed in 1861, Prime Minister Cavour issued a famous instruction to his successors to rule the South 'with liberty'. He repeatedly warned against the use of military force in the South and the declaring of a 'state of siege' (a form of martial law).[4] Even as Cavour issued these instructions, however, the use of exceptional measures to bolster up the new government in the South was becoming a reality. Indeed, the first clear sign of official unease over conditions in Southern Italy came from Cavour himself, when in 1861 he shelved plans to give administrative autonomy to the newly acquired Southern provinces. Instead, the new provinces were simply incorporated into the existing, centralized, Piedmontese system of administration.

Even more indicative of the escalating difficulties of the government was its increasing use of military powers to maintain a semblance of authority. Centralized political authority broke down in Southern Italy in the early 1860s, making any kind of systematic law-enforcement impossible there. Faced with this situation, the central government responded with military force. In 1862, during another attempt by Garibaldi to seize Rome from the Pope, the whole of the Southern mainland and Sicily was placed under a state of siege. Starting with the Pica law in 1863, the Italian parliament approved a series of special laws which gave the police and military extensive powers of arrest and trial, and which were used to pursue a protracted military campaign against brigandage on the Southern mainland. In Sicily between 1860 and 1866, the period covered by this book, the same powers were used in various attempts to enforce the conscription laws, to collect taxes, to break up criminal conspiracies, and to repress a revolt in the city of Palermo.

Yet the use of these emergency measures served simply to emphasize the government's weakness and isolation, its inability to enforce its authority by any other means. The sad truth was that the South represented a challenge to the identity and *raison d'être* of Italian liberalism. Liberal policy did not seem to work in the Southern half of the peninsula as it had, with apparent success, in Piedmont. Thus, the prevailing disorder and political opposition in the South came to reflect more general anxieties about the territorial integrity of united Italy and the capacity of its new ruling class. Furthermore, the government's use of military coercion in the South after unification seemed

---

[4] E. Artom, 'Il conte di Cavour e la questione napoletana', *Nuova Antologia*, 180 (1901), 152.

flatly to contradict the English model of 'self-government' and *laissez-faire* which many Italian liberals had claimed as their own.[5]

More serious still was the fact that, in Sicily in particular, military powers and emergency legislation did not seem to work either. Although by 1865 brigandage on the mainland was more or less under control, this was not the case in Sicily. As we shall see in the chapters which follow, neither the campaigns against recalcitrant conscripts nor operations to destroy criminal conspiracies produced anything like the desired results. Despite having requested additional force, local authorities were in practice often unwilling to assist the military, while the population seemed bitterly resentful of its presence. For every *mafioso*, bandit, or recalcitrant held in custody, there always seemed to be two or more ready to take his place. New problems produced by the campaigns themselves—severe overcrowding in Sicilian prisons, a series of cholera outbreaks brought in by the troops, the interruption of harvests and commerce—also undermined law and order. Partly because repression was ineffective and produced only disruption, it led to a cycle of local resistance leading to further repression and, in turn, to local resistance on a greater scale still.

Until 1860, the political identity of Northern Italian liberals was defined in reference to North and North–Central Italy. What familiarity the *garibaldini* and moderate liberals had with Sicily was through classical literature, travel-writing, and art. Thus, their immediate perceptions of the island were conditioned by a powerful mythology linked to nature and history—classical ruins, fertile agriculture, dramatic landscapes, and a geographical position closer to Africa and the Middle East than to Northern Europe.[6] Equally dramatic, however, was the evidence of Sicily's present-day decline (*decadenza*). In this respect, nothing was more shocking than the poverty and ignorance of its inhabitants. Giorgio Asproni, a Mazzinian from Sardinia, admired Palermo's poor for being 'bold, lively and ready at any time for a punch-up or bloodletting', but few Northern liberals were as impressed by the exuberant behaviour of the island's inhabitants.[7] One envoy, in a refrain that was to become all too familiar in subsequent years, bemoaned the fact that 'the

---

[5] For a discussion of Italian attitudes to different models of liberalism, see R. Gherardi, *L'arte del compromesso: la politica della mediazione nell'Italia liberale* (Bologna, 1993), 115–40, 154–61. [6] Giarizzo, 'Per una storia della Sicilia', 4–7.

[7] 10 Aug. 1860, in G. Asproni, *Diario politico, 1855–1876* (7 vols.; Milan, 1974–91), ii. 506.

people . . . prefer personal vendetta to the arm of the law'.[8] The Sicilian landscape, in other words, may have been regarded as romantic and exotic, but its inhabitants were seen as politically dangerous and, quite often, personally threatening.[9]

It was, as a result, relatively easy for officials sent to the Sicilian provinces after 1860 to blame illiberal Sicilians rather than Italian liberals for the difficult situation there. Sicilians, according to an increasingly accepted official orthodoxy, were not ready for liberalism; they languished instead in some brutal and far-off 'dark age'. In 1862, the prefect of Girgenti (Agrigento), Enrico Falconcini from Tuscany, baldly informed his new provincial council that 'the new institutions so brilliantly adapted to the civil education of Italians from the upper provinces of the kingdom are, for those from the lower provinces, premature and inappropriate'.[10] He went on to write of his horror at the 'barbarism' of Sicilians, 'in the island which I had heard described so poetically as an earthly paradise'.[11] Members of the military, sent to back up liberal rule in Sicily 'using, if necessary, physical force', argued that their presence was necessary because conditions in Sicily were unsuitable for liberalism.[12] One Piedmontese general, Raffaele Cadorna, told the Minister of War that the inhabitants of Palermo had a naturally 'violent character'.[13] In 1863, General Giuseppe Govone told the Italian parliament that the harsh measures adopted by his army to enforce the conscription laws in Sicily were entirely unavoidable. The situation in Sicily was, in his words, 'really something out of the Middle Ages'; Sicilians had not yet developed beyond a stage of primitive 'barbarity' and were thus not yet able to enjoy the benefits of civilization.[14]

Two years later, the prefect of Palermo, Filippo Gualterio (an

---

[8] 10 Oct. 1861, from Diomede Pantaleone to the Minister of the Interior, G. Scichilone, *Documenti sulle condizione della Sicilia dal 1860 al 1870* (Rome, 1952), 96.

[9] Giarrizzo, 'Per una storia della Sicilia', 9.

[10] Quoted in P. Pezzino, 'Un prefetto "esemplare": Enrico Falconcini ad Agrigento (1862–63)', in P. Pezzino, *Il paradiso abitato dai diavoli: società, élites, istituzioni nel Mezzogiorno contemporaneo* (Milan, 1992), 234.

[11] E. Falconcini, *Cinque mesi di prefettura in Sicilia* (Florence, 1863), 68.

[12] The phrase is Cavour's, in a letter to the king, describing the government's aims in Southern Italy. *Il carteggio Cavour-Nigra dal 1858 al 1861* (4 vols.; Bologna, 1926–9), iv. 290–3.

[13] 10 March 1861, *Il generale Raffaele Cadorna nel Risorgimento italiano*, ed. L. Cadorna (Milan, 1922), 196.

[14] A political outcry ensued and Govone apologized for his remarks the next day. The relevant passage is published in D. Mack Smith (ed.), *The Making of Italy, 1796–1866* (London, 1968; 2nd edn., 1988), 371–3.

Umbrian liberal), remarked upon the 'exceptional criminal tendencies' of the local inhabitants. He also drew attention to the presence of an organized gang of criminal conspirators which had 'even its own statutes', which was supported by the most powerful members of local society, and which made its presence felt through violence and the fear of violence. This 'so-called mafia' (*la cosidetta 'maffia'*) was, according to Gualterio, responsible for the failure of liberal policy in Sicily. The mafia openly assisted the government's political enemies and through its secretive, brutal methods undermined the morality of Palermo's citizens. For the mafia in Sicily to be defeated, exceptional measures were called for.[15] Implicitly, Gualterio blamed (at least a section of) the Sicilian population, rather than the weakness of liberal government, for his decision to suppress judicial rights and deploy military force.[16]

Official reactions to the 'barbarous' conditions in Sicily were also affected by the situation elsewhere in the South. The brigands' war on the mainland produced its share of official anxiety; and here, too, the immediate response was to blame the population for its lack of 'morality'. In 1863, an ex-Garibaldian general working with the parliamentary enquiry into brigandage wrote, 'This is a country that should be destroyed or at least depopulated and its inhabitants sent to Africa to get themselves civilized!'[17] 'It is not we who benefit from the union,' the former Prime Minister, Massimo d'Azeglio, wrote on a more benevolent but equally condemnatory note, 'but this wretched population without morals, without valour, without learning.'[18] On the mainland too, Northerners were struck by the contrast between the beauty and apparent richness of the landscape and the 'weakness' of its people. The South, according to a saying popular at this time, was 'a paradise

[15] 25 Apr. 1865, in Archivio Centrale dello Stato, Roma (henceforth, ACSR) Ministero dell'Interno (henceforth, Interno), b. 7, f. 4, n. 4. For other, contemporary descriptions of the mafia which include an extract from Gualterio's report see P. Pezzino (ed.), *Mafia: industria della violenza* (Florence, 1995), 3–68.

[16] Paolo Pezzino has written extensively on the political context within which what he calls the 'mafia paradigm' developed. See, in particular, 'Stato violenza società: nascita e sviluppo del paradigma mafioso', in M. Aymard and G. Giarrizzo (eds.), *La Sicilia* (Turin, 1987); also in P. Pezzino, *Una certa reciprocità di favori: mafia e modernizzazione nella Sicilia postunitaria* (Milan, 1990). For a different analysis of Gualterio's 1865 report, see C. Duggan, *Fascism and the Mafia* (London, 1989), 26–7.

[17] Quoted in J. Dickie, 'A Word at War: The Italian army and Brigandage', *History Workshop Journal*, 33 (1992), 8.

[18] Quoted in N. Moe, '"Altro che Italia!": il Sud dei piemontesi (1860–61)', *Meridiana*, 15 (1992), 67.

inhabited by devils' (*un paradiso abitato da diavoli*).[19] It seemed, in the words of one Piedmontese general, 'impossible' that where 'nature had done so much for the land', it could not have produced better inhabitants.[20]

Neither historical nor contemporary understandings of what has come to be called the 'Southern Question' can be separated from the circumstances and outcome of Italian unification.[21] The Right's fall from power at the hands of Southern deputies in 1876, the numerous official and private inquiries detailing Southern problems, and the severe economic and political crises of the 1880s and 1890s all combined to keep the Southern Question at the forefront of political and academic debate throughout the liberal period.[22] The South in these debates was cast, according to Daniel Pick, 'as a form of other world, racially different, a space to be explored, penetrated, contained, colonised'.[23]

Early generations of Southernists stressed various sources of Southern difference. Villari and Turiello blamed moral corruption and peasant ignorance; Leopoldo Franchetti pointed to the anti-liberal tendencies and *prepotenza* of the Southern middle classes. Cesare Lombroso developed in the 1890s a theory of racial degeneracy which accounted for the 'natural' criminality of the South.[24] What they all held in common was an image of the South trapped by its past, a sense of the South as a subversive, atavistic presence within the 'resurgent' Italian nation.

[19] 'Seven centuries before Christ a Greek lyric sang of Calabria as "the happiest land in the world"—poor tragic Calabria, which will always be one of the most sterile lands of Europe . . . Literature was the involuntary artisan of the legend of the happy southerner, scarcely deigning to garner the fruits of the earth which grew in wild profusion about him.' C. Sforza, *Contemporary Italy* (New York, 1944), 98. See also B. Croce, 'Il "paradiso abitato da diavoli"', in *Uomini e cose della vecchia Italia* (Bari, 1943). For a recent commentary, see Pezzino, *Il paradiso abitato dai diavoli*, 9–10.

[20] 12 December 1860, in C. Cavour, *La liberazione del mezzogiorno e la formazione del regno d'Italia: carteggi di Camillo Cavour con Villamarina, Scialoja, Cordova, Farini ecc* (5 vols.; Bologna, 1949–54), v. 231–2. For a more detailed analysis, see Moe, '"Altro che Italia!"', 68.

[21] Although Southernists often disagreed about the extent to which the 'Sicilian Question' could be subsumed into the broader Southern Question. Giarrizzo, 'Per una storia della Sicilia', 10.

[22] Giarrizzo, *Mezzogiorno senza meridionalismo*, p. ix; P. Bevilacqua, *Breve storia dell'Italia meridionale* (Rome, 1992), 33–58.

[23] D. Pick, *Faces of Degeneration: A European Disorder, c.1848—c.1918* (Cambridge, 1989), 114.

[24] For a discussion see Salvadori, *Il mito del buongoverno*. On Lombroso, Pick, *Faces of Degeneration*, 109–52, is particularly useful. Rosario Villari's *Il Sud nella storia d'Italia* (Rome and Bari, 1961; 3rd edn., 1988) is still the best anthology of Southernist writing. For Sicily, Giarrizzo, 'Per una storia della Sicilia', analyses fiction as well as the different approaches of social theorists and historians.

Since unification, the Southern Question has been largely a question of whom to blame. Initial perceptions of Southern 'immorality' also tended to be reinforced, rather than undermined, by mounting evidence of other problems. The increasingly visible contrast between an apparently capitalist prosperity in the North and the feudal poverty of the South merely confirmed existing notions of Southern difference. When, in the 1880s and 1890s, Giustino Fortunato broke with tradition by describing the problems of climate, soil, and geography which the deceptively picturesque Southern landscape caused its inhabitants, he did so in order to explain another failure—the absence of economic growth in the South.[25] Indeed, the difference in rates of economic growth between the industrializing North and the more agrarian South was to become the most enduring symbol of Southern difference after unification.[26] Economic backwardness further defined an understanding of South and North as 'a symbolic polarity of barbarity and civilization, bourbonism and liberalism, a feudal style of life in the South, and a bourgeois one in the North'.[27] In this way the Italian nation was constructed as, in John Dickie's words, 'the opposite of its South'.[28]

II

For historians of nineteenth-century Sicily, therefore, the problem of 'ungovernability' cannot be fully distinguished from more general perceptions of Southern 'difference'. Similarly, and particularly since the late 1940s, historical interpretations of this problem have also been tied to broader questions about national unification and the nature of Italian liberalism. As a result of these debates, the focus of blame for the South has shifted dramatically, away from the immorality of its 'wretched population' and towards the inadequacies of the national leadership.[29]

The debate among historians about Italian liberalism was prompted by the publication in 1949 of Antonio Gramsci's historical writings,

---

[25] On Fortunato, see Salvadori, *Il mito del buongoverno*, 146–83.

[26] The literature on economic development in the South is vast and continues to grow. A good introduction is L. Cafagna, 'La questione delle origini del dualismo economico italiano', in *Dualismo e sviluppo nella storia d'Italia* (Venice, 1989).

[27] Giarrizzo, *Mezzogiorno senza meridionalismo*, p. xv. For a discussion of the application of terms such as 'dualism', 'differential', or 'divide' to the Italian economy see L. Cafagna, *Nord e Sud: non fare a pezzi l'unità d'Italia* (Venice, 1994), 25–49.

[28] Dickie, 'A Word at War', 7.

[29] For a discussion, see L. Riall, 'Elite Resistance to State Formation: The Case of Italy', in M. Fulbrook (ed.), *National Histories and European History* (London, 1993), 48–56, and L. Riall, *The Italian Risorgimento: State, Society and National Unification* (London, 1994), 1–5.

widely interpreted as a response to Benedetto Croce's *History of Italy*, published during the Fascist period.[30] In fact, both Croce and Gramsci were driven by the need to redefine and re-evaluate Italian liberalism in the light of its collapse into Fascist repression. Croce, however, defended the parliamentary system of liberal Italy as the 'antithesis' of Fascism, whereas Gramsci saw a logical progression between the compromises of this 'retrograde' system and the later practices of Fascist Italy.[31] 'Is it not', Gramsci asked, 'precisely the Fascist movement which in fact corresponds to the movement of conservative and moderate liberalism in the last century?'[32]

Croce had nothing but praise for the efforts of moderate liberals in bringing about a united Italy. The liberal leadership was, in his words, 'a spiritual aristocracy of upright and loyal gentlemen . . . a permanent source of moral and political education'.[33] Faced, he argued, with the destabilizing challenges of consolidating national unity after 1871, successive liberal governments had not hesitated to do what was necessary to safeguard progress and freedom. What defined Italian liberalism was its flexibility, what Rosario Romeo calls 'the elasticity of institutions and the good sense of its ruling class'.[34] Gramsci disagreed. Liberal Italy's instability was, for Gramsci, more serious and involved a more fundamental social conflict than Croce admitted.[35] Liberal Italy's instability was a direct product of the way in which the liberals had come to power during the Risorgimento. Gramsci described the Risorgimento as a 'passive revolution', as a revolution without mass participation where the revolutionary leadership is inadequate and 'the old society resists and secures itself a breathing space'.[36] Since the Italian bourgeoisie was,

---

[30] A. Gramsci, *Il Risorgimento* (Turin, 1949), substantial extracts of which are translated as 'Notes on Italian History' in *Selections from the Prison Notebooks of Antonio Gramsci* (London, 1971), eds. Q. Hoare and G. Nowell Smith, and B. Croce, *A History of Italy from 1871 to 1915*, trans. C. M. Ady (Oxford, 1929). Gramsci refers specifically to Croce's work in *Selections from Prison Notebooks*, 114–20.   [31] Ibid. 108.

[32] Ibid. 119.   [33] Croce, *A History of Italy*, 5.

[34] R. Romeo, *Dal Piemonte sabaudo all'Italia liberale* (Turin, 1963), 134.

[35] Gramsci questioned in particular Croce's periodization: 'Is it possible to write a history of Italy in modern times without a treatment of the struggles of the Risorgimento? . . . is it fortuitous, or is it for a tendentious motive, that Croce begins his narratives from . . . 1871? I.e. that he excludes the moment of struggle; the moment in which the conflicting forces are formed, are assembled . . . the moment in which one system of social relations disintegrates and falls and another arises and asserts itself?' *Selections from Prison Notebooks*, 118–19.

[36] Ibid. 185. On Gramsci's concept of passive revolution in the Risorgimento, see J. A. Davis, 'Introduction: Antonio Gramsci and Italy's Passive Revolution', in J. A. Davis (ed.), *Gramsci and Italy's Passive Revolution* (London, 1979).

as Gramsci put it, 'incapable of uniting the people around itself', it had been unable to overthrow the existing feudal order and to create a basis for the new Italian state.[37]

For the problem with the Risorgimento, which explained the subsequent problems of liberal Italy, was its lack of a revolutionary 'Jacobin' party to lead the bourgeoisie and peasantry in a conquest of the feudal order. Gramsci drew an unfavourable comparison between a model bourgeois revolution—the French Revolution, in which the Jacobins 'forced' the revolution 'in the direction of real historical development'—and the failed Italian version.[38] In Italy, the Mazzinian democrats were frightened by the violence of the rural masses and were therefore unable to establish an independent, leading ('hegemonic') role in the revolution. This role fell instead to the moderate liberals who, far from being solely the representatives of the Italian bourgeoisie, were also the 'organic vanguard' of exclusively Piedmontese interests, and even of the landed upper classes.[39] 'Those men', Gramsci wrote, 'were not capable of leading the people, were not capable of arousing their enthusiasm and their passion . . . They made the people-nation into an instrument, into an object, they degraded it.'[40]

The Piedmontese moderates came to their position of power in Italy not by revolutionary struggle but by a 'gradual and continual absorption' of the groups most hostile to them. In contrast to adversarial, 'bi-partisan' parliamentary systems, opposition in the Piedmontese parliament was 'transformed' and co-opted (diluted by enticements and favours).[41] The moderates also used the Piedmontese—and, later, the Italian—state, rather than popular support, to further their interests and ambitions.[42] Their leadership created a political system in Italy based on coercion and 'domination' rather than, as in the more stable bourgeois governments of France and

---

[37] *Selections from Prison Notebooks*, 53.

[38] Ibid. 79. For a critical analysis of Gramsci's use of the French revolution as a model for bourgeois revolutions, see P. Ginsborg, 'Gramsci and the Era of Bourgeois Revolution in Italy', in Davis (ed.), *Gramsci and Italy's Passive Revolution*, 31–45, 53–7.

[39] *Selections from Prison Notebooks*, 60.   [40] Ibid. 90.

[41] The term *'trasformismo'* usually refers to the period of Left government after 1876; Gramsci's use of the term is novel in so far as he dates it back to the Cavourian period; ibid. 58–9.   [42] Ibid. 59, 105.

Britain, consent and 'hegemony'.[43] The sources of liberal Italy's instability were thus to be found in the failure of democratic revolution. They said, Gramsci wrote in a celebrated passage:

that they were aiming at the creation of a modern State in Italy, and they in fact produced a bastard. They aimed at stimulating the formation of an extensive and energetic ruling class, and they did not succeed; at integrating the people into the framework of the new State, and they did not succeed. The paltry political life from 1870 to 1900, the fundamental and endemic rebelliousness of the Italian popular classes, the narrow and stunted existence of a sceptical and cowardly ruling stratum, these are all the consequences of that failure.[44]

Thus, with Gramsci, the Risorgimento was finally stripped of its heroes and the glorious myths surrounding them. Italian unification, described by none other than Gladstone as 'the most stupendous fabric . . . ever . . . erected on the basis of human integrity', became instead the 'paltry' reflection of a 'cowardly' ruling class.[45]

Gramsci, together with another Marxist historian, Emilio Sereni, also argued that the failure of democratic revolution in the Risorgimento could explain the Southern Question.[46] Specifically, the absence of agrarian reform allowed the Southern nobility to survive alongside a weak middle class, thereby curtailing the process of democratization in the South. An alliance, or 'historic bloc', was established between the Southern nobility and Northern industrialists which acted as a powerful constraint on political development in liberal Italy.[47] The failure of democratic revolution also established a dispossessed, disenfranchised and permanently discontented peasant class in

---

[43] The opposing concepts of 'hegemony' (leadership) and 'domination' (coercion) are central to Gramsci's innovative analysis of bourgeois power, although they are not without their problems. See P. Anderson, 'The Antinomies of Antonio Gramsci', *New Left Review*, 100 (1976), 1–78, which provoked a new, more critical approach to Gramsci's political philosophy. Gramsci's discussion of the moderate party's hegemony in the Risorgimento is usefully analysed by J. Femia, *Gramsci's Political Thought: Hegemony, Consciousness and the Revolutionary Process* (Oxford, 1981), 47–50, and by Ginsborg, 'Gramsci and the Era of Bourgeois Revolution', 50–3.   [44] *Selections from Prison Notebooks*, 90.

[45] Quoted in M. Urban, *British Opinion and Policy on the Unification of Italy, 1856–1861* (Scottsdale, Pa., 1938), 604.

[46] E. Sereni, *Il capitalismo nelle campagne (1860–1900)* (Turin, 1947; 1968 edn.). Sereni and Gramsci actually developed their arguments independently of each other. Sereni discusses the historiographical debate in the introduction, 'Al lettore', to the 1968 edition.

[47] J. A. Davis, 'The South, the Risorgimento and the Origins of the "Southern Problem"', in Davis (ed.), *Gramsci and Italy's Passive Revolution*, 67.

the South, a threat to political stability rather than a source of support for the new regime.[48]

The origins of the Southern Question were thus to be found in the creation of the Italian nation state. Both the shortcomings of Italian liberalism and the existence of an impoverished, rebellious South were linked to Italy's 'passive revolution'. Within united Italy, the relationship between North and South was structurally unbalanced. Gramsci described the relationship between the urban, industrializing North and the rural South as a 'city countryside relationship': the North exercised a 'locomotive function' and the South was dragged along behind regardless.[49] This subordination of South to North had devastating economic consequences for the South. Sereni argued that the creation of a national market in Italy based on the needs of capitalist development in the North damaged the more fragile rural economy of the South. Furthermore, the lower standard of living amongst the Southern peasantry considerably reduced the demand for Northern manufactured goods, thus slowing Italian industrialization as a whole.[50]

Anglo-Saxon histories of the Risorgimento and liberal Italy have also been affected by this debate. Mack Smith insists in a recent preface to *Cavour and Garibaldi* that these controversies were 'quite extraneous' to his work.[51] Yet his careful demythologizing of the events of 1860 contributed to a general sense of disillusionment with the Risorgimento and its outcome. Subsequent generations of British historians—notably Ginsborg writing on the 1848 revolution in Venice—were influenced directly by Gramsci.[52] In Italy too, more than one generation of historians was inspired by this persuasive analysis to delve into the relationship between leadership and class in the Risorgimento. Della Peruta's influential work on the democrats in Lombardy, Scirocco's work on democrats in the mainland South, and Romano's on Sicilian democrats all emphasize the centrality of class conflict—particularly the middle-class fear of peasant violence—

[48] Gramsci's analysis of the Southern peasantry is developed extensively in the pre-prison article 'Some Aspects of the Southern Question', in A. Gramsci, *Pre-Prison Writings*, ed. R. Bellamy, trans. V. Cox (Cambridge, 1994).

[49] *Selections from Prison Notebooks*, 90–102. Davis, 'The Risorgimento and the "Southern Problem"', 68.   [50] Sereni, *Il capitalismo nelle campagne*, 36–9.

[51] Mack Smith, *Cavour and Garibaldi*, p. xi.

[52] P. Ginsborg, *Daniele Manin and the Venetian Revolution of 1848–49* (Cambridge, 1979).

in the decline and defeat of the democratic movement.[53] Similarly, historians explain government policy after unification as a desperate effort to prevent revolution from below. Even Alberto Caracciolo, who is much more sympathetic to the Right than some other historians, accepts that a form of 'temporary dictatorship' was set up by the government in an attempt to defeat the democratic opposition and control the South.[54] The failure of bourgeois leadership and a consequent use of coercive 'domination' thus explains why Italian unity was built on the basis of a centralized, quasi-authoritarian state with, it is argued, little involvement from Italian civil society. A narrow suffrage, heavy-handed policing, and state intervention in society and the economy also seem to reflect a political system where the coercive power of the state was more important than social and cultural hegemony.[55]

The 'statism' or 'dictatorship' of the liberal Right is the starting-point for Franco Molfese's seminal study of the brigands' war of the 1860s, and for Paolo Alatri's meticulous account of political struggle in Sicily after unification.[56] Alatri shows how readily the government was prepared to use brutal and, often, unconstitutional methods in order to defeat the Left in Sicily. Focusing on the new Italian army, Molfese notes that from the beginning it exercised 'indiscriminate reprisals, especially arson accompanied by looting and vandalism' against those suspected of collusion with the opposite side.[57] Maintaining government stability was, it is concluded, always a higher priority for members of the Right than obeying the constitutional guarantees which they had sworn to uphold.

Dominating this approach is a sense that Italian liberalism is different, and less successful, than liberalism elsewhere in Europe. It is these so-called 'exceptionalisms', moreover, which account for the persistent problem of the South. They are traced to the character of Italian national leadership, to its tenuous relations with civil society, and

---

[53] F. della Peruta, 'I contadini nella rivoluzione lombarda del 1848' and 'Aspetti sociali del '48 nel Mezzogiorno', in *Democrazia e socialismo nel Risorgimento* (Rome, 1977); A. Scirocco, *I democratici italiani da Sapri a Porta Pia* (Naples, 1969); S. F. Romano, *Momenti del Risorgimento in Sicilia* (Messina, 1952).

[54] A. Caracciolo, *Stato e società civile: problemi dell'unificazione italiana* (Turin, 1959), esp. 68–9.

[55] *Problemi dell'unità d'Italia: atti del II convegno di studi gramsciani* (Rome, 1962); C. Pavone, *Amministrazione centrale e amministrazione periferica da Rattazzi a Ricasoli* (Milan, 1964); E. Ragionieri, *Politica e amministrazione dello stato unitario* (Bari, 1967).

[56] F. Molfese, *Storia del brigantaggio dopo l'unità* (Milan, 1964); P. Alatri, *Lotte politiche in Sicilia sotto il governo della Destra, 1866–76* (Turin, 1954).

[57] *Storia del brigantaggio*, 189.

even to a closet sympathy with more authoritarian ideologies. Perhaps most of all, the 'peculiarities' of Italian liberalism are traced to the middle classes. The Italian middle classes are condemned both for being bourgeois and for harbouring aristocratic tendencies. As Raffaele Romanelli comments, they are accused of 'a bourgeois failing' and also of 'a failure to be bourgeois'.[58]

However, this consensus was not shared by all historians. One in particular, the Sicilian historian Rosario Romeo, who received his training at Croce's *Istituto per gli studi storici* in Naples, took issue with the assumptions made by Gramscian historians.[59] Romeo's aim and main methodological innovation was to counter what he saw as the economic determinism of Marxist historiography on empirical as well as on theoretical grounds.[60] Indeed, all of Romeo's major works—*Il Risorgimento in Sicilia*, *Risorgimento e capitalismo*, *Cavour e il suo tempo*—are characterized by an almost unparalleled depth of statistical and textual research as well as by a strident anti-Marxism.[61]

At the heart of Romeo's dispute with Gramsci is his insistence that Italian unification should be seen as a progressive step which ultimately benefited the whole nation. Far from being a 'passive revolution' imposed arbitrarily from above, moderate liberal leadership in the Risorgimento, as Romeo seeks to show, had deep roots. He attributes the predominance of Piedmontese moderate liberalism in Italy to four main factors: the cultural links established between Piedmontese aristocrats and European liberals in the early nineteenth century, the rapid development of Piedmontese agriculture in the same period, the emergence of a new middle class in the Piedmontese countryside, and the sweeping liberal reforms of the late 1840s and 1850s.[62] Cavour and his

---

[58] R. Romanelli, 'Political Debate, Social History, and the Italian *borghesia*: Changing Perspectives in Historical Research', *Journal of Modern History*, 63/4 (1991), 718.

[59] For an analysis of the intellectual influences on Romeo, see G. Pescosolido, *Rosario Romeo* (Rome and Bari, 1990), 4–15.

[60] Although Romeo had absorbed Croce's philosophical idealism (and anti-Marxism) from his teachers at Naples, he was also familiar with current economic theory and was enthused by the possibilities of empirical research. See R. Romeo, 'Introductory Essay', in K. R. Greenfield, *Economics and Liberalism in the Risorgimento: A Study of Nationalism in Lombardy* (Baltimore, 1934; 1965 edn.), p. xiii; G. Mori, 'Rosario Romeo: un grande storico per una grande illusione?' *Passato e Presente*, 13 (1987), 3–4; and Pescosolido, *Rosario Romeo*, 4.

[61] *Il Risorgimento in Sicilia* (Bari, 1950), *Risorgimento e capitalismo* (Bari, 1959), *Cavour e il suo tempo* (3 vols.; Bari, 1969–84). Derek Beales describes Romeo's method as 'defending idealist historians with a barrage of statistics', in a review of *Risorgimento e capitalismo*, *Economic History Review*, ser. ii, 12, 1–3 (1959–60), 338.

[62] Romeo describes and analyses this process in his multi-volumed *Cavour e il suo tempo*, particularly in the two parts of vol. ii.

followers were, Romeo argues, as passionate as other liberals when it came to political freedom, and more passionate than most when it came to free trade.[63] Where their policies took an authoritarian direction, as in the South, this was a decision supported by the Left as well as the Right.[64] Moreover, although Cavour had always to move cautiously in his reform programme, 'a substantial sphere of new civil and political liberties separated the liberal regime from the arbitrary absolutism of the Carloalbertine monarchy' (1831–49, i.e. the period immediately preceding liberal government).[65]

For Romeo, the 'peculiarities' of Italian liberalism—which he might more easily call 'instabilities'—can be attributed to an environment which was in some respects hostile to its development.[66] He thus praises the *connubio*, the 'unlawful union' between centre-Left and centre-Right in the Piedmontese parliament, which was so criticized by Gramsci. As Romeo sees it, the *connubio* was a remarkably effective and progressive response to the problem of uniting the various liberal factions in Piedmont. Indeed, for Romeo, the 'passive revolution' becomes a virtue:

the love of wisely-guided and gradual progress, the respect for individual rights, the rational evaluation of the risks and sacrifices involved in gaining the end desired and, in short, the capability of uniting Italy without the excesses and the violence which characterized so many similar movements at the time and subsequently.

Reform without revolution, in other words, was the central achievement of moderate liberalism.[67]

For Romeo, the concern of Marxist historians with revolution in the present distorted their judgement of democratic revolution in the nineteenth century.[68] In reality, there was no possible alternative to moderate liberal leadership:

the moderate solution . . . was based on the hegemony of the most cultured and economically active classes of Central–Northern Italy, and they tended to subordinate the demands of the rest of the country to their demands.[69]

---

[63] *Cavour, ii.* 703.   [64] Ibid. iii. 828–9, 872.

[65] Romeo, *Dal Piemonte sabaudo all'Italia liberale*, 137.

[66] Romeo particularly singles out financial constraints and an unwelcoming foreign situation; see *Cavour,* ii. esp. 480, 497, 556, 676–7, 694–5, and 732.

[67] Ibid. 572–80.

[68] Here Romeo picks up and develops the argument of his teacher in Naples, Federico Chabod, in 'Croce storico', *Rivista Storica Italiana,* 64 (1952), 473–530.

[69] *Cavour, iii.* 879.

Moreover, the Italian economy would not even have profited from an agrarian revolution in the South. According to Romeo, the needs of Italian industrialization demanded the subordination of the peasant economy, 'the sacrifice imposed for so many decades on the countryside and on the *Mezzogiorno*'.[70] But Romeo also points to genuine efforts, made by Cavour and his successors, to bring about economic reform and restructure political life in the South.[71]

The defence mounted by Romeo of moderate liberalism and its achievements was hugely controversial. Arguably, this was always his intention.[72] What has tended to be obscured by the often furious polemic between Romeo and other historians is that, in important respects, they agree about the problems of the South. Romeo may disagree about the character of moderate liberalism; but his descriptions of the South, of its 'inertia', 'traditional parasitism', and 'deep-rooted backwardness', are little different from those of Gramsci and Sereni.[73]

Romeo agrees with Marxist historians that Southern backwardness in this period can be identified with the weakness of the Southern bourgeoisie.[74] His description of the Sicilian middle class in the Risorgimento, while more sympathetic than most, reaches broadly the same conclusions as the Gramsci-inspired studies of Renda and Brancato.[75] In *Il Risorgimento in Sicilia* Romeo refers to the 'intrinsic weakness' of the Sicilian agrarian bourgeoisie:

---

[70] *Risorgimento e capitalismo*, 197–8.   [71] *Cavour*, iii. 865–6.

[72] *Risorgimento e capitalismo* in particular provoked fierce debate. See A. Gershenkron, 'Rosario Romeo and the Original Accumulation of Capital', in *Economic Backwardness in Historical Perspective* (Cambridge, Mass., 1966), on Romeo's use of statistical evidence. The contributions of Eckhaus, Romeo, and Tosi in A. Caracciolo (ed.), *La formazione dell'Italia industriale* (Bari, 1973) discuss the North–South divide. The controversy surrounding *Cavour e il suo tempo* was caused in part by Romeo's personal attacks on the views of other historians (already apparent in *Risorgimento e capitalismo*). On the polemical aspect of Romeo's work, see Mori, 'Rosario Romeo', 5–6, 12.

[73] *Cavour*, iii. 865, 876.

[74] Davis, 'The Risorgimento and the "Southern Problem"', 69–70.

[75] F. Renda, *Storia della Sicilia dal 1860 al 1970*, i (Palermo, 1984), F. Brancato, *La Sicilia nel primo ventennio del Regno d'Italia* (Bologna, 1956). Giarrizzo writes, 'Romeo's judgement on the Southern "middle class" is always critical, and he does not make much of a distinction between Sicily and the Mezzogiorno. But he never participated in the *bagarre* against the Sicilian bourgeoisie and petite-bourgeoisie'. Giarrizzo, 'Per una storia della Sicilia', 27. Franco Benigno argues that the dominant interpretation of Sicily's role in the Risorgimento—the one established by Romeo—was steeped in an 'anti-Sicilian polemic'. F. Benigno, 'Introduzione', in F. Benigno and C. Torrisi (eds.), *Élites e potere in Sicilia dal medioevo ad oggi* (Rome, 1995), p. xi.

whose own economic backwardness and resulting inability to overthrow completely the rule of the old aristocracy meant that they squeezed closer to them . . . on which basis the unity of the dominant agrarian class was reconstructed . . . remaining therefore tied to the continuation of the *latifondo* as the fundamental economic organism in the interior zone.[76]

Many smaller proprietors 'blindly' eschewed a commercial exploitation of their property, preferring to ape the 'lazy' and 'parasitical' activities of their former lords, and lead 'an idle and shabby existence'.[77] Brancato and Renda concur; the weakness of the Sicilian middle class frustrated economic development and allowed a system of feudal relations between 'baron' and peasant to survive in the countryside.[78]

Romeo tends to dismiss Sicilian peasant movements as mere agitation without any possibility of further development. He suggests, however, that this reflects the weakness of the middle class: 'in its incapacity and reluctance to ally itself with the masses . . . lies the principal proof of the fundamental insufficiency of the Southern intellectual bourgeoisie'.[79] Even Romeo's analysis of the middle class's political aims and achievements is not unlike that of Gramscian historians such as Romano. For both Romeo and Romano, the Risorgimento in Sicily is a political movement devoid of economic or social aims. They also agree that it was the inability, particularly after 1848, to lead a successful revolution against the Bourbons in Naples which led Sicilian liberals to throw in their lot with—and to subordinate themselves to—the Northern moderate Liberals.[80]

There is, in other words, a paradigm of backwardness which, since the time of unification, has guided all analyses of the South. While the problems of Italian liberalism have been constantly rebutted and reevaluated, the same cannot be said of Southern problems. In the modern period, the history of the South has been almost entirely a history of the Southern Question, a history of the failure of modernization and an analysis of whom or what to blame for Southern difference. The history of the Southern Question has been described appropriately

---

[76] *Il Risorgimento in Sicilia*, 195.   [77] Ibid. 197.

[78] Brancato, *a Sicilia*, 23; Renda, *Storia della Sicilia*, 82.

[79] *Il Risorgimento in Sicilia*, 384.

[80] However, Romeo concludes that the alliance with Northern liberals 'saved' the Risorgimento in Sicily, while Romano argues that this alliance frustrated social revolution and permanently subjugated Sicily to the needs of Northern Italy. Romeo, *Il Risorgimento in Sicilia*, 286–7, 338–68; Romano, *Momenti del Risorgimento in Sicilia*, 65–7. See also Pescosolido's comments in *Rosario Romeo*, 20.

by Piero Bevilacqua as a 'kind of non-history, the frustrating tale of all that could not have been'.[81]

More recent historical research, however, has begun to uncover a rather different set of Southern realities. In so doing, it suggests that understandings both of Southern 'difference' and of Italian liberalism's 'peculiarities' may need to be readdressed.[82] Perhaps the most important conceptual change in recent research is the recognition that there is more than one South. Local and regional studies have begun to show that no single South existed in economic terms. Rather, dynamic, export-led sectors coexisted alongside non-commercial, subsistence ones. Southern provinces had their own internal 'dualisms' between commercial and non-commercial sectors—each Southern province, Franca Assante suggests, had its own 'South'.[83] Thus, the simple North–South dichotomy which assumes a single, homogenous South, with its 'simple opposition between backwardness and modernization', may, in Adrian Lyttleton's words, hide 'more than it reveals'.[84]

In the first number of *Meridiana*, the periodical which has acted as the forum for new research and debate on the South, the South is defined as a 'society in motion', undergoing a profound process of modernization.[85] The South, it is argued, experienced a 'difficult' process of modernization, or a 'modernization without growth'.[86] Explanations for the South's economic problems now look at such factors as the loss of overseas markets, the worldwide fall in grain prices, long-term environmental changes, and the lack of a modern infrastructure. Bevilacqua notes that many Southern exports (grain, citrus fruits) were particularly vulnerable to fluctuations in the world

---

[81] Bevilacqua, *Breve storia dell'Italia meridionale*, p. viii.

[82] There are a number of useful articles which assess the significance of 'revisionist' historiography in the South: A. Lyttleton, 'A New Past for the Mezzogiorno', *Times Literary Supplement*, 4618 (4 October 1991), 14–15, and J. A. Davis, 'Changing Perspectives on Italy's "Southern Problem"', in C. Levy (ed.), *Italian Regionalism* (Oxford, 1996). A. Massafra, 'La ragioni di una proposta', in A. Massafra (ed.), *Il Mezzogiorno preunitario: economia, società, istituzioni* (Bari, 1988) is one of the clearest statements of the revisionist agenda.

[83] F. Assante, 'Le trasformazioni del paesaggio agrario', in Massafra (ed.), *Il Mezzogiorno preunitario*, 22.   [84] Lyttleton, 'A New Past for the Mezzogiorno', 14.

[85] 'Presentazione', in *Meridiana*, 1 (1987), 14. Giarrizzo even suggests that the South is the part of Italy most revolutionized by the process of modernization. Giarrizzo, *Mezzogiorno senza meridionalismo*, p. xxviii.

[86] Or 'modernization without development', the phrase used by anthropologists Jane and Peter Schneider in their study of a Western Sicilian *latifondo* community, *Culture and Political Economy in Western Sicily* (New York, 1976).

economy. The weak international role of Southern Italy also disadvantaged Southern merchants and entrepreneurs who had little or no control over the international terms of trade.[87] The South's economic problems now tend to be dated to the agrarian crisis of the 1880s rather than to national unification.[88]

The significance of this kind of explanation is that it refers to externally mediated problems rather than to internal political, social, or cultural disadvantages. The emergence of a North/South divide is seen as an accident of geography, the world economy, and/or international politics. It is not seen as the outcome of economic unification, a failed democratic revolution, or Southern 'corruption', but more as a symptom of Southern economic disadvantages than as a cause. Thus, the revisionism of economic historians has been, as John Davis puts it, 'the essential jumping-off point for the revisionist agenda' more generally.[89] Crucially, by distinguishing the causes of Southern economic problems from the causes of its political or social ones, historians have dissolved the established connections between the South's economic backwardness, its archaic social structure, and its corrupt politics.

Deeply rooted notions of Southern immorality and violence have recently come into question. Non-historians, more sensitive to the uses and power of language and visual imagery, have encouraged historians to regard established representations of Southern criminality with more scepticism. In this analysis, traditional depictions of Southern difference lose much of their explanatory force; they no longer account for the Right's failure in the South, but simply reflect it. What Dickie terms 'the myths and lurid metaphors' surrounding banditry are, he argues, part of the process whereby the army—the repressor—'made banditry make sense'.[90] The image of a violent South which was, according to Moe, established at the time of unification, formed part of a justification for its violent treatment at the hands of the Italian state.[91] Southern immorality and violence, according to this analysis, can be seen as an imagined product of the encounter between North and

---

[87] Bevilacqua, *Breve storia dell'Italia meridionale*, 11–13, 31–2, 52–8.

[88] M. Petrusewicz, *Latifondo: economia morale e vita materiale in una periferia dell'ottocento* (Venice, 1989); G. Giarrizzo, 'La Sicilia e la crisi agraria', in *Mezzogiorno senza meridionalismo*.

[89] J. A. Davis, 'Remapping Italy's Path to the Twentieth Century', *Journal of Modern History*, 66/2 (June 1994), 293.   [90] Dickie, 'A Word at War', 5.

[91] Moe, '"Altro che Italia!"', 54.

South, as a symptom of political and economic problems rather than as a cause.[92]

Historical perceptions of the Southern bourgeoisie have also changed drastically. Local studies, less dominated by the notion of a North–South 'divide', have yielded some interesting results. Research based on electoral lists, for example, reveals that in many rural communes in both Sicily and the Southern mainland there was a substantial and rapid transfer of wealth and land from an old-established nobility to a new, agrarian bourgeoisie. In some of the coastal Sicilian cities, particularly Trapani, Catania, and Messina, there was also a significant growth in the numbers of merchants, entrepreneurs, and professionals. In the 1960s Giarrizzo published a study of Biancavilla (an agrarian community on the slopes of Mount Etna) which described the emergence of a new 'ambitious and active' middle class, intent on challenging the nobility for control of the commune.[93] His conclusions have been backed up by more recent research. During the first half of the nineteenth century new 'middling' groups began to make concerted inroads into local politics in many parts of Sicily and the mainland South, occupying key positions in local councils, police forces, and the judiciary.[94]

The new approach to the South challenges the monolithic image of Southern backwardness, and suggests instead a more 'complex', 'varied', 'open', and 'changing' picture of Southern history.[95] It has, in short, tended to break down the previous orthodoxies of the Southern Question; although, problematically, it also offers very little to take its place. Revisionists attempt to reach beyond the confines of the Southern Question, but often without a clear sense of what a new 'South-

[92] Certain reservations regarding this kind of analysis are expressed in L. Riall, 'A proposito di John Dickie, "Una parola in guerra: l'esercito italiano e il brigantaggio 1860–1870"', *Passato e Presente*, 27 (1991), 195–8. John Dickie replies to these criticisms in 'Una risposta sul "brigantaggio"', ibid. 28 (1993), 193–5. Paolo Pezzino objects more strongly to Moe's analysis in 'Risorgimento e guerra civile: alcune considerazioni preliminari', in G. Ranzato (ed.), *Guerre fratricide: le guerre civili in età contemporanea* (Turin, 1994), 59. In a later article, he states unequivocally, 'It is impossible to sustain that the perception of the Mezzogiorno as a "diverse" reality . . . has nothing to do with historical reality but is only a representation.' 'L'oggetto misterioso: Mezzogiorno d'Italia e revisionismo storiografico', *Società e Storia*, 68 (1995), 381.

[93] G. Giarrizzo, *Un comune rurale nella Sicilia etnea (Biancavilla 1810–1860)* (Catania, 1963), 167.

[94] See, in particular, the contributions of Moricola, Benigno, Civile, Iachello, and di Ciommo in Massafra (ed.), *Il Mezzogiorno preunitario*. See also G. Oddo, *Lo sviluppo incompiuto: Villafrati 1596–1960* (Palermo, 1986), 81–185.

[95] Giarrizzo, *Mezzogiorno senza meridionalismo*, p. ix.

ernism' should consist of or of what it should be identified with.[96] And, while economic analyses of the South have toyed with various explanations for the absence of sustained economic growth, there have been far fewer attempts to account for its persistent political instability. Biagio Salvemini has suggested that all attempts to locate the 'peculiarities' of the South are misconceived and should be abandoned.[97] Hardly surprisingly, some historians have expressed considerable hostility to aspects of the revisionist agenda; Paolo Pezzino, for instance, suggests that Southern revisionism leads logically to a denial of Southern difference 'altogether'.[98]

To make matters more complicated, revisionists have also been at work on Italian liberalism and its much-maligned ruling class. Recent studies have emphasized the strength of Italian liberalism—the liberal convictions of Cavour and his successors, and the impact of liberal ideas on the new middle classes. Raffaele Romanelli argues that the 'dictatorship' of the Right has been greatly overestimated. The Right's use of administrative centralization to unite Italy was seen by them as a temporary expedient; moreover, in practice, it was considerably more open and flexible than it appeared, and was driven forward by the most liberal of intentions.[99] Raffaella Gherardi also insists that the sense of 'poverty' which pervades Italian liberalism is misplaced. Italy's parliamentary system was stabilized by a remarkable degree of compromise, by the ability of liberal statesmen to establish a working majority irrespective of Left–Right divisions in the Chamber.[100] Thus, for Gherardi and others like her, the 'peculiarities' of the Italian political system are positive advantages.[101] To a considerable extent, in other words, recent analyses of moderate liberalism and the Historic Right favour the more positive interpretation established by Romeo.

An even more striking process of revisionism has occurred with regard to the middle classes and middle 'orders' (both Northern and

---

[96] For a critical analysis which defends the 'dualistic' account of the Italian economy, see Cafagna, *Nord e Sud*, esp. 82–4.

[97] B. Salvemini, 'Sulla nobile arte di cercare le peculiarità del Mezzogiorno', *Società e Storia*, 68 (1995), 353–72. For some general reflections on the implications of revisionist research on the South, see A. M. Banti, 'Il Sud come problema della storia italiana', ibid. 341–52, and Pezzino, 'Mezzogiorno d'Italia e revisionismo storiografico', ibid. 373–84.

[98] P. Pezzino, 'Quale modernizzazione per il Mezzogiorno?', in *Il paradiso abitato dai diavoli*, 10.

[99] R. Romanelli, *Il comando impossibile: stato e società nell'Italia liberale* (Bologna, 1988). [100] Gherardi, *L'arte del compromesso*, esp. 8–9.

[101] For a discussion see L. Riall, 'Progress and Compromise in Liberal Italy', *Historical Journal*, 38/1 (1995), 205–13.

Southern).[102] Studies of bourgeois sociability and mentalities, of their political engagements and economic activities have proliferated. From such studies an alternative picture of the Italian middle classes has emerged, a more varied but also a more positive one than has hitherto existed. Moreover, the strength of this new perspective lies precisely in its attention to local and regional differences and in its focus on the diverse (often non-economic) ways of becoming middle-class.[103] Through a sensitivity to specific historical contexts and what Romanelli calls 'the options available to individuals', it challenges the application of externally derived sociological models of modernization to the Italian middle classes and the resulting sense of their failure to conform to these models.[104] As a result, the new approach has also shaken the sense of Italian 'exceptionalism' on which the Gramscian analysis of liberal Italy was based.

Italian exceptionalism has also been profoundly undermined by the (often controversial) revision of the stereotypical models themselves. In Britain, the model for successful industrialization against which Italy is unfavourably compared, historians have developed an alternative 'gentlemanly capitalism thesis' to explain the 'peculiarities' of English economic development and of the English middle class.[105] Explaining the formation of a modern élite, British historians now stress the enduring power of landed interests and the presence of 'entrenched pre-modern elements' giving 'legitimacy to anti-modern sentiments' in an industrial, capitalist society.[106] Thus Martin Daunton writes of the consensus surrounding 'the apparent failure of a self-confident middle

[102] For differing definitions of the Italian middle classes, see A. Lyttleton, 'The Middle Classes in Liberal Italy', in J. A. Davis and P. Ginsborg (eds.), *Society and Politics in the Age of the Risorgimento: Essays in Honour of Denis Mack Smith* (Cambridge, 1991), 218–19, 233.

[103] There are three excellent analyses in English of new approaches to the Italian bourgeoisie: Lyttleton, 'The Middle Classes in Liberal Italy', Romanelli, 'The Italian *borghesia*', and Davis, 'Remapping Italy's Path to the Twentieth Century', esp. 301–10.

[104] Romanelli, 'The Italian *borghesia*', 737.

[105] On the 'gentlemanly-capitalism thesis' deriving from a debate between Anderson and Thompson in the 1960s, see P. Anderson, 'Origins of the Present crisis', *New Left Review*, 23 (1964), 26–53, and E. P. Thompson, 'The Peculiarities of the English', in *The Poverty of Theory and Other Essays* (London, 1987).

[106] M. J. Weiner, *English Culture and the Decline of the Industrial Spirit, 1850–1980* (Cambridge, 1981), 7. See also L. Stone and J. Stone, *An Open Elite? England, 1540–1880* (Oxford, 1984), W. D. Rubinstein, 'New Men of Wealth and the Purchase of Land in Nineteenth-Century England', in *Elites and the Wealthy in Modern British History: Essays in Social and Economic History* (Brighton, 1987), and P. J. Cain and A. G. Hopkins, *British Imperialism: Innovation and Expansion, 1688–1914* (London, 1993).

class to emerge and seize power and social prestige' in nineteenth-century Britain.[107]

Research in the last few decades also suggests that British liberalism's strength and solidarity has probably been overestimated by Italian historians; the British Liberal Party, like its counterparts elsewhere in Europe, seems to have been built on the basis of alliances and compromises.[108] Even the concept of bourgeois revolution has been under attack since the 1960s. In France, the *locus classicus* for bourgeois revolution, historical interest has shifted entirely away from a class model. If anything, the Revolution is now seen to provide striking elements of continuity; historians tend to downplay the outward—often misleading—appearance of dramatic change, and to deny that a revolutionary bourgeoisie ever existed at all.[109]

Even more illuminating are the challenges to other models of 'national exceptionalism': in Germany, to the so-called 'structural-continuity thesis', a Marxist explanation of Germany's 'missing' bourgeois revolution which, referring to the incapacity of a weak bourgeoisie to assert itself over a dominant aristocracy, has much in common with Gramsci's concept of passive revolution; and, in Spain, to the concept of a failed bourgeois revolution. Blackbourn and Eley have suggested, with reference to Germany, that the concept of bourgeois revolution needs to be reformulated.[110] A bourgeois revolution can occur without the assertion of bourgeois political power; a process of economic reform suited to the needs of a commercial bourgeoisie can take place without the development of liberal democracy. Blackbourn describes a 'silent bourgeois revolution' in Germany. The 'real strength and power' of the German bourgeoisie was, he suggests, 'anchored in the capitalist mode of production and articulated through dominance in civil society' rather than through the emergence of 'one specific state-form'.[111] Alternatively, as Adrian Shubert suggests of the Spanish case, a liberal revolution can take place even if revolutionary change was 'overseen by the

[107] M. Daunton, '"Gentlemanly Capitalism" and British Industry 1820–1914', *Past and Present*, 122 (1989), 119.
[108] For an instructive comparison of British and German liberalism see G. Eley, 'Liberalism, Europe and the Bourgeoisie 1860–1914', in D. Blackbourn and R. J. Evans, *The German Bourgeoisie* (London, 1991), esp. 298–308.
[109] F. Furet, *Interpreting the French Revolution* (Cambridge, 1981), 1–79.
[110] D. Blackbourn and G. Eley, *The Peculiarities of German History* (Oxford, 1984). See also R. J. Evans, 'The Myth of Germany's Missing Revolution', in *Rethinking German History* (London, 1987).   [111] *The Peculiarities of German History*, 175.

"wrong" social group' (that is, the landed nobility).[112] This echoes a suggestion made by Alan Knight in relation to Latin American revolutions that 'the relations between state and civil society under developing capitalism . . . permit a variety of regimes'.[113] Thus, on the one hand, the failure of the bourgeoisie to lead a liberal revolution does not necessarily imply the failure of liberal revolution as a whole. Nor, on the other hand, is there anything necessarily inconsistent about the rise of the middle classes and the persistence of an authoritarian political system. Judged in terms of their ability either to overthrow the nobility or to create a liberal democracy, the middle classes in nineteenth-century Italy seem no more of a variant on a European norm than most of their contemporaries.

The reconceptualization of bourgeois revolution and of bourgeois identity undermines the power of a class analysis to explain Italian political exceptionalism. Together with the empirical rehabilitation of both the Italian middle classes and Italian liberalism, it also suggests that there was nothing inherently 'peculiar' about the liberal leadership's beliefs, methods, or identities. More importantly for our purposes, it implies that there was nothing so peculiar about Italian liberalism as to explain by itself the failure of liberal policy in the South. Taken with the revisionist attempt to reconceptualize the Southern Question, it makes the question asked at the beginning of this chapter—why was Sicily ungovernable?—particularly difficult to answer.

The new, revisionist picture of an economically dynamic South means that probably the most striking feature of Southern difference, the inability of successive administrations to govern peacefully and effectively, to guarantee law and order, raise taxes, organize conscription, or hold elections has become much more difficult to explain. What, then, was the reason for Sicily's social and political instability? Why were the Sicilian élites apparently unable to control the violence of the rural poor? Why, if Italian liberalism was not very different from its European equivalents, did the liberal government resort more readily than most to the use of military repression and of exceptional, often unconstitutional, laws? And why were the government's various attempts to establish a liberal administration in Sicily unsuccessful?

---

[112] A. Schubert, *A Social History of Modern Spain* (London, 1990), 5.

[113] A. Knight, 'Social Revolution: A Latin American Perspective', *Bulletin of Latin American Research*, 9/2 (1990), 182.

What was it, to repeat the question asked at the outset, that made Sicily different from Piedmont?

III

One reason why these questions are difficult to answer is that, traditionally, historians of nineteenth-century Europe have been interested in liberal forms of political change, in industrial economic growth, and in urban societies. Thus, until recently, nineteenth-century European historians have been conceptually blinkered to other kinds of political and economic modernization and, particularly, to the effects which such modernization had on the countryside. In the Sicilian case, they have focused unduly on major urban areas on the coast (Palermo, Catania), where there was either considerable economic development or a significant growth in liberal public opinion (or both). By contrast, since the outcome of modernization in rural Sicily during the nineteenth century was neither particularly capitalist nor particularly liberal, the forms of modernization which did occur there have never merited much attention. This is an unfortunate omission, because it seems that much of Sicily's political instability in the nineteenth century was caused by the experience and outcome of modernization in rural areas; specifically, by changes to landownership and land-usage, and by changes in the political relationship between central and local power.

Historians of liberal Italy have often assumed that Italian liberals were the first to attempt a programme of modernization in Sicily. This assumption seems to derive from the general tendency to associate the Bourbon monarchy with reaction and corruption. More recent research, however, suggests that this process of modernization began much earlier: during the period of 'Enlightened Absolutism' in the mid- to late eighteenth century, and continuing after the Restoration of 1815.

Bourbon reformers had two related objectives: to undermine the economic and political power of the Sicilian barons, and to replace them with the rule of a single, centralized administrative authority based in Naples. At least some of the 'peculiarities' of Sicilian modernization seem to derive from the fact that the Bourbons were far more successful in the former objective than they were in the latter.[114] The reforms largely destroyed the old particularistic relationship between monarchy, nobility, and local notables, which had been based on perso-

---

[114] E. Iachello, 'Centralisation étatique et pouvoir local en Sicile au xixe siècle', *Annales, Histoire, Sciences Sociales*, 1 (1994), 241–66.

nal loyalty, reciprocal obligations, and special privileges. Yet although the reforms weakened the old nobility, by creating new sources of resentment between central and local power they also weakened the power of the state. In Sicily, where these privileges had been especially jealously guarded, noble opposition to Bourbon rule grew steadily from the end of the eighteenth century. And, after 1815, the nobility's resentment of the Bourbon monarchy was accompanied and, at times, fuelled by the agitation of new groups who based their opposition on liberalism and nationalism.[115]

There is considerable evidence from other Restoration states in Italy that protest over political change and economic reform, as much as unrequited demands for it, fuelled the constitutional and nationalist demands of the early nineteenth century.[116] In the Two Sicilies, even before the rise of a liberal opposition, the new system of government which the Bourbons sought to establish seems to have been in considerable trouble. To succeed in their objective, the Bourbons needed either some new basis for political consent or considerably more coercive resources than they had at their disposal; all they actually managed to do was to destroy the old regime, with its old bases of support and stability, without constructing anything to take its place.[117]

However, if reform did little to enhance the exercise of power at the centre, it did have a dramatic impact on the structure of power within local communities. The new landowning class brought into being by the reforms began to challenge the old for control of the local community.[118] Since the local bureaucracy grew in size as a result of administrative centralization, it created new employment and patronage opportunities in many of the smaller towns and villages. By acquiring

[115] On the complexities and contradictions of this relationship, see A. de Francesco, 'Cultura costituzionale e conflitto politico nell'età della restaurazione', in Benigno and Torrisi (eds.), *Élites e potere in Sicilia*.

[116] See A. de Clementi, *Vivere nel latifondo: le comunità della campagna laziale fra '700 e '800* (Milan, 1989), M. Caffiero, 'Usi e abusi: comunità rurale e difesa dell'economia tradizionale nello stato pontificio', *Passato e Presente*, 24 (1990), 73–93, and F. Rizzi, 'Pourquoi obéir a l'état? Une communauté rurale du Latium aux XVIIIe et XIXe siècles', *Etudes Rurales*, 101–2 (1986), 271–87.

[117] Steven Hughes makes the same comment about reforms carried out during this period in the Italian Papal States: S. Hughes, *Crime, Disorder and the Risorgimento: The Politics of Policing in Bologna* (Cambridge, 1994), 65.

[118] Giarrizzo, *Un comune rurale nella Sicilia etnea*, chs. 1–2, A. de Francesco, *La guerra di Sicilia: il distretto di Caltagirone nella rivoluzione del 1820–21* (Catania, 1992), 35–137, E. Iachello, 'Potere locale e mobilità delle élites a Riposto nella prima metà dell'Ottocento', in Massafra (ed.), *Il mezzogiorno preunitario*.

these bureaucratic responsibilities, members of the local élite also acquired new sources of power in their community. In this way, political reform accelerated a process of social mobility in rural communities.[119]

The process of state formation and the reaction of rural élites to it can be considered two of the key elements in explaining Sicilian 'difference'. Nevertheless as John Davis rightly points out, however significant the problems caused by a weak state and the blurring of public and private power were, they were also far from being unique to Sicily or even to the South. Indeed, these problems were often as prominent a feature of the relatively more stable rural areas of Northern and Central Italy as they were of the South.[120] Thus, the inability of the liberal state, after the collapse of the Bourbon monarchy, to rebuild the political consensus in Sicily on the basis of representative government still remains unexplained.

The failure of the Liberal government to establish a political consensus in Sicily is the problem which this book investigates. It focuses in particular on the countryside of Western and Central Sicily—the Sicilian 'interior'. One of the most positive aspects of recent revisionist writings is that it obliges us to look at Southern Italy not as a single region but as a collection of different localities. Despite its obvious notoriety for crime and disorder, Sicily was probably not the most violent or politically unstable part of Southern Italy in this period. Notwithstanding its traditional image as a place dominated by grain production and ruled over by feudal rentiers, by 1860 it was neither. Nor was Sicily the most economically 'backward' or politically neglected region of Southern Italy. Within Sicily, there was in fact a huge variation in levels of commercial development and in kinds of political activity.

There are, nevertheless, a number of reasons why politics in Sicily were of particular significance in this period, and are of particular importance to this kind of study. The political upheaval which took place in Sicily in the mid-nineteenth century was of a particularly complex nature. It involved a multi-cornered and overlapping struggle among traditional and not-so-traditional élites, liberals, democrats, autonomists, Bourbons, clerics, and the urban and rural poor. Furthermore, it was a struggle that took place, and was experienced, at both a

---

[119] P. Pezzino, 'Monarchia amministrativa ed élites locali: Naro nella prima metà dell'Ottocento', in Pezzino, *Il paradiso abitato dai diavoli*, 106–20.
[120] Davis, 'Changing Perspectives on Italy's "Southern Problem"', 60.

national and a communal level. It was in Sicily that the revolution against
the Bourbons started, and it was here that the collapse of political and
administrative authority in 1860 was most dramatic. After 1860 the
situation in Sicily posed especially severe problems for a liberal government whose primary aim was to restore political authority and establish
administrative 'normalization'. It was, finally, in the countryside of
Western and Central Sicily—the main focus of the later chapters—
that the military campaigns of 1862 to 1866 were concentrated.

One word of caution is, however, necessary. The confusion and bitter
rivalries of Sicilian politics are also present in the government reports of
the period. Lack of personal contacts and a misunderstanding of the
politics of rural communities undermined central government attempts
to control them. The reports which reached Palermo, Naples, and
Turin were often extremely tendentious, and those in the capital had
no means of gauging their accuracy. In attempting to describe the
situation in Sicilian rural communities, we too are at the mercy of these
reports. In many respects, the documents from this period tell us far
more about the problems of government than they do about the problems of rural communities, and this emphasis is reflected in the
chapters which follow.

In what follows, a comparison is made of the attempts of the Bourbons, *garibaldini*, and the Piedmontese liberals to grapple with the
problems of controlling the Sicilian countryside. This analysis offers
an alternative view of the 'peculiarities' of Italian liberalism. It is a
remarkable fact, often neglected by historians, that although the regimes
which ruled Sicily in the course of the nineteenth century (the Bourbon
monarchy from 1815 to 1860, Garibaldi's dictatorship during the summer and autumn of 1860, and the Italian nation-state after 1860) were
bitterly opposed to each other, they all pursued broadly similar policies
towards Sicily, and all pursued them equally ineffectually. They all
sought, and were unable, to establish greater control from the centre
by substituting formal bureaucratic power for informal bargains with
local élites. They all sought, and were unable, to bring about a programme of land reform which could resolve the conflicts in the countryside. These common experiences suggest that the long-term failure
of political leadership in modern Sicily—not just the specific failure of
liberal leadership—is what really needs to be addressed and explained.

A study of central-local politics can clarify much about the ungovernability of Sicily. It also offers an opportunity to study Risorgimento
and post-Risorgimento politics from a new perspective. When looked at

from a local as well as from a national perspective, the political instability which characterized much of the Risorgimento period in Italy seems to be characterized as much by resistance to political and economic change as by a revolutionary demand for liberty and nationhood. Liberals, seen in this light, were little different from their predecessors. They were merely able to take advantage of the prevailing political and social instability to seize control in the South. Once in power, however, they were ill-equipped to cope with the demands which they had initially encouraged.

In turn, a study of Sicily's 'ungovernability' shows the whole process of modern state formation to be a much less straightforward and much more compromised process than is often assumed. Rather than being a two-way struggle between centre and periphery, state formation in Sicily was a multi-cornered fight involving intense internal rivalries and producing a series of ambivalent outcomes. Political modernization in Sicily strengthened the power of traditional élites at the expense of liberal government, and it also accentuated the bitter factional and class conflict within rural communities. It produced substantial changes in rural communities, but these were not always the changes desired by, or beneficial to, the central government, the local élites, or the rural poor. In all these respects, political change in Sicily before and during the period of Italian unification offers an interesting case-study of the many and diverse roads to the modern political world.

I

Restoration Sicily: Poverty, Protest, and Power, 1815–1849

I

In 1815, upon returning to Naples from its exile in Sicily during the Napoleonic wars, the Bourbon government declared its intention of upholding the innovations of the so-called *decennio francese* (the 'French decade', 1806–15). The French administration had destroyed the administrative, juridical, and financial structures of the *ancien régime* in Naples. Feudalism was officially abolished in 1806 and, in a series of additional laws, the political privileges of the Church and nobility were eradicated. In its place, Napoleonic administrators had begun to build a centralized and bureaucratic state.[1] After 1815 the Bourbon government accepted that the administrative innovations dating from the *decennio francese* were irreversible. More importantly, members of the restored government also realized that the modern state which the French revolutionaries had begun to construct could actually be used to assist in the reconstruction of absolutism.

Between 1815 and the first wave of revolutionary opposition to the Bourbon government in 1820–1, the chief Bourbon minister and the figure most associated with these reforms was Luigi de' Medici. De' Medici hoped to use principles of bureaucratic rationality to unify the Bourbon kingdom and to promote economic and civil progress. His ideal was that of an 'administrative monarchy', a state where power was shared between the monarch and the bureaucracy, thus obviating the need for representative government. He sought, in brief, to 'amalgamate' the Napoleonic administrative system with the principle of dynastic legitimacy.[2]

---

[1] The reforms of the *decennio* have recently attracted considerable attention. For recent discussions, see P. Villani, 'Il decennio francese', in *Storia del Mezzogiorno*, 4 (Rome, 1986), A. Scirocco, *L'Italia del Risorgimento* (Bologna, 1990), 11–27, and J. A. Davis, 'The Napoleonic Era in Southern Italy: An Ambiguous Legacy?', *Proceedings of the British Academy*, 80 (1993), 133–48.

[2] R. Romeo, 'Momenti e problemi della restaurazione nel regno delle Due Sicilie (1815–1820)', in *Mezzogiorno e Sicilia nel Risorgimento* (Naples, 1963), 51–69.

Thus, in common with other Restoration rulers in Italy, the Bourbon monarchy attempted after 1815 to create a modernized form of absolutism.[3] The most far-reaching of these reforms were of an administrative nature. All of the territories of the Two Sicilies were divided into provinces with identical administrative and judicial structures. Each province was ruled by an intendant (*intendente*) who was appointed by central government. The intendant was assisted by a substantial staff, which included secretaries with specific portfolios and provincial councillors elected by the wealthiest members of the province. Each province was, in turn, divided into districts, under the administrative control of a sub-intendant, and communes, presided over by a mayor. The mayor was appointed by the intendant; he was usually a local man, and was assisted by a local bureaucracy and by an elected council.[4] Responsibility for compiling the list of electors rested with the intendant and sub-intendants; property-ownership was the main criterion for eligibility.[5] Judicial and police powers were also increasingly controlled by the centre. Although local interests were represented through the system of elected councils, all significant powers of decision and execution were confined to central government and its representatives.

It was with regard to Sicily that the Bourbons' newly acquired modernizing zeal found its most dramatic expression. Yet it was also in Sicily that this process provoked the fiercest opposition. Sicily had a long and jealously guarded tradition of political and administrative autonomy. At the end of the eighteenth century the Sicilian nobility had managed largely to frustrate attempts by the Sicilian Viceroy Marchese Caracciolo to abolish noble privileges and establish more direct rule from Naples.[6] Furthermore, Sicily had largely escaped the political, judicial, and administrative upheavals of the revolutionary

[3] For a useful comparison with similar policies pursued in Austria's Italian provinces, see M. Meriggi, *Il regno Lombardo-Veneto* (Turin, 1987) and the same author's earlier *Amministrazione e classi sociale nel Lombardo-Veneto* (Bologna, 1983). There is also a good discussion of Restoration reform in B. Montale, *Parma nel Risorgimento: istituzione e società (1814–1859)* (Milan, 1993), and of the police reforms of de' Medici's counterpart in the Papal States, Cardinal Consalvi, in S. C. Hughes, *Crime, Disorder and the Risorgimento: The Politics of Policing in Bologna* (Cambridge, 1994).

[4] G. Candeloro, *Storia dell'Italia moderna, ii: dalla restaurazione alla rivoluzione nazionale* (Milan, 1958), 64–5; Scirocco, *L'Italia del Risorgimento*, 40, 45–6, 49.

[5] G. Giarrizzo, 'La Sicilia dal Cinquecento all'unità d'Italia', in V. d'Alessandro and G. Giarrizzo, *La Sicilia dal vespro all'unità d'Italia* (Turin, 1989), 670–1.

[6] On the reforms of the Marchese Caracciolo, see F. Renda, *Baroni e riformatori sotto il ministero Caracciolo (1786–1789)* (Messina, 1974) and E. Pontieri, *Il riformismo borbonico nella Sicilia* (Rome, 1945).

period. Between 1805 and 1815 the island had been occupied by the British army, and the Bourbon royal family had taken refuge there. The British had actually affirmed Sicily's traditional autonomy: in 1812 the Sicilian parliament of nobles was re-convened and a separate Sicilian constitution promulgated.[7]

After 1815 Bourbon policy aimed to eradicate this long tradition of Sicilian separatism. Gaetano Cingari writes that de' Medici's policy towards Sicily was guided by three basic principles: anti-constitutionalism, anti-separatism, and hostility to the nobility.[8] All three principles reaffirmed the importance of centralization and administrative uniformity. As de' Medici wrote, 'the political union with Sicily is the only policy which we must pursue with every effort. We must make whatever sacrifice is necessary for Sicily to achieve this aim: but there must be a single government.'[9] In 1816, Ferdinando I abolished the Sicilian constitution and established direct rule from Naples. Palermo lost much of its importance as a separate administrative capital, as well as its monopoly of the courts and most of its privileges as a free port. Between 1816 and 1820, in a series of decrees, the Bourbon government integrated the administration of Sicily into the new, uniform, and centralized system based in Naples; the new judicial and financial structures of the Bourbon kingdom were also extended to Sicily. By a decree of October 1817, Sicily was divided for administrative purposes into twenty-three districts under the control of seven provincial intendants.[10]

In an image which has endured to this day, liberal opposition in Palermo depicted Bourbon government as corrupt, reactionary, and oppressive. The reality was, however, more complex. Depending on whose influence prevailed in Naples, Bourbon policy towards Sicily

---

[7] On this period, see J. Rosselli, *Lord William Bentinck and the British Occupation of Sicily* (Cambridge, 1956).

[8] G. Cingari, 'Gli ultimi Borboni: dalla restaurazione all'unità', in *Storia della Sicilia*, 8 (Naples, 1977), 5.

[9] Quoted in Romeo, 'Momenti e problemi della restaurazione', 89.

[10] The new provinces (often called *valli* in official records) were Palermo (districts of Palermo, Cefalù, Corleone, Termini), Messina (Messina, Castroreale, Mistretta, Patti), Catania (Catania, Caltagirone, Nicosia), Girgenti (Girgenti, Bivona, Sciacca), Siracusa (Siracusa, Modica, Noto), Trapani (Trapani, Alcamo, Mazara), and Caltanissetta (Caltanissetta, Piazza, Terranova). See Giarrizzo, 'La Sicilia dal Cinquecento all'unità d'Italia', 667. For a more detailed analysis of the administrative changes introduced in 1817 see E. Iachello, 'Centralisation étatique et pouvoir local en Sicile au xixe siècle', *Annales, Histoire, Sciences Sociales*, 1 (1994), 241–66 and 'La trasformazione degli apparati periferici dello stato nel xixe secolo: la riforma amministrativa del 1817', in F. Benigno and C. Torrisi (eds.), *Élites e potere in Sicilia dal medioevo ad oggi* (Rome, 1995).

made a series of shifts between reaction and modernization (represented in the early Restoration in the rival views of de' Medici and Canosa). In administrative policy, the government oscillated between granting greater or lesser political autonomy to Sicily. The revolutions of 1820, 1837, and 1848–9 were all followed by a period of repression. Yet for a period in both the 1820s and 1830s the central government also set up an additional administrative body, albeit with limited responsibility, for Sicilian affairs. During the early 1830s the new king, Ferdinando II, introduced a number of administrative, economic and infrastructural reforms intended to improve relations between Naples and Sicily, a programme which was quickly abandoned when a severe outbreak of cholera in 1837 led to a number of uprisings in Siracusa and other Sicilian cities. Thereafter Ferdinando concentrated on enhancing central government's control over Sicily and improving the way in which the island was policed. During the decade prior to the outbreak of revolution in 1848 Bourbon policy further confirmed the end of Sicily's separate status within the Bourbon kingdom.[11]

If there was a single consistent strand to Bourbon policy in Sicily during the period 1815 to 1848 it was to attack noble privilege. The abolition of feudalism (ordered by the Sicilian parliament in 1812) was confirmed in two additional laws (of 1818 and 1824) eradicating feudal entails and customary rights, and implementing other measures intended to create a new class of non-noble landowners in the countryside.[12] Like their eighteenth-century 'Enlightened' predecessor, the Marchese Caracciolo, both de' Medici and Ferdinando II saw the Sicilian nobility as the enemy of progress and modernization in the island. De' Medici had also developed an intense personal dislike of the Sicilian nobility and the whole system of *baronaggio* whilst in exile in Sicily with the Bourbon royal family.[13] The Sicilian nobility was not, in his view, interested in 'the happiness of Sicily' ('the good of Sicily is closer to my heart than to all Sicilians');[14] he felt that the Sicilian nobility was interested only in maintaining their privileged relationship with Naples, and was directly responsible for the island's poverty and economic backwardness. De' Medici also anticipated that the nobility would use their hold over the local political system to frustrate his reforming initiatives. It was for this reason that he gave substantial

[11] Giarrizzo, 'La Sicilia dal Cinquecento all'unità d'Italia', 692–708, 720–33, Scirocco, *L'Italia del Risorgimento*, 152–3, and Cingari, 'Gli ultimi Borboni', 28–31.

[12] Candeloro, *Storia dell'Italia moderna*, ii. 66–8.

[13] Romeo, 'Momenti e problemi della restaurazione', 94.   [14] Ibid. 89.

powers over local government to the provincial intendants. Administrative centralization was thus the means and the end of de' Medici's policy in Sicily.[15] Together with a process of economic modernization, administrative centralization would be, he hoped, both the means of destroying the traditional, feudal authority of the nobility and of replacing it with the enlightened rule of a modern state.

De' Medici's assessment of how the Sicilian nobility would react to his policy was largely accurate. The solution he proposed, however, was fundamentally flawed. Like many of his contemporaries in Restoration Italy, de' Medici was unable to adapt to the different requirements of post-Napoleonic politics; he was, in Luigi Blanch's words, 'a better statesman than politician'.[16] De' Medici seems never to have appreciated the overriding necessity of securing goodwill and support for the sweeping administrative changes he proposed. On the one hand political reactionaries, led by the powerful Prince Canosa, strongly opposed de' Medici's reforms and, after 1820, succeeded in reversing many of them. On the other hand, the anti-constitutional stance of both de' Medici and his successors alienated liberal sources of support.[17] During the 1820s and 1830s, a powerful—and eloquent—movement for Sicilian autonomy developed, led by the nobility and wealthy bourgeoisie. Carbonarist conspiracies and, later, Mazzinian insurrectionary movements also contributed to a growing climate of political hostility to the Bourbons in Sicily.

Romeo attributes the survival of the Bourbon monarchy until the final crisis of 1860 to the weakness of its enemies.[18] The real significance of the Sicilian opposition movement, for Romeo, was intellectual and cultural rather than political. Sicilian autonomists asserted a separate Sicilian identity (sometimes referring to its classical heritage, sometimes to the assertion of autonomy in the medieval period), primarily against the corrupting influence of Naples.[19] Yet, as we shall see in the following chapters, the Sicilian opposition was unable to agree about a future form of government or about important aspects of social and economic policy. In this respect, de' Medici's main mistake was not to

[15] Romeo, 'Momenti e problemi della restaurazione', 92–3.
[16] L. Blanch, 'Luigi de' Medici come uomo di stato e amministratore', in *Scritti Storici,* ii: *il regno di Napoli dalla restaurazione borbonica all'avvento di Re Ferdinando II (1815–1830)* (Bari, 1945), 119.
[17] On the difficulties of navigating between the extremes of Right and Left, see M. Broers, *Europe after Napoleon: Revolution, Reaction and Romanticism, 1814–1848* (Manchester, 1996), 15–18.   [18] Romeo, 'Momenti e problemi della restaurazione', 113.
[19] R. Romeo, *Il Risorgimento in Sicilia* (Bari, 1950), 257–90.

look beyond the barons. By not seeking the support of the new middle classes, particularly in those cities outside Palermo (particularly Messina and Catania) which were developing economically and which had always opposed the baronial privileges of Palermo, he failed to win over those potentially most attracted by his programme of economic modernization.[20] Fearing Sicilian separatism and aristocratic reaction, he opposed constitutional reform which might also have provided the basis for middle-class support in Sicily. In addition, de' Medici and his successors were hampered by serious financial constraints and by a series of economic crises, notably in 1816–17.[21] Economic problems meant that they were unable significantly to broaden the popular basis for Bourbon rule. By introducing higher taxation and by attempting to bring in military conscription, the government actually became extremely unpopular among both the urban and rural poor.[22]

In the words of Luigi Blanch again, the Bourbon government found itself 'unloved by those who looked to the future and unloved by those who clung to the past'.[23] Bourbon attempts at modernization destroyed the legitimacy of the Bourbon monarchy, but failed to establish a new legitimacy for the Bourbon state. Like his counterpart in the Papal States, Cardinal Consalvi, de' Medici found that political modernization was a double-edged sword. The government gave itself the appearance of greater power, but at the price of greater responsibility; as Hughes argues of Consalvi's reforms, administrative centralization 'centralized responsibility' for the administrative system, and centralized the blame if the system did not work properly.[24] In Sicily (and in parts of the mainland as well) the system did not work at all as envisaged. The implementation of a reform programme was hampered by immense practical difficulties. Particularly in the remote districts of the Sicilian interior, central government often lacked the financial and administrative resources to train and/or to employ an efficient, loyal bureaucratic staff in sufficient numbers to help its provincial administrators. Poor communications and the isolation of rural communities also gave tremendous power to local élites with an intimate knowledge of the area,

[20] Romeo, 'Momenti e problemi della restaurazione', 94. De Francesco argues that initially many Sicilian democrats supported the administrative reforms, precisely because it was seen as a way of undermining the power of the barons. A. de Francesco, 'Cultura costituzionale e potere politico', in Benigno and Torrisi (eds.), *Élites e potere in Sicilia*, 131.

[21] Giarrizzo, 'La Sicilia dal Cinquecento all'unità d'Italia', 672–5, 698–708.

[22] Cingari, 'Gli ultimi Borboni', 10–11.   [23] Blanch, *Scritti Storici*, ii. 111.

[24] Hughes, *Crime, Disorder and the Risorgimento*, 3.

and it hindered the provincial intendants whose power came from outside the communes.

Such practical problems meant that the intendant, for all his nominal control over a province, was in practice dependent on the willingness of local élites to implement government policy. Unfortunately, in some areas the new administrative system was very unpopular—or, at best, ignored—so that this support could rarely be relied upon. Enrica di Ciommo writes, of the process of administrative modernization on the mainland, that it 'drastically reduced traditional rights, autonomies and prerogatives which had been established for a long time'.[25] Spagnoletti writes that, in peripheral provinces of the mainland, the process provoked a deluge of petitions and complaints.[26] In Sicily the impact of these reforms was probably even more drastic. Local representatives of the old nobility were angered by the loss of their fiscal powers and privileges. Magistrates were irritated by the appropriation of their judicial powers by the centre. By depriving local communities of many of their administrative, judicial, and fiscal powers, the central government affected important, and entrenched, economic interests.

In this way the provincial intendant, the main symbol of the Bourbon government's zeal for modernization in Sicily, also became a symbol of its unpopularity. According to one study of a commune in Sicily's southern interior, the provincial intendant lacked either enough bureaucratic leverage or a sufficient level of local support to carry out the administrative functions assigned to him by Naples.[27] Since he was the state representative for the province, he was also offically prevented from manipulating the more informal relations of power. What influence he managed to establish was derived from his ability to mediate in the quarrels and factional rivalry which, as we shall see, often divided Sicilian rural communities. Thus, as the new administrative system adapted to these conditions and as the rural communities adapted to the new system, the intendant also became a symbol of central government's weakness in the face of local power.[28] For the first time after

[25] E. di Ciommo, 'Élites provinciali e potere borbonico: note per una ricerca comparata', in A. Massafra (ed.), *Il Mezzogiorno preunitario: economia, società, istituzioni* (Bari, 1988), 967.
[26] A. Spagnoletti, 'Centri e periferie nello stato napoletano del primo ottocento', ibid.
[27] P. Pezzino, 'Monarchia amministrativa ed élites locali: Naro nella prima metà dell'ottocento', in *Il paradiso abitato dai diavoli: società, élites, istituzioni nel Mezzogiorno contemporaneo* (Milan, 1992), 134.
[28] This was also the case on the Southern mainland. See Spagnoletti, 'Centro e periferie nello stato napoletano', 390.

1815, central power in Naples took responsibility for controlling the Sicilian countryside. If anything, this shift of responsibility led to it losing what little leverage it had hitherto possessed.

II

The countryside was in many respects the mainstay of the Sicilian economy in the early nineteenth century. Within the countryside, there was a great variety in systems of agriculture, levels of commercialization, forms of land tenure, and social structure. Sicily was historically divided into an Eastern and a Western region, separated by the river Salso; and this distinction persisted as a cultural perception well into the nineteenth century. Until the reforms of the early Restoration, Sicily was also divided for administrative purposes into three *valli* (val di Mazara, val Demone, and val di Noto) which, over time, had developed distinct political and economic characteristics.[29] By the nineteenth century a further regional distinction had emerged, between the commercialized, mixed agriculture of the coastal plains and foothills, and the extensive grain monoculture of the area Giarrizzo calls 'African Sicily'—the arid uplands of the Central and Western interior.[30]

Undoubtedly the most visible signs of economic growth were to be found in the vineyards and orchards of the coastal plains and foothills. In many cases substantial investment had resulted in the development of new production methods and the opening of new export markets. During the British occupation of Sicily in the Napoleonic wars, a group of English entrepreneurs established a substantial wine industry in Marsala, near Trapani.[31] On the plain of Catania and in the famous *conca d'oro* ('golden shell') region around Palermo, the cultivation of citrus fruits for export markets also increased enormously during this period. By the 1830s wine was Sicily's second largest export, at 16.7 per cent of total exports, while citrus fruits and dried fruits together represented 18.2 per cent.[32]

[29] For a useful summary, see S. R. Epstein, *An Island for Itself: Economic Development and Social Change in Late Medieval Sicily* (Cambridge, 1992), 25–33.

[30] Giarrizzo, 'La Sicilia dal Cinquecento all'unità d'Italia', 611.

[31] R. Trevelyan, *Princes under the Volcano* (London, 1972). Not all the investment was foreign; the famous Florio dynasty had its origins in the wine industry. See S. Candela, *I Florio* (Palermo, 1986), M. d'Angelo, 'Vincenzo Florio, mercante-imprenditore', in Massafra (ed.), *Il Mezzogiorno preunitario*.

[32] These figures are given in Romeo, *Il Risorgimento in Sicilia*, 214–15. On citrus-fruit production in Sicily, see S. Lupo, *Il giardino degli aranci: il mondo degli agrumi nella storia del Mezzogiorno* (Venice, 1990).

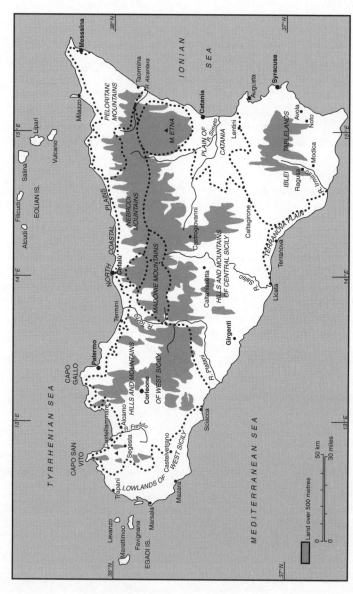

MAP 1. Geographic Divisions of Sicily (adapted from S. R. Epstein, *An Island for Itself: Economic Development and Social Change in Late Medieval Sicily*, Cambridge, 1992, 28)

In the coastal regions and, more generally, in the Eastern provinces of Messina, Catania, and Siracusa/Noto, the landholdings tended to be considerably smaller and more commercially oriented than elsewhere. Peasant ownership of land (often on fixed-rent leases or *enfiteusi*), if not particularly widespread, was much more common here than in the interior. The growth in size and wealth, during the nineteenth century, of cities like Trapani and Catania was also based largely on the production for export of vines and citrus fruits in the nearby countryside. Although silk-manufacturing in Messina and Catania had been affected by foreign competition and was in decline, a fairly substantial mercantile and entrepreneurial class began to make its presence felt in these cities during the early decades of the nineteenth century.[33]

By contrast, in Sicily's capital, Palermo, there was much less evidence of economic growth or of social diversification. In this way the traditional political rivalry between Palermo and Messina (and, increasingly in the nineteenth century, Catania) was intensified by a growing sense of economic difference. In Palermo the Sicilian nobility continued to live lives of sophistication and ostentation based on the rent from their landed estates in the interior.[34] For Goethe, who came to Palermo in 1787, the city was a 'paradise' and its public gardens 'enchanted'.[35] Palermo, according to an English naval officer visiting in 1824, still offered a 'picture of incomparable beauty' filled with 'gaiety and animation'.[36] Yet by the nineteenth century (and arguably before) the wealth of Palermo had begun to decline: its economy was particularly badly hit by the reduction of its role as an administrative capital after 1815. Palermo's decline as an administrative centre affected the nobility and the large number of middle-class professionals formerly employed in

---

[33] There were some large factories associated with the influx of foreign capital which existed alongside much smaller workshops. On the substantial silk manufacturing industry which existed in north-eastern Sicily until the mid-nineteenth century, see S. Laudani, *La Sicilia della seta: economia, società e politica* (Rome, 1996), Romeo, *Il Risorgimento in Sicilia*, and O. Cancila, *Storia dell'industria in Sicilia* (Rome and Bari, 1995), 73–7, 87–95. On the growth of commercial élites in Messina see R. Battaglia, *Mercanti e imprenditori in una città maritima: il caso di Messina (1850–1900)* (Milan, 1992); in Trapani, see F. Benigno, 'Fra mare e terra: orizzonte economico e mutamento sociale in una città meridionale: Trapani nella prima metà dell'Ottocento'; and in Sicily as a whole, see R. Battaglia, 'Qualità e trasformazione del ceto mercantile siciliano a metà dell'Ottocento': both in Massafra (ed.), *Il Mezzogiorno preunitario*.

[34] For a description see O. Cancila, *Palermo* (Rome and Bari, 1988), 9–18.

[35] J. W. Goethe, *Italian Journey*, trans. W. H. Auden and E. Mayer (London, 1962), 236, 258.

[36] *Travels through Sicily and the Lipari Islands in the Month of December 1824 by a Naval Officer* (London, 1827), 159.

the government administration.[37] Although a growing number of rich (sometimes foreign) merchants and entrepreneurs came to live in Palermo during this period, their numbers remained relatively modest, and their impact was cultural rather than economic.[38] Efforts were made, particularly after the 1848 revolution, to improve the urban environment of Palermo through the construction of new public gardens and wide boulevards. Although these plans were partly success-ful—the rich began to move northward towards Monte Pellegrino into smart new suburbs—these changes also led to the gradual degradation of the older quarters in the centre of the city.[39] In these quarters, close to some of the most splendid seventeenth- and eighteenth-century *palazzi* in the whole of Europe, there grew up some of the worst nineteenth-century slums.

Pontieri describes Palermo as 'a nineteenth-century feudal city, a city in which 40,000 proletarians lived, whose livelihood was dependent on the whims and wishes of the great'.[40] After 1815, Palermo's artisans, simultaneously affected by government attempts to abolish their guilds, were particularly harmed by the rapid fall in demand for luxury goods and services by the élite of the city. The slums of Palermo, in the Albergheria and Kalsa quarters of the city, also appalled visitors. For one observer, even more remarkable than 'the grimness of the sur-roundings . . . from which there is no escape except through vice and sin, is the wretched, miserable and emaciated condition of most of the population to be seen swarming through filthy courtyards'.[41] The slums of Palermo also had a fearsome reputation for their high levels of violent crime and for their low standards of 'morality'. In Palermo, rates of infant mortality and illegitimate births (both important indices of pov-erty) were much higher than in the cities of Northern Europe: illegi-timate births reached a high point during the cholera epidemic of 1837, at some 16.8 per cent of all births. The average life expectancy was 32

---

[37] A sense of the importance of government bureaucracy as a source of employment in Palermo can be gained from comparing the electoral lists for Palermo and Catania: in 1851, some 39.7 per cent of those registered to vote in Palermo were public employers and 26.6 per cent were professional; only 13.9 per cent of voters in Catania were public employees. These figures are given in E. Iachello and A. Signorelli, 'Borghesie urbane dell'Ottocento', in M. Aymard and G. Giarrizzo (eds.), *La Sicilia* (Turin, 1987), 120–1.

[38] Cancila, *Palermo*, 18–29.

[39] C. di Seta and L. di Mauro, *Palermo* (Bari, 1981), 156.

[40] E. Pontieri, *Il riformismo borbonico nella Sicilia* (Rome, 1945), 224.

[41] Quoted in F. Brancato, *La Sicilia nel primo ventennio del regno d'Italia* (Bologna, 1956), 64.

years, compared to over 40 years in England, France, and Switzerland.[42] Palermo was by no means alone in being affected by cholera epidemics (in 1837 and 1854), but the slow growth of its population in this period was matched only by Rome.[43] Increasingly, according to Cancila, there grew up in Palermo 'next to the nobility . . . a mass of wretched and under-employed people who were always at the heart of every revolt'.[44]

Although the wealth of economically expanding cities like Trapani and Catania was partly due to relations with a rich agrarian hinterland, this was much less the case in Palermo. Elsewhere, and most notably in the grain-producing interior, the isolation between city and countryside was striking. Despite the rapid expansion of sulphur-mining (with a virtual world monopoly, sulphur was Sicily's largest single export)[45] in the Central and Southern interior, even by the mid-nineteenth century the mining and export of sulphur had failed to transform the hitherto impoverished cities of Caltanissetta and Girgenti (Agrigento) into significant commercial centres.

The Sicilian sulphur-mining industry was particularly hampered by poor transport facilities and by backward technology. Efforts made by the Bourbon government in the 1830s to break the hold of English merchants over its export and trade and to develop a chemical industry in Sicily also came to nothing.[46] Problems of extraction and transport meant that the first sulphur to be extracted was from smaller mines near Girgenti, where the sulphur was easier to extract and the mines closer to the sea (although Girgenti itself lacked a proper port). There were much richer mines near Caltanissetta, which began to be exploited during the 1840s and 1850s. However, only after unification, and once the Catania–Caltanissetta–Girgenti railway was completed, was it possible to extract the sulphur on a much larger scale and with greater efficiency.[47] Conditions in the mines themselves were harsh even by the standards of the early nineteenth century. They were also extremely hazardous and, it was suggested, injurious to personal morality (workers stripped naked due to the extreme heat). Workers

---

[42] Cancila, *Palermo*, 52.   [43] Ibid. 5.   [44] Ibid. 51.

[45] In 1815 there were 15 sulphur mines in Sicily; by 1850 this had increased to 196. Even more impressive was the increase in tonnage exported, rising from 38,136 tons in 1833 to 77,814 only 5 years later. J. A. Davis, 'Palmerston and the Sicilian Sulphur Crisis of 1840: An Episode in the Imperialism of Free Trade', *Risorgimento*, 1/2 (1982), 8.

[46] Ibid. 5–10; D. W. Thomson, 'Prelude to the Sulphur War of 1840: The Neapolitan Perspective', *European History Quarterly*, 25 (1995), 163–80.

[47] G. Canciullo, 'Ferrovie e commercio zolfifero', in G. Barone and C. Torrisi (eds.), *Economia e società nell'area dello zolfo* (Caltanissetta and Rome, 1989).

suffered severe health problems from the pollution produced by the sulphur.[48] However, a recent study of conditions in the sulphur mines has suggested that the workforce (by 1860 some 16,000 individuals) enjoyed a better standard of living than their peasant counterparts: they had a higher income, ate meat more regularly, and enjoyed more leisure time.[49]

The technical and geographical problems confronting the sulphur-mining industry reflect what were more general obstacles to the economic development of the Sicilian interior during this period. Above all, the absence of internal communications was a feature of Sicily which travellers constantly complained of.[50] In 1860 Sicily had only 618 kilometres of trunk roads, 1,390 of provincial roads, and 460 of local roads. The figure for local roads is especially significant in that it suggests the extent to which smaller rural communities were cut off from any contact with each other or the outside world. Particularly in the interior, communications between communities and with the surrounding countryside were extremely scarce.[51] The few roads that did exist were in a poor state of repair; the hilly terrain of the interior and the problem of flooding in bad weather further compounded the problems of communication. Even the journey between Palermo and Girgenti could take two days; Mack Smith writes that as late as 1860 it still involved fording a river in bad weather.[52] There were no railways in Sicily until after unification.

The isolation of the interior was also reflected in the pattern of settlement. 'In Sicily,' de Tocqueville wrote in 1827:

there are no villages, there are only towns and these are even quite substantial. Having travelled in almost total solitude for about eight or ten leagues it is quite startling suddenly to enter a town of twenty thousand souls.[53]

Only in the market-gardening zones of the East, and in similar zones of the provinces of Trapani and Palermo, did the population live

---

[48] Cancila, *Storia dell'industria in Sicilia*, 25.

[49] Peter Schneider, interviewed in 'Changes in Rural Society: Piedmont and Sicily', BBC Open University, 1996. The figures are given in F. Renda, *Storia della Sicilia dal 1860 al 1970*, i (Palermo, 1984), 103.

[50] Goethe gives a fearsome description of leaving the major town of Castrogiovanni (Enna) by a tiny and steep path, so steep that they had to dismount and lead their mules. Goethe, *Italian Journey*, 242.   [51] Renda, *Storia della Sicilia*, 240.

[52] D. Mack Smith, *A History of Sicily, ii: Modern Sicily after 1713* (London, 1968), 474.

[53] A. de Tocqueville, *Voyages en Sicile et aux États Unis*, quoted in Giarrizzo, 'La Sicilia dal Cinquecento all'unità d'Italia', 686.

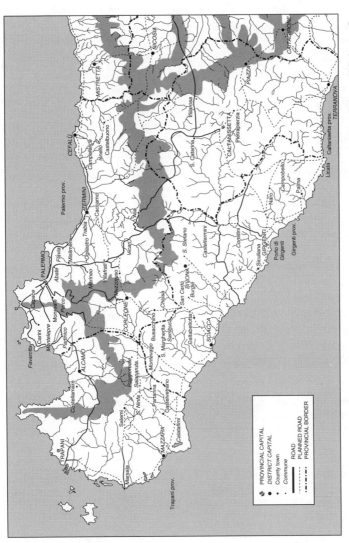

MAP 2. Western and Central Sicily *c.*1840: Administrative Divisions, Communications (Archivio di Stato di Palermo, Luogotenente Generale, Lavori Pubblici, Piante Topografiche, progetti ecc, nn. 270, 271)

permanently in the countryside. In the West and Central regions of the Sicilian interior people lived instead in large, nucleated settlements known as *paesi* (or 'agrotowns', as they are now called by anthropologists).[54] The surrounding countryside, as de Tocqueville testified, appeared almost entirely devoid of human habitation. Although, during the harvests, men would leave their homes and spend weeks working in the fields, sleeping in either isolated *masserie* (large farmhouses) or temporary straw huts, they never brought their families with them. Women seem rarely to have worked in the fields, or ever to have left town at all. As Giarrizzo writes of Biancavilla, outside feast and market days Sicilian rural towns could be 'sleepy' and 'dull' (*poco animata*); women and the occasional lawyer or notary appeared to be the only full-time inhabitants.[55]

The Tuscan reformer Leopoldo Franchetti, visiting the Sicilian interior in the early 1870s, described it as a 'vast desert' where 'neither tree nor house breaks up the monotonous desolation of solitude'.[56] His companion, Sidney Sonnino, noted that the land was given over entirely to 'the cultivation of grain . . . alternated with natural pasture and early hay . . . [with] no cultivation of trees and fruit bushes'.[57] During the rainy seasons the problem of soil erosion due to water run-off was dramatic; while during the long, hot summer, water shortages were equally acute. This remarkable landscape was largely man-made. Starting in the sixteenth century, the formerly wooded uplands of the Sicilian interior were gradually 'colonized'—with devastating ecological consequences—for the purposes of grain-cultivation. The *paesi* or agrotowns had also been established at this time, largely to house agricultural labourers mostly brought in from the coast (but sometimes from overseas) to work on the vast grain-estates.[58]

In Lampedusa's celebrated novel about the declining Sicilian nobility,

[54] Iachello and Signorelli, 'Borghesie urbane dell'Ottocento', 94. For a definition of an 'agro-town' see A. Blok, 'South Italian Agro-Towns', *Comparative Studies in Society and History*, 11 (1969), 121–35.

[55] G. Giarrizzo, *Un comune rurale nella Sicilia etnea (Biancavilla 1810–1860)* (Catania, 1963), 17.

[56] L. Franchetti, *Condizioni politiche e amministrative della Sicilia* (1876; Rome, 1993 edn.), 22–3.

[57] S. Sonnino, 'I contadini in Sicilia', in L. Franchetti and S. Sonnino, *Inchiesta in Sicilia* (1876; Florence, 1974 edn.), 410.

[58] On the expansion of grain-cultivation in the interior during this period see O. Cancila, *Barone e popolo nella Sicilia del grano* (Palermo, 1983). On demographic changes see F. Benigno, 'Aspetti territoriali e ruralizzazione nella Sicilia del Seicento: note per una discussione', in *La popolazione della campagne italiane in età moderna* (Bologna, 1993).

The Leopard, the Salina family leaves Palermo in the height of summer to visit the family estate at Donnafugata in the *latifondo*—'the real Sicily . . . the one compared to which baroque towns and orange groves are mere trifles.'[59] Their journey lasts more than three days through a blazing landscape: 'never a tree, never a drop of water: just sun and dust'.[60] Like Lampedusa's fictional family, the noble élites of Palermo undertook the arduous journey to visit their estates only once or twice a year. And although the visits to Donnafugata gave Don Fabrizio Salina a sense of 'everlasting childhood', most Sicilian nobles spurned what they saw as the ignorance and isolation of rural life.[61] Even in the early nineteenth century the towns and the system of agriculture in the Sicilian interior still reflected the process of colonization which had taken place two centuries before. The empty, arid, roadless countryside of the Sicilian interior constituted a vast natural barrier which isolated the latifundist communities both from the outside world and from each other. Sicily was an urban society in a rural setting. The countryside was a source of wealth; but it was left largely to itself.

According to one estimate, 82 per cent of the island's agricultural land in this period was used either for cereal cultivation or for pasture.[62] Yet ownership of the *latifondo* was traditionally confined to a small, privileged élite made up largely of the nobility and the Church. Their landholdings were often extraordinarily extensive. Although exact figures for the size of landholdings in the period before unification are not available, contemporary descriptions testify to their vastness. Sidney Sonnino estimated in 1876 that most estates were between 500 and 1,000 hectares in size, and that some covered more than 6,000 hectares. It is likely that these estates were larger still at the beginning of the century.[63] 'Travelling through Sicily,' the agricultural reformer Paolo Balsamo wrote in a study published in 1845, 'one invariably goes from one *feudo* to another, that is, from the land of one large landowner to that of another.'[64] Landowners were absentees, living, as we have seen, in the cities. They relied on *gabelloti* (rent-collectors) and other agents (shepherds, carters, and field-guards) to manage their estates and gather rents from peasant families. During sowing and

[59] T. di Lampedusa, *The Leopard*, trans. A. Colquhoun (London, 1960), 124.
[60] Ibid. 66.   [61] Ibid. 74.   [62] Renda, *Storia della Sicilia*, 93.
[63] Sonnino, 'I contadini in Sicilia', 24. There is a useful description of landholdings in the *latifondo* in A. Blok, *The Mafia of a Sicilian Village: A Study of Violent Peasant Entrepreneurs* (Oxford, 1974), 58–84.
[64] P. Balsamo, *Memorie inedite di pubblica economia ed agricoltura* (Palermo, 1845), 190.

harvest the *gabelloti* would base themselves in large farmhouses in the countryside; this gave them control over the workforce and over access to markets and to supplies. Over the years, these *gabelloti* had become enormously powerful figures in latifundist communities, largely as a result of acting as middlemen between the noble landowner and his far-away estates.[65] By contrast, and particularly by the early years of the nineteenth century, the noble landlords had begun to lose their grip on the countryside, as mounting debts undermined their economic power.

The cultivation of the *latifondo* required the use of a large labour force, but only at certain times of the year, during sowing and the harvest. Although the bulk of most peasants' income came from working as labourers in the grain fields, almost all of them also rented or owned tiny plots of land (of between less than one hectare to four or five hectares). They also had access to grazing rights on common land. A variety of contracts were made between the peasant and the landlord: peasants could be sharecroppers, tenants-in-kind, or simply day-labourers (and were sometimes all three).[66] However, what all these contracts reflected was the need of the landlord (or, more accurately, his *gabelloto*) to keep a tight control over the labour force so that enough men would be available to bring in the harvest.[67] For the most part, the wages given to the peasants were insufficient to sustain a family through the year. The peasants' own rented holdings were rarely large enough to be economically viable; and the peasants also lacked either the technical knowledge or the means to increase productivity.

One contemporary reformer, the marchese Francesco Accordino, compared the Sicilian peasantry to 'the savages of New Holland and the poorest natives of North America, without clothes, without houses . . . without any resources to protect them from famine'.[68] Most peasants were heavily reliant on loans to sustain them from one harvest to the next. These loans were usually obtained at a high interest from a local *gabelloto*, a situation which left them chronically in debt and, in effect, subservient to the *gabelloti*. 'The Sicilian peasant,' Sidney Sonnino commented in 1876, 'is sober, industrious and works hard'; but, he

[65] For an analysis of the importance of these men, often linked to another powerful figure, that of the *mafioso*, see Blok, *The Mafia of a Sicilian Village*, 32–4, and J. Schneider and P. Schneider, *Culture and Political Economy in Western Sicily* (New York, 1976), 66–72.

[66] Ibid. 59.

[67] M. Verga, 'Il "Settecento del baronaggio": l'aristocrazia siciliana tra politica e cultura', in Benigno and Torrisi (eds.), *Élites e potere in Sicilia*, 93–4.

[68] Quoted in F. della Peruta, 'La conoscenza dell'Italia reale alla vigilia dell'unità', in *Realtà e mito nell'Italia dell'Ottocento* (Milan, 1996), 74.

continued, 'usury makes it impossible for the Sicilian peasant to save anything, to improve his position in any way'.[69] This unequal situation also increased the demand for—and conflict over—land, as peasants saw the acquisition of land as the only means of improving their lot.

III

To outsiders, the rural communities of early-nineteenth-century Western Sicily, and the deserted grain-fields which surrounded them, may well have appeared timeless and unchanging. In reality, nothing could have been further from the truth. A series of rapid changes had begun to affect the *latifondo* by the early nineteenth century. Pressure on pastoral land from grain-farming was considerable and growing. This was partly due to an increase in Sicily's population, which grew by some 19 per cent between 1814 and 1861. Declining yields caused by soil erosion also created an increasing demand for good arable land which, in turn, gave rise to widespread conflict over land-usage between herdsmen and arable farmers.[70] Conflict over land was also affected by sulphur-mining. Although sulphur-mining was hugely profitable, the levels of pollution which it produced were so high as to make the presence of mines incompatible with any kind of agricultural activity. This too increased tensions over land-usage.[71]

Perhaps most of all, the *latifondo* was affected by the abolition of feudalism by the Sicilian parliament in 1812. As we have seen, this legislation was followed by a series of additional laws relating to property and its inheritance, the most important of which abolished primogeniture (1818) and which released property from restrictions on sale (1824).[72] Taken together, and given the indebtedness of many noble landowners, these laws transformed the nature of land-ownership in the Western Sicilian *latifondo*. Instead of landholdings taking the form of feudal tenure with attendant rights and obligations, estates now

---

[69] 'I contadini in Sicilia', 104, 107.

[70] Schneider and Schneider, *Culture and Political Economy in Western Sicily*, 65–6, 140–8. Much of the South was affected by the pressure from arable farmers: see J. A. Davis, *Conflict and Control: Law and Order in Nineteenth-Century Italy* (London, 1988), 43–5, and, for a detailed study of similar conflicts in Lazio in the Papal States, A. de Clementi, *Vivere nel latifondo: le comunità della campagna laziale fra '700 e '800* (Milan, 1989).

[71] On these conflicts see the comments of R. Mangiameli, 'Dalle bande alle cosche: la rappresentanza della criminalità in provincia di Caltanissetta', in Barone and Torrisi (eds.), *Economia e società nell'area dello zolfo.*

[72] O. Cancila, 'Dal feudo alla proprietà borghese: la distribuzione della terra', in *L'economia della Sicilia: aspetti storici* (Palermo, 1992), 107–18.

assumed the status of 'unfettered private property' which the owner
could use and dispose of as he saw fit.[73] This conversion of feudal land
to private property was accompanied by the abolition in 1812 of customary rights (*usi civici*), such as grazing rights and access to wood and
water, which the peasantry had possessed over the estates. In 1817, the
grazing rights on common land were abolished and the division of
common land into private hands was ordered. As a result of these
laws, common land was rapidly enclosed and converted from pastoral
to arable use.

The land reforms had a devastating effect on the peasantry's economic position. Illegal 'usurpations', whereby landowners who were
keen to add to their holdings simply took *de facto* possession of common
land, worsened their position.[74] Provision had been made, in the 1817
law, for common land to be partitioned up among the peasantry; these
instructions were reaffirmed in laws of 1839 and 1841, which stated that
where proof could be established of traditional use of land, one-fifth of
the land would be given to the peasant as sole owner.[75] However, the
Bourbon government, under pressure from Sicilian ministers, was
eventually persuaded to make possession of land sufficient evidence
of title to it. In practice, this meant that the burden of proof was left to
the peasants to show that illegal usurpations had taken place.[76] Some of
the common land which was made available was simply appropriated by
powerful landowners. Conflicts developed over access to land, land
usage, and property boundaries. Communities frequently became
involved in unending litigation in attempts to determine the original
title to a piece of land and to resolve claims over the kinds of rights
which had 'traditionally' existed over it. Compensation, when ordered
by the courts, was also the subject of substantial litigation, as wildly
contrasting estimates were frequently submitted.[77]

However, although the dominance of the rural economy by large
landholdings did not diminish significantly, the reforms did have a
marked effect on social relations in the *latifondo*. Whereas, before the
abolition of feudalism, ownership of landed estates was confined to a

[73] D. Mack Smith, 'The Latifundia in Modern Sicilian History', *Proceedings of the
British Academy*, 51 (1965), 93.
[74] Cancila, 'Dal feudo alla proprietà borghese', 118–20; G. Fiume, *La crisi sociale del
1848 in Sicilia* (Messina, 1982), 121–2.
[75] Cancila, 'Dal feudo alla proprietà borghese', 118–23.
[76] Mack Smith, 'The Latifundia in Modern Sicilian History', 96.
[77] Cingari, 'Gli ultimi Borboni', 21–2.

privileged noble and clerical élite, afterwards anyone with enough money could buy into the market. The freeing of property rights was all the more significant because many nobles were heavily in debt and were very keen to sell their land to raise money. As a result, land changed hands very rapidly. By the first decades of the nineteenth century, a new class of non-noble/non-ecclesiastical landowners had emerged and had begun to take control of the *latifondo* economy.

One of the original intentions of the Bourbon programme of land reform had been to improve the economy of the *latifondo* by ending the concentration of land in very few hands. The division of common land was meant to create a new class of smallholders, thereby solving the problem of absenteeism, offering the rural poor a stake in improving the land, and, it was hoped, providing a new source of support for the Bourbon government. In the event, almost the reverse happened. The reforms above all, benefited, a growing middle or 'gentry' class.[78] A substantial number of this gentry class had acted as *gabelloti* for the old nobility, and had been the first to profit from their increasing indebtedness. They were also quick to adopt the inclinations, habits, and customs of their noble predecessors. Like the nobles before them, the gentry tended to spend their rental income on conspicuous consumption.[79] Unlike their noble predecessors, however, they tended to spend it in the latifundist communities themselves. Giarrizzo describes the 'pretensions' of the newly rich in Biancavilla. They spent huge sums on impressive houses and on extensive urban improvements such as public gardens, road-widening, and theatres.[80] This seems to have been a feature of many Sicilian rural communities: often, more money was spent on theatres and public gardens than on improving the landed estates.

The most striking element of continuity in these communities was provided by its relationship with the land. While the number of large landowners increased rapidly during this period (from an estimated 2,000 to 20,000),[81] landownership continued to provide the basis of wealth, status, and power throughout much of Sicily, in the same way that it always had done. Lawyers, merchants, and other professionals were all anxious to invest their money in the purchase of land.

---

[78] Bevilacqua, *Breve storia dell'Italia meridionale* (Rome, 1992), 5.

[79] Romeo, *Il Risorgimento in Sicilia*, 194–5.

[80] *Un comune rurale nella Sicilia etnea*, 9–15.

[81] D. Gambetta, *The Sicilian Mafia: The Business of Private Protection* (Cambridge, Mass., 1994), 91.

Effectively, the long-term result of the opening up of land for sale and purchase after 1812 was an increase in competition over landownership. In this way, the land reforms also intensified other existing rivalries within rural communities. The acquisition of land was partly achieved through marriage and the maintenance of family and kinship ties which, in the early decades of the nineteenth century, was the means by which local élites were formed throughout the South. Landholdings were accumulated through family and marriage, and this was safeguarded through a system of inheritance which was based on the male line.[82]

In 1838, the procuratore del Re in Trapani, Pietro Calà Ulloa, wrote to the king in Naples describing the factionalism of Sicilian rural communities. There were, he wrote, in many communities:

> unions or *fratellanze*, types of sects, which are called parties but without a political aim or affiliation, without meetings, without any link other than loyalty to a leader, who in one place might be a property-owner and in another an archpriest. A common fund serves their occasional needs to have a functionary exonerated at one moment . . . at another to protect an accused or, then again, to find an innocent man guilty. These are many kinds of little Governments within the Government.[83]

In the Western *latifondo*, and in the more mixed agricultural areas of the North-Eastern uplands as well, conflicts over land acquired even more importance because they were part of a broader factional struggle within rural communities. Typically, these factions were based on a powerful family (or families), whose control over territory, the market, or local government (or all three) 'gave them a considerable advantage over other social groups'.[84] Barone writes that 'family alliances and kinship relations gave "form" and stability to the political élites'.[85] In turn, rivalries over land were all the more intense because they were rooted in family and kinship structures. The Church, one of the largest landowners in Sicily (Corleo estimates that the Church owned one-tenth of agricultural land in Sicily at the time of national unification)

---

[82] P. Macry, 'Le élites urbane: stratificazione e mobilità sociale, le forme del potere locale e la cultura dei ceti emergenti', in Massafra (ed.), *Il Mezzogiorno preunitario*, 801–8.

[83] This letter is reproduced in Pontieri, *Il riformismo borbonico*, 224.

[84] Schneider and Schneider, *Culture and Political Economy in Western Sicily*, 71; and for a general discussion of the sources of power available to what they call 'rural entrepreneurs', ibid. 66–79.

[85] G. Barone, 'Dai nobili ai notabili: note sul sistema politico in Sicilia in età contemporanea', in Benigno and Torrisi (eds.), *Élites e potere in Sicilia*, 169; see also the comments of E. Iachello in 'Potere locale e mobilità delle élites a Risposto nella prima metà dell'Ottocento', in Massafra (ed.), *Il Mezzogiorno preunitario*, 918–24.

was also sometimes involved in these factional struggles.[86] Members of the 'high clergy' (with family and personal links to the Sicilian nobility) even found themselves in conflict with the 'low clergy'—local priests—who owned little land and were often very poor. The local clergy were often so poor that they were obliged to seek other employment, in the service of the commune or as *gabelloti*. On more than one occasion agitation over land was led by impoverished local priests, in part out of frustration at their exclusion from the ranks of the 'high' clergy and in part out of anger at the vast landholdings and power of the same.[87]

The factionalism of Sicilian rural communities was also affected by the administrative changes introduced to local government, justice, and the police after 1815. In particular, these administrative changes played a crucial role in determining who came out on top in the conflicts between élites. On occasion, administrative reforms could produce a sense of collective local solidarity against the central power. In a study of Naro (in the province of Girgenti), Paolo Pezzino notes the tendency for the rural nobility to 'fuse' with sections of the rural middle class, and suggests that this may have been caused by the process of administrative centralization. He finds, for instance, that in Naro the immediate effect of the reforms was to bring about a cessation of factional conflict. Indeed, the new laws produced an alliance of rival families around the defence of local autonomy. This allowed a degree of power-sharing and the development of common political attitudes between the old and the new élites.[88]

However, this alliance between élites was far from being a stable one. Even Pezzino admits that in Naro there were other moments (he pinpoints the turbulent cholera years of the late 1830s) when relations between rival élites were dominated by 'difference'.[89] Although the evidence available is sketchy, studies of rural communities elsewhere in Sicily and Southern Italy confirm that, particularly by the 1830s, there was growing competition amongst élites for the key positions in local government. Giarrizzo describes a growing 'appetite' among the

---

[86] S. Corleo, *Storia dell'enfiteusi dei terreni ecclesiastici di Sicilia*, ed. A. li Vecchi (Caltanissetta and Rome, 1977), 329. There are other details about the Church's land-holdings in Cancila, 'Dal feudo alla proprietà borghese', 111–18.

[87] Fiume, *La crisi sociale del 1848*, 150–5. For a discussion of the political implications of this division between 'low' and 'high' clergy in Sicily, see R. Composto, 'Fermenti sociali del clero minore siciliano prima dell'unificazione', *Studi Storici*, 5 (1964), 263–80, and F. Brancato, 'La partecipazione del clero alla rivoluzione siciliana del 1860', in *La Sicilia e l'unità d'Italia* (Palermo, 1960), esp. 9–16.

[88] Pezzino, 'Monarchia amministrativa ed élites locali', 174–5.   [89] Ibid. 175.

middle class of Biancavilla for administrative power; they saw administrative office as a means of asserting their independence from the old nobility as well as the 'culmination of their success as a separate class'.[90] In the commune of Villafrati (in the province of Palermo), two rival factions developed after 1812 based around shifting loyalties to a local family and to the government. Although a degree of power-sharing did exist ('each one took a slice of power for itself'), there was never sufficient agreement to guarantee political stability.[91] In Lercara Friddi, a sulphur-mining town, there was considerable rivalry between the established Sartorio family and the relative newcomers, the Nicolosi family (whose activities are discussed in more detail below). This rivalry was focused on control of the key administrative positions of the commune as well as management of the sulphur mines.[92]

Along with land and family, politics thus became an important means of accumulating wealth and acquiring status in the Sicilian countryside.[93] It is not hard to understand why this came about. Since the Bourbon administrative reforms were largely unsuccessful, they left what Pezzino refers to as a 'legal and institutional vacuum' at the communal level, which members of the local élite scrambled to fill.[94] And, in significant respects, control of local government was the key to controlling the local economy. The local administration controlled the division of common land, decided the amount of common land to be divided, and decided who was to be the ultimate beneficiary of the division.[95] The local administration also controlled the budget for the commune which, in turn, gave it control over allocation of public works and the contracts connected to them. Those in charge of the local administration could decide on forms and methods of taxation, and they were responsible for the drawing up of electoral lists. Finally, those in charge of the local administration held control over most bureaucratic appointments within the local administration. Crucially, they also controlled the flow of information between the commune and the provincial and central administrations.

Thus, the extensive powers offered by control of local government meant that an ambitious mayor or councillor could do more than simply

[90] *Un comune rurale nella Sicilia etnea*, 167.
[91] G. Oddo, *Lo sviluppo incompiuto: Villafrati 1596–1960* (Palermo, 1986), 81–91.
[92] R. Mangiameli, 'Banditi e mafiosi dopo l'unità', *Meridiana*, 7–8 (1990), 83.
[93] For an analysis see Macry, 'Le élites urbane', 806–8.
[94] 'Monarchia amministrativa ed élites locali', 175.
[95] Cancila, 'Dal feudo alla proprietà borghese', 122–5.

enrich himself. He could make control of local government a powerful instrument of patronage within a given community. He could benefit his family and his friends by awarding them public works contracts, employing them in administrative positions, or making sure they, and not their rivals, profited from the division of common land. He could use the local police or militia as a means of defending this wealth against peasant violence. In this way, local politics in Western Sicily developed around vertical ties of patronage and clientelism: factions formed around the 'spoils' of an administrative system, and supporters of the faction in power would be rewarded with government offices and contracts. As Fiume suggests in her study of Marineo, the object of factional struggle was 'the monopoly of communal offices, run to accumulate, supplement, and consolidate family wealth through the looting of the public purse'.[96]

Administrative centralization may have deprived local élites of their political autonomy, but it also offered them new opportunities for acquiring wealth, status, and power. Hence it is not surprising that struggle for control of local government was such an important feature of the factional conflicts between élites.[97] However, probably the most striking feature of this factionalism, of these 'little governments within the government', was the use of violence. The threat of violence was one of the principal means by which the *gabelloti* ensured payment of rents and of debts owed to them. Violence was one way in which the new élites gained control of local government. What Stephen Wilson calls 'blood vengeance' remained an important system of sanctions and social control.[98]

Factionalism also played a role in the organization of crime: many of the armed gangs in the Sicilian countryside who engaged in cattle-rustling, kidnapping, and extortion had links with the élites and with the economic and political rivalries between them. Giovanna Fiume suggests that bandits tended to be 'strong men', who often worked for the new élites in a variety of guises. They were employed to guard a landowner's property (particularly his cattle) or to steal the property of another landowner. They were used to protect goods on their way to market and, in areas with sparse communications, to control access to

---

[96] G. Fiume, 'Introduzione', in G. Rampolla, *Suicidio per mafia* (Palermo, 1986), 17.

[97] Iachello, 'Potere locale e mobilità delle élites', 915. On similar conflicts in the province of Bari, see di Ciommo, 'Elites provinciali e potere borbonico', in Massafra (ed.), *Il Mezzogiorno preunitario*, 978–90.

[98] S. Wilson, *Feuding, Conflict and Banditry in Nineteenth-Century Corsica* (Cambridge, 1988), 268–9.

the market itself. They were available to settle scores or extort money or favours; and they served to protect 'their' landowner from the violence of others.[99]

This link between the activities of armed gangs and the aspirations of local élites also suggests that, in Sicily, bandits were far from being 'the champions of the poor' described by Eric Hobsbawm.[100] Pezzino points out that the areas shown by Fiume to be the most 'infested' (the phrase used in government reports) by banditry—the sulphur-mining regions of the *latifondo*, the hills around Palermo—were areas of rapid economic development, not of economic stagnation.[101] The sulphur-mining areas were particularly notorious for crime and violence; the caves, according to one German businessman visiting them in the 1880s, made an excellent hide-out for bandits.[102] Indeed, it is probably more helpful to see banditry in Sicily—and in many other parts of the South as well—as a form of upward mobility rather than as an expression of collective protest against poverty.[103] Fiume writes that bandits in Sicily were used as 'an instrument in the power struggles between rival sections of the rural élites'.[104] The bandits themselves may have been young, impoverished males, but they worked for powerful people: 'bandits worked for somebody and only secondarily for themselves . . . behind an invincible bandit there was always an aristocrat, a judge, a mayor, a *capitano d'arme* [local policeman]'.[105] Both for the peasants who made up the bands, and for the *prepotenti* who controlled them, banditry was part of the everyday struggle for survival, wealth, and/or power.

Violence thus played an integral part in the emergence of new rural élites and in the conflicts between them. Certain kinds of criminal

---

[99] G. Fiume, *Le bande armate in Sicilia, 1819–1849* (Palermo, 1984).

[100] E. Hobsbawm, *Primitive Rebels* (1959; Manchester, 2nd edn., 1971), 28. For a fuller analysis see the same author's *Bandits* (1969; London, 2nd edn., 1985).

[101] P. Pezzino, 'Stato, violenza, società: nascita e sviluppo del paradigma mafioso', in *Una certa reciprocità di favori: mafia e modernizzazione nella Sicilia postunitaria* (Milan, 1990), 96.

[102] A. Schneegans, *La Sicilia nella natura, nella storia e nella vita* (Florence, 1890), 287.

[103] In Salerno, for example, it was said that men of violence 'did not rob to survive but to get rich'. R. Marino, 'Nuova borghesia e amministrazione locale nelle cronache giudiziarie del Principato Citra', in Massafra (ed.), *Il Mezzogiorno preunitario*, 1101. For a general discussion of these activities and their rationale, see Davis, *Conflict and Control*, 80–90.

[104] G. Fiume, 'Bandits, Violence and the Organization of Power in Nineteenth-Century Sicily', in J. A. Davis and P. Ginsborg (eds.), *Society and Politics in the Age of the Risorgimento: Essays in Honour of Denis Mack Smith* (Cambridge, 1991), 77.

[105] Fiume, *Le bande armate in Sicilia*, 68.

activity became part of the process of economic mobility, and their perpetrators were protected by the most powerful members of local society. The comparison between these 'strong men' and their more famous later nineteenth-century counterparts, the mafia, seems unavoidable. Some historians see the mafia developing directly from bandit organizations. D'Alessandro, for instance, sees bandits coming 'down from the mountain, where their struggle had been direct, brutal and primitive, to the coast . . . [where] they now chose indirect action as more useful and advantageous', and where working for the state seemed the most profitable option.[106] In the nineteenth century, however, the distinction between bandits and *mafiosi* seems much more blurred. Even in the judicial records relating to bandits and *mafiosi*, the terms are used interchangeably, along with other descriptions such as '*manutengoli*' ('aiders and abetters'), '*facinorosi*' ('the lawless'), and '*malviventi*' ('wrongdoers').[107] As late as 1876 Leopoldo Franchetti admitted that it was difficult to tell the 'infinite variety' of bandits, *mafiosi*, and conspirators apart.[108]

Perhaps the most useful way of understanding the importance of organized violence in this society is not to make arbitrary distinctions between those involved but to analyse their motives. Diego Gambetta argues that the mafia developed in parts of Sicily as a means of policing the peasantry, of enforcing property rights over land and livestock, and of controlling routes to the market. The mafia, according to Gambetta, was in the 'business of private protection'; it reflected rather than contributed to conditions of acute insecurity.[109] Salvatore Lupo suggests that 'the threat of brigandage was used to convince landowners that the protection of their land should be entrusted to *mafiosi*'.[110] Thus, the way in which rural élites used violence reveals how little the Bourbon government was able to police the countryside; *mafiosi* provided, in Robert Putnam's words, 'a kind of privatized Leviathan'.[111] Even more importantly, the need for private protection suggests that Sicilian rural élites were in reality far weaker than they appeared, having

---

[106] V. d'Alessandro, *Brigantaggio e mafia in Sicilia* (Messina, 1950), 135.

[107] See the comments of Valeria Pizzini, 'La storia della mafia tra realtà e congetture', *Studi Storici*, 35/2 (1994), 436.

[108] Franchetti, *Condizione politiche e amministrative della Sicilia*, 26.

[109] Gambetta, *The Sicilian Mafia*, 90–6.

[110] S. Lupo, *Storia della mafia dalle origini ai giorni nostri* (Rome, 1993), 11.

[111] R. D. Putnam, *Making Democracy Work: Civic Traditions in Modern Italy* (Princeton, 1993), 147.

both a fragile hold over their newly acquired property and a tenuous grip on the workforce.

There are few detailed historical studies of specific rural communities in the Sicilian *latifondo*, but what evidence there is points to great instability and flux. Putnam identifies the problems of the South with the lack of a 'civic tradition' and, while his analysis probably overstates the case,[112] there appears to have been relatively few associational groups or other manifestations of élite sociability which might have given the Southern élites a sense of solidarity and security. Some historians (most explicitly Pagden) have attributed this 'distrust' directly to Bourbon policies, which promoted friction and tension between élites as means of controlling them.[113] Evidence gathered by anthropologists also suggests that, in the words of one study, new élites 'experienced many swings of fortune'.[114] An analysis of social mobility in Riposto—a commercial centre in Eastern Sicily—suggests that, at least in this type of community, there were moments of rapid mobility followed by periods of stagnation.[115] In the sulphur-mining town of Lercara Friddi, control of the commune shifted between the Nicolosi family and their arch-rivals, the Sartorio family.[116] While custom and culture continued to subordinate the ex-*gabelloti* to their feudal lords, and the peasantry to both, the wealth, position, and social legitimacy of the new rural élites could be lost with remarkable speed.[117] The usurpation of common land added to their wealth, but it also undermined their authority over the peasantry.[118] In this situation, where, as Franchetti remarked, 'the instinct of self-preservation made everyone ensure the help of someone stronger', clientelism provided a form of security: 'it fell to clientelism to provide the force which held society together'.[119]

There was, moreover, one significant new source of tension and insecurity in many communities. This was the rising tide of peasant

---

[112] Ibid. 121–62. For a criticism of Putnam, see S. Lupo, 'Usi e abusi del passato: le radici dell'Italia di Putnam', *Meridiana*, 18 (1993), 151–68.

[113] A. Pagden, 'The Destruction of Trust and its Economic Consequences in the Case of Eighteenth-Century Naples', in D. Gambetta (ed.), *Trust: Making and Breaking Co-operative Relations* (Oxford, 1988). See also A. M. Banti, 'Il Sud come problema della storia italiana', *Società e Storia*, 68 (1995), 344–9.

[114] Schneider and Schneider, *Culture and Political Economy in Western Sicily*, 150.

[115] Iachello, 'Potere locale e mobilità delle élites', 924, 930–1.

[116] Mangiameli, 'Banditi e mafiosi dopo l'unità', 83–4.

[117] Bevilacqua, *Breve storia dell'Italia meridionale*, 6.

[118] Di Ciommo, 'Élites provinciali e potere borbonico', 986.

[119] Quoted in Putnam, *Making Democracy Work*, 146.

unrest. Rosario Romeo describes the Sicilian land-reforms and enclosures of the early nineteenth century as a 'vast plundering (*spolazione*)
of the Sicilian peasantry'.[120] Like the acquisition of land by new élites,
this process was rapid, destabilizing, and, often, extremely violent. For
the peasantry the loss of customary rights and the enclosure of common
land was a devastating blow which left them without access to a water
supply, grazing for their animals, or wood for fuel. At the same time, the
peasants remained tied to the land and to the landowner by the old
forms of agrarian contract which left them permanently in debt.
Indeed, the problem of peasant indebtedness was probably considerably
worsened by the tendency of new landowners to charge even more
usurious rates of interest than their predecessors; landowners, according to one contemporary, were 'no longer poor aristocrats as much as
grasping usurers'.[121] Added to these problems, high levels of taxation
(particularly the hated *macinato* or grist tax) made the economic position of the peasantry increasingly precarious.[122]

Starting from what Romeo calls a 'peaceful state of mind', by the mid-
nineteenth century the peasants in Sicily had become a revolutionary
force.[123] Widespread, and often ferocious, peasant unrest was perhaps
the most frightening feature of the revolutions of 1820–1, 1848–9 and
1859–60. Its focus was the partition of common land and taxation. Direct
action by the peasantry—where they 'invaded' enclosed common land
with their livestock, destroyed planted crops, and 'devastated' enclosed
woodland—had a tendency to spill over into more open forms of violence
against the landowners themselves. During 1820 parts of the *latifondo*
were in a state of virtual civil war; in many communes peasant violence
was caught up in a general armed struggle for control of local administrations.[124] Angered by repeated enclosures of common land, bands of
peasants in 1848 (so-called *comunisti*, because they were upholding the
rights of the commune over common land) came together and 'usurped'
the common land for themselves.[125] In Biancavilla, where the communal
administrators had 'usurped' the common land, peasants attacked and

[120] Romeo, *Il Risorgimento in Sicilia*, 187.
[121] Quoted in D. Mack Smith, 'The Peasants' Revolt in Sicily, 1860', in *Victor Emmanuel, Cavour and the Risorgimento* (London, 1971), 191.
[122] Fiume, *La crisi sociale del 1848*, 109–11.   [123] *Il Risorgimento in Sicilia*, 171.
[124] A. De Francesco, *La guerra di Sicilia: il distretto di Caltagirone nella rivoluzione del
1820–21* (Catania, 1992), 141–66.
[125] See the descriptions of land occupations in 1848 in Fiume, *La crisi sociale del 1848*,
122–9.

burnt down the municipal treasury.[126] In the relatively more peaceful town of Villafrati the mayor was forced by an 'exultant throng' to hand over all the tax and land records, which were then publicly burned.[127]

Peasant violence was one means by which the fortunes of liberal revolution in the cities became caught up with revolution in the countryside. De Francesco writes, of the 1820 revolution in Caltagirone, that popular unrest became an integral part of the struggle for supremacy between newly rich, often younger, democrats, and supporters of the Bourbon administration.[128] During 1820 and 1848–9, many radical democrats sought to encourage and give direction to peasant discontent over land, organizing peasants—and often bandits—into 'guerrilla' bands (in 1820) or *squadre* (in 1848–9).[129] In 1848–9, groups of democrats and peasant *squadristi* formed an irregular military force against the Bourbons, often forcibly ousting local power-holders from their positions in the communes.

However, attempts to organize rural unrest were not successful. The apparent encouragement of crime and violence alarmed the more moderate liberals within the opposition movement in Sicily. In January 1848, right at the beginning of the revolution, the revolutionary government in Palermo formed a National Guard 'to protect property and persons', to prevent revolutionary 'excesses', and, effectively, as a means of controlling the rural *squadre*.[130] But, by its very nature, peasant violence was difficult to control; and even the radical democrats in Palermo had a tenuous hold over these activities. More generally, the democrats failed to establish any direction over the politics in rural communes. These seem to have been guided overwhelmingly by local considerations and interests. In 1848, factions declared themselves as 'liberals' and accused their rivals of being 'bourbons' or 'royalists'. Yet these seem largely to have been terms of convenience, used, as Fiume puts it, 'arbitrarily so as to cover up vendettas of a personal nature'.[131]

IV

Throughout the Restoration period, Sicily posed problems to its Bourbon administrators. Between the return of the Bourbons to Naples in 1815 and the final collapse of Bourbon government in 1860, there

---

[126] Giarrizzo, *Un comune rurale nella Sicilia etnea*, 285–6.
[127] Oddo, *Lo sviluppo incompiuto*, 101.   [128] De Francesco, *La guerra di Sicilia*.
[129] On the attitude of democrats towards popular unrest, see Romano, *Momenti del Risorgimento in Sicilia*, 171–92.   [130] Cingari, 'Gli ultimi Borboni', 52–3.
[131] Fiume, *La crisi sociale del 1848*, 134.

was a series of revolutionary upheavals in Sicily. Two major revolutions took place in 1820–1 and in 1848–9; both demanded autonomy from Naples. These revolutions were also marked by widespread popular violence in the countryside and towns. An additional number of more localized (but no less violent) revolts against Bourbon rule were organized, most notably in 1837. Moreover, these revolutions were merely the most visible sign of political and social instability. Behind them lay broader problems with the way Sicily was governed. The activities of bandits, the occupation of landed estates by peasants, and the prevalence of violence in local government were all indications of the central administration's failure to maintain law and order on a day-to-day basis.

It is, of course, worth remembering that many aspects of this political crisis were far from being unique to Sicily. To an extent, the crisis in Sicily reflected broader problems of legitimacy and power which affected many other Restoration states in Italy after 1815. Like most other rulers in Restoration Italy, the Bourbon government was unable to establish lasting support for its attempted compromise between the old order and the new. At different times between the revolutions of 1820 and 1848–9, the government either pursued a reactionary line which alienated its more moderate supporters or attempted to introduce progressive reforms which seem to have satisfied no-one. In addition, structural constraints, particularly of a financial and economic nature, hampered Bourbon reformers. The distance between the central government and its Sicilian provinces also raised huge practical problems of implementation and surveillance.

These general problems notwithstanding, many of the problems which the government faced in Sicily were of its own making. Specifically, its policy of political modernization was largely counter-productive. Since the policy was aimed against the established political élite in Sicily, it should not have been surprising that it provoked resentment among them and fuelled a movement of opposition to rule from Naples. At the same time, Bourbon policy unleashed a process of social and political change which ultimately undermined not just the established élites but the central government as well. As John Davis comments, 'ironically, the institutions which had been created in order to weaken the autonomy of élites ended up by reinforcing their power at the expense of the state'.[132] Indeed, the political instability and the

---

[132] J. A. Davis, 'Lo stato e l'ordine pubblico nel Mezzogiorno e in Sicilia nella prima metà del XIX secolo', in *Contributi per un bilancio del regno borbonico, 1815–60*, ed. F. Pilliteri (Palermo, 1990), 30.

widespread social disorder which were a striking feature of Sicily in this period can perhaps be best explained by reference to the weakening of the old regime and, in particular, to the effect which this had on the social and political structure of the Sicilian countryside. In the countryside, rural élites made a mockery of Bourbon pretensions, proving far more capable than central government in controlling the local administration.

The crisis of Bourbon rule in the Sicilian countryside, which culminated in the revolution of 1859–60, was partly caused by these rapid shifts in political relations between central and local power. Changes taking place within local communities also undermined Bourbon rule. The political changes introduced by the Bourbon government in an attempt to modernize its provincial and local administration combined with a process of economic change to destabilize relations within the countryside. The effect both of administrative reform and of the abolition of feudalism created a new élite of non-noble property-holders in the countryside. This process also intensified a long-standing problem of peasant impoverishment and indebtedness. A series of conflicts then developed among new and established élites over landownership, and between élites and peasants over access to land and land-usage. In turn, these conflicts were accentuated by the conflict between local and central power for control of the countryside and of its wealth.

In the *latifondo* the effect of political modernization was to destroy the structures of the old regime along with its old bases of support. Traditional social relations, with their attendant rights, obligations, and privileges, were undercut by the abolition of feudalism and administrative centralization. The reforms introduced by the Bourbon government weakened the old nobility and alienated the Church. They also undermined what loyalty had existed to the Crown. Crucially, however, few stable social and political relationships developed to replace those of the old regime. Although social mobility occurred throughout the South, and new individuals and families came to prominence, this process did not bring with it major alterations in the forms of agrarian contracts. In general, the new élites were also no more loyal (perhaps a great deal less so) to the Crown. Peasant poverty meant that the threat of popular unrest increased enormously. Modernization meant, in other words, that the Bourbons had less control over the countryside than hitherto, and that the countryside itself became much more unstable.

What were the broader political consequences of this crisis in the countryside? The Risorgimento in Sicily was traditionally defined in terms of a political struggle between the liberal nobility/middle class in Palermo and Sicily's Bourbon rulers in Naples. However, it is clear from more recent, revisionist work that the extent of political and social instability experienced in this period cannot be explained simply by reference to the tensions between urban élites and the central government in Naples. Equally important was the developing conflict between central and local power in the countryside, and the explosive social and political conflicts within rural communities themselves.

The transition from feudal monarchy to modern bureaucratic state in Sicily took place very rapidly. Partly because of this perhaps, this process was neither peaceful nor clear-cut. Indeed, it could be argued that the two systems coexisted: élites were able to use the new bureaucratic 'public' powers to pursue their own personal, and more traditional, goals. What this meant, however, was that no autonomous political movement, based on defence of local rights, developed in the provinces. In a sense, rural élites came to need the protection of the state, and the 'spoils' which working for the state provided, to maintain their wealth and status and to guard against the threat of peasant revolt. In this respect, the introduction of a new administrative system actually intensified factional conflicts within communities. One of the most obvious consequences of these conflicts was to undermine the liberal struggle against the Bourbons. The problems of maintaining a regular administrative system in Sicily persisted and, if anything, intensified during the revolutions of 1820 and 1848-9. In practice, as we shall see only too clearly in the chapters which follow, liberals were to prove no more capable of controlling the countryside than the Bourbons had been.

2

From Risorgimento to Revolution, 1849–1860

I

After the repression of the 1848 revolutions, the Bourbon government never fully recovered its authority in Sicily. Prince Filangieri led the army which occupied Palermo in May 1849, and he was given full military and civil powers by the king to re-establish government authority. Initially, Filangieri sought to gain public support for the regime. Ferdinando II conceded greater administrative autonomy with the organization of a separate Sicilian ministry and made a series of popular fiscal concessions. There was some investment in infrastructural improvements. However, Filangieri's efforts were unpopular with the government in Naples, and were too timid to win him many friends among Sicilian liberals. Financial constraints, the famine of 1853–4, and a cholera outbreak in 1855 undermined Filangieri's earlier successes: and when he resigned in 1855, he was replaced by the more straightforwardly reactionary Prince Castelcicala.[1]

Both Filangieri and Castelcicala shared a common determination to repress any sign of political conspiracy. Special responsibility for this was given to Salvatore Maniscalco, the Bourbon chief of police from 1849 to 1860. Maniscalco became the symbol of Bourbon rule in this period, and he came to symbolize Bourbon cruelty, corruption, and misgovernment. He was, one French commentator wrote:

blamed for a great deal of violence. I am not referring to torture, which is difficult to prove, but I do know that it is his police who are held responsible for the practice of throwing the father, mother, wife or children in prison and holding them there until the wanted man gives himself up.[2]

[1] On Filangieri's policies in Sicily and his replacement by Castelcicala, see A. Scirocco, *L'Italia del Risorgimento* (Bologna, 1990), 331, 335, G. Candeloro, *Storia dell'Italia moderna*, iv: *dalla rivoluzione nazionale all'unità* (Milan, 1964), 38–41, and R. de Cesare, *La fine di un regno* (3 vols.; Milan, 3rd edn., 1909), i. 50–60.

[2] M. Monnier, *Garibaldi: histoire de la conquête des Deux-Siciles* (Paris, 1861), 89.

Maniscalco also quickly acquired notoriety for his use of professional criminals as spies against revolutionaries and as policemen to combat smuggling and the sale of contraband. In fact, this alliance between reactionaries and criminals was one sustaining element behind the government's survival until the crisis of 1859–60.

However, the lack of any effective reform and the dubious measures adopted by Maniscalco's police meant that the Bourbon government became increasingly unpopular in Sicily. After 1848–9 many of the leaders of the 1848 revolution were sent into exile or languished in prison, yet anti-Bourbon political activity actually intensified during the 1850s. Alongside these conspiracies, popular discontent in the countryside grew and the numbers of peasant *squadre* also increased. In 1856 this activity resulted in a major revolt. One of the members of the Mazzinian central committee in Sicily, Francesco Bentivegna, organized a *squadra* from Corleone to attack the towns of Mezzojuso and Villafrati; and similar disturbances took place in Cefalù, led by Salvatore Spinuzza.[3] While these revolts were easily suppressed (and both Bentivegna and Spinuzza executed), they provided striking evidence of the growing number of anti-government conspiracies in Sicily.

In 1859 another series of disturbances, centred on Bagheria to the east of Palermo, greeted the news of Austria's defeat by the coalition of France and Piedmont. According to Castelcicala, 'a gang of around 30 men from Bagheria stole the arms from a customs' boat, committed a series of thefts and two murders and, the gang having grown somewhat larger during the night, with cries of "*Viva Napoleone, Viva la libertà*" attacked various communes'. The disturbances in Bagheria were followed by an attempted revolt in Girgenti and, in November 1859, an attempt on Maniscalco's life.[4] At around the same time, many of Sicily's most famous revolutionary exiles—Francesco Crispi, Saverio Friscia, Rosolino Pilo—returned to Sicily and began to organize revolutionary conspiracies against the Bourbon government. Pilo established important links with the popular leader, Giovanni Corrao, and through him made contact with various bandits in the Madonie mountains. Preparations began for a larger insurrection.

The mounting unrest in Sicily during 1859 was all the more serious

---

[3] Candeloro, *Storia dell'Italia moderna*, iv. 256–7.

[4] R. Moscati, *La fine del regno di Napoli: documenti borbonici del 1859–60* (Florence, 1960), 133. For a detailed description of the revolt and the attack on Maniscalco, see de Cesare, *La fine di un regno*, ii. 186–9. On the conspiracy in the province of Girgenti see G. Berti, *I democratici e l'iniziativa meridionale nel Risorgimento* (Milan, 1962), 740.

since it coincided with a growing crisis of Bourbon government in Naples. In May 1859, king Ferdinando II—known pejoratively as '*Re Bomba*' since his bombardment of Messina and Palermo at the end of the 1848–9 revolution—died after a painful illness. His last act as monarch had been to declare his country's neutrality in the war in Northern Italy between the Austrian Empire and the Franco–Piedmontese coalition. Ferdinando's 23-year-old son, Francesco, became king on his death. The historical consensus on Francesco II seems to be that despite his best efforts he was not, in Candeloro's words, 'the right man to overcome the crisis that confronted the kingdom'.[5] He was, by all accounts, a kind and gentle man; but he was also pious, timid and unimaginative. Until 1859 he had lived in the shadow of his ebullient father, who had done little to prepare him for the immense task that was to befall him. Even Harold Acton, in his spirited defence of the 'last Bourbons of Naples', admits that Francesco was the wrong man for the job, a monarch who spent his time in prayer while his kingdom collapsed around him.[6]

The crisis which Francesco II's kingdom faced was threefold. The first problem was a diplomatic one. Since the end of the Crimean War in 1856, the international reputation of the Two Sicilies had declined along with that of its closest ally, the Austrian Empire. At the Congress of Paris in 1856, the French Foreign Minister, Count Walewski, denounced the 'intolerable despotism' of the Neapolitan administration; this and similar remarks led to the severing of diplomatic relations with France and Britain.[7] During the 1850s British public opinion also turned increasingly against the Bourbon monarchy, a shift marked decisively by the publication in July 1851 of Gladstone's 'Letters to Lord Aberdeen', denouncing the Bourbon administration as 'the negation of God erected into a system of government' and calling for 'forcible intervention by the authority of Europe' to end it.[8] One of Francesco's first decisions upon becoming king in 1859 was to uphold his kingdom's neutrality in the Austrian war; he did so in the face of strong pressure from the Piedmontese to form an anti-Austrian coalition. This decision finally cemented the diplomatic isolation of the Two Sicilies. When Austria was defeated, the territorial sovereignty of the Two Sicilies (and, incidentally, all of Italy's absolutist states) was seriously compromised; in turn, Austria's defeat came to undermine the Bourbon state's authority over its own subjects.[9]

The second problem which Francesco faced was financial. The repression of the 1848 revolution had been extremely costly. Yet, during the 1850s, Ferdinando II continued to spend extravagantly on his army and navy. Increasing amounts of money were required to service the public debt; there was, by contrast, very little government expenditure on either education, welfare, or public works. According to figures given by Scirocco for government expenditure in 1854, out of a total of 31.4 million ducats, 14 million was spent on the armed forces, 6.5 million went to service the public debt, and only 1.2 million was used for education, welfare, and public works.[10] By 1859, the size of the public debt had considerably narrowed the choices open to Francesco and his ministers. Financial constraints meant that, during the crisis of 1859–60, the government was unable to win any popular support for itself by cutting taxes or through investment.

Despite the decisive victory won over the liberals in 1848 and 1849, the Bourbon government floundered in its aftermath. Whereas government policy in the 1830s had been characterized by substantial public investment and economic reforms, government policy in the 1850s seemed to lose direction. In the Two Sicilies no process of renewal or reconciliation followed the shock of 1848; instead, Ferdinando engaged in a repression so severe as to shock even firm supporters of his regime. Police surveillance increased, the Church's control of education was reinforced, and censorship was tightened.[11] The same ministers from the pre-1848 period held onto the same jobs; in terms of years and ideas, the government aged visibly after 1848.[12] Hence, the third problem which Francesco II faced on his accession to the throne in 1859 was a problem of legitimacy. Furthermore, since much residual loyalty to the Crown was lost with Ferdinando's death, this problem grew rapidly much worse during 1859.

Seen with the benefit of hindsight, the new and inexperienced king made a series of errors which brought the downfall of his kingdom much closer. Francesco failed to grasp either the significance of Austria's defeat by Piedmont in 1859 or the importance of the subsequent risings in the Central Italian duchies, where moderate liberals seized control of their governments and declared their intention to unite with

---

[9] Scirocco, *L'Italia del Risorgimento*, 416.   [10] Ibid. 335.   [11] Ibid. 325–30.
[12] R. Moscati, *Il Mezzogiorno d'Italia ed altri saggi* (Messina, 1953), 94–5.

Piedmont. Instead, Francesco chose to emphasize the continuity between his reign and that of his father's. He appointed Filangieri, now
75 and a man of immense experience but still associated indelibly with
the old regime, as Prime Minister. Francesco also used the army to
quell popular demonstrations celebrating the Franco–Piedmontese victory over the Austrians at the battle of Magenta. Subsequently he
disbanded the Bourbon army's best troops, the Swiss regiments in
Naples, after an attempted mutiny over pay. This action deprived the
Bourbon monarchy of its most effective means of defence against
revolution; de Cesare remarks that the disbanding of the Swiss regiments 'marked the first real misfortune for the dynasty'.[13]

In the year between his accession to the throne in May 1859 and
Garibaldi's invasion of Sicily in May 1860 Francesco vacillated ineffectually between a policy of reform and one of repression. Francesco and
Filangieri tried to revive Ferdinando II's policy from the 1830s, where
demands for political reform were defused by the offer of administrative
improvements. In a gesture of reconciliation, a number of political
prisoners were amnestied and the list of *attendibili* (political suspects
under police surveillance) was abolished. Unfortunately, all these efforts
merely made the government look incompetent; the bureaucracy
blocked all attempts at modernization and, in an act of pure humiliation
for the government, the Bourbon chief of police, Casella, successfully
countermanded the order abolishing the *attendibili*.[14] As late as the
spring of 1860 the government also ignored the mounting problems
in Sicily and, instead, sent the bulk of its troops North to protect
against the threat of Piedmontese invasion from the Romagna.[15]

II

It was in these circumstances of general political and financial crisis, and
of mounting political and popular discontent in Sicily, that a revolutionary conspiracy was hatched in Palermo during March 1860. The
conspiracy was led by a young Sicilian Mazzinian, Francesco Riso, and
included members of the Palermo nobility and bourgeoisie. Once discovered, the conspirators took refuge in the Gancia convent in Palermo,
and attempted an insurrection from there at the beginning of April.

[13] De Cesare, *La fine di un regno*, ii. 17.
[14] Scirocco, *L'Italia del Risorgimento*, 400–1; Acton, *The Last Bourbons of Naples*, 394.
[15] Scirocco, *L'Italia del Risorgimento*, 401.

Although quickly suppressed, the failed but celebrated 'Gancia' insurrection quickly spread to the surrounding countryside.[16]

It also provoked a massive crackdown by a panicked Bourbon administration.[17] A state of siege was declared, and thirteen of the conspirators were arrested and shot. An atmosphere of fear and general confusion prevailed. One British businessman in Palermo complained that it was dangerous to venture outdoors 'in the midst of an infatuated mess of unexperienced soldiers consisting chiefly of raw recruits, few of whom have ever had a musket in their hands before this day week'.[18] In other cities, such as Catania, Messina, and Trapani, where revolutionary committees were known to be operating, there were numerous arrests and executions. Between 8 and 15 April Messina was under constant artillery fire.[19]

The severity of this repression provoked protests from many of the foreign consuls in Sicily, above all from the British.[20] Consul Goodwin criticized the behaviour of Bourbon troops in a strongly worded letter to Elliot, his superior in Naples. He contrasted the crowd around the Gancia convent wearing 'tricoloured cockades and crying "*Viva l'Italia e Vittorio Emanuele*"' with the 'fury' of the troops as they 'rampage[d]' through the area around the convent.[21] Elliot wrote to London that the Bourbons had used 'unnecessary cruelty and severity' in bombarding Messina.[22] However, it is also possible that the government would have been less unpopular had it been more effective. Throughout April 1860, conspiratorial activity intensified. One of the major leaders in the unfolding drama, Rosolino Pilo, arrived back in Sicily on 10 April. He immediately re-established his links with the *squadre* and began to plan new insurrections in the Palermo countryside. An even more important figure in revolutionary circles in Sicily, the republican lawyer

[16] S. F. Romano, *Momenti del Risorgimento in Sicilia* (Messina, 1952), 123–33.

[17] See the long report of 17 Apr. 1860 from Castelcicala to the minister in Naples which describes the conspiracy. Archivio di Stato di Palermo (henceforth ASP), Ministero e R. Segretaria di Stato per gli Affari di Sicilia presso S. M. Ripartimento Polizia (henceforth Min. Affari Sicilia, Polizia), b.1238.

[18] Extract of a letter, dated 11 April 1860, from a Mr Morrison sent to the British envoy, Elliot, in Naples. Public Record Office, London (henceforth PRO) Foreign Office (henceforth FO), 70/315.

[19] For a description of these events, see de Cesare, *La fine di un regno*, ii. 205–25.

[20] See the letter detailing these complaints from the Bourbon foreign secretary, Carafa, to the Sicilian minister in Naples; 20 April 1860, in ASP, Min. Affari Sicilia, Polizia, b.1238. See also the collective protest from all the vice-consuls in Messina to the Bourbon commander, Russo, 13 April 1860, PRO, FO 70/315.

[21] 18 April 1860, PRO, FO 651/7.   [22] 17 April 1860, PRO, FO 70/315.

Francesco Crispi, also began to make elaborate plans for an expeditionary force from Northern Italy to help the revolutionaries in Sicily.
After considerable effort, he managed to persuade Giuseppe Garibaldi—the 'Hero of Two Worlds' and of the 1849 Roman Republic—
to lead it.[23]

In a famous study of the Sicilian peasantry in the 1860 revolution,
Denis Mack Smith describes vividly the chaos and unrest prevailing on
the eve of Garibaldi's arrival.[24] Although the April revolution could not
have succeeded without Garibaldi's assistance, its effect was to contri-
bute enormously to Garibaldi's success. News of the Gancia insurrection in Palermo led to numerous uprisings and disturbances elsewhere.
On 9 April, the British vice-consul in Girgenti, Boates, wrote to vice-
consul Rickards in Messina that since communications with Palermo
had been interrupted 'great excitement prevails here and if news from
Palermo be favourable we shall have a revolution here'.[25] According to
the *luogotenente generale*, Castelcicala, in some towns in the province of
Palermo (he named Bagheria, Misilmeri, Carini, Partinico, Piana dei
Greci, and Capaci), 'the lawless [*i facinorosi*] rose up in a crowd unfurl-
ing the tricolour flag'. There was an instant and dramatic increase in
the number of *squadre*, both in the mountains surrounding Palermo and
further afield. Their presence, Castelcicala wrote, exhausted and
demoralized his troops and interrupted supplies of food to the capital.
There were, he added, so many bandits in the vicinity that their mules
had contaminated Palermo's water supply.[26]

Revolt spread in waves to surround Palermo on all sides. In Collesano, near Cefalù, an armed band entered the town in the dead of night
and looted the tax offices and the house of the local judge.[27] In Petralia
Sottana in the Madonie mountains, 'a handful of bandits [*ladroni*]'
opened fire on the local watch and killed a number of notables, including the mayor. These disturbances often led to the opening of prisons
and the freeing of dangerous criminals. The opening of prisons in Piana
dei Greci in the mountains above Palermo, and in Castellamare on the
coast between Palermo and Trapani, swelled the ranks of armed gangs

---

[23] Acton, *The Last Bourbons of Naples*, 427; Candeloro, *Storia dell'Italia moderna*, iv.
429–31.
[24] Mack Smith, 'The Peasants' Revolt in Sicily: 1860', in *Victor Emmanuel, Cavour and
the Risorgimento* (London, 1971), 197–202.   [25] PRO, FO 70/315.
[26] 6 April 1860, ASP, Min. Affari Sicilia, Polizia, b.1238.
[27] April 1860, report from the local judge to Maniscalco, ASP, Minstero e Segretaria di
Stato presso il Luogotenente Generale, Ripartimento di Polizia, 1819–63 (henceforth
Luog. Polizia), b.1503. f. affari diversi Cefalù.

which continued to trouble this area throughout April and May.[28] In the heart of the *latifondo*, Don Onofrio Guggino of Bivona was inspired by the news of the Gancia revolt to arm himself, loot the Bivona tax office, and open up the prisons in nearby Prizzi and Corleone. He then formed an armed gang with the prisoners and proceeded to create havoc locally. Shortly afterwards, however, Guggino—who was the son of a wealthy notable—was taken hostage by a rival gang. He was eventually rescued by another gang of armed men led by his father and brothers.[29]

The main effect of the insurrection in Palermo was that government representatives became increasingly unable to control events in the surrounding countryside. Armed bands proliferated, and interrupted communications between Palermo's districts and the central administration in Palermo.[30] Both the mail and the telegraph service were halted for most of April, cutting off communications with the other Sicilian provinces. The government reports which did get through (by steamship from Messina, Catania, and Girgenti) spoke of the isolation of officials, their fear of worse to come, and the difficulty of enforcing their authority against the 'criminals'. The intendant of Girgenti wrote that there was great agitation among the poorer classes in the town: only a lack of weapons stopped them from attacking government forces. In many communes, he went on, attempts to collect the *macino* tax had been 'abandoned'.[31]

In the province of Trapani many officials—including even the intendant Stazzone—seemed to have 'abandoned' the business of government entirely. According to Trapani's procurator general, agitation started with the news of the Gancia insurrection, and culminated in his being forced by an angry mob to release prominent republican conspirators from Trapani's prisons on 7 April. Although the arrival of troops had calmed the situation, intendant Stazzone steadfastly refused to take any further action, particularly against the local police, who by this time had themselves become a threat to public order. 'We remain,' the procurator general went on:

[28] The incident took place on 29 Apr.; the report is dated 8 May 1860, Castelcicala to the minister in Naples. ASP, Min. Affari Sicilia, Polizia. b.1238.

[29] 28 April 1860, Sub-intendant of Bivona to Maniscalco, ASP, Luog. Polizia, b.1504, f. affari diversi Bivona.

[30] 11 April 1860, Castelcicala to the minister in Naples, ASP, Min. Affari Sicilia, Polizia, b.1238.

[31] Two reports refer to particular problems in Girgenti: the first sent by Castelcicala to Naples on 18 April 1860, in ASP, Min. Affari Sicilia, Polizia, b.1238, the other dated 23 April 1860 in ASP, Luog. Polizia, b.1504, f. affari diversi Girgenti.

in a state of disorder under the false appearance of order. The intendant is with a few wily employees and does all they tell him to do. To deceive him they hide the truth and tell him falsehoods.[32]

Much of the district of Alcamo (in Trapani province) was, in mid-April, taken over by the *squadre*. 'In Alcamo,' Castelcicala reported to Naples on 11 April:

the rebellion prevails. The police, the companions-at-arms [*compagnia d'armi*] have been disarmed, the official authorities dismissed and held under house arrest, the people hold sway. . . . the countryside is infested with lawless people.[33]

Many other reports also referred to employees keeping irregular hours, not doing their job, or fleeing their posts.[34] When Collesano was invaded by an armed band, most officials were so 'frightened and intimidated' that they fell back 'to escape with their lives'.[35] Many government officials were, in Mack Smith's words, simply 'too terrified to remain in their jobs'.[36]

Even before the arrival of Garibaldi's volunteers in Sicily, any semblance of normal government had, for all intents and purposes, broken down. Although, at the end of April, there was evidence of a return to order in the provinces, rumblings of revolt continued, particularly in the province of Palermo. Mack Smith writes that while 'Garibaldi was indeed to arrive none too soon, since the revolt was near the point of collapse . . . the most important fact was that the government could never altogether extinguish the forces of disorder'.[37] On 26 April Castelcicala reported a rumour that 'thousands of exiles [*emigrati*] have disembarked with arms and money'; this rumour, he noted, was preventing a return to order in the province. In Palermo itself, he wrote, 'from yesterday onwards there have been murmurings of disturbances . . . to take place together with an insurrection of sectarians [*i faziosi*] in the nearby towns so as to trap the troops between two lines

[32] 22 Apr. 1860, from the *procura generale* in Trapani to Castelcicala, in ASP, Min. Affari Sicilia, Polizia, b.1238; 20 Apr. 1860, from Castelcicala to the minister in Naples in ibid.   [33] Ibid.

[34] See above from the intendant of Girgenti, 23 Apr. 1860, ASP, Luog. Polizia, b.1504, f. affari diversi Girgenti. On 30 Apr. information from the *giudice reggio* of Bagheria was sent to Maniscalco that officials of the telegraph service were not doing their job: ASP, Luog. Polizia, b.1502.

[35] No date; from the judge of Collesano, ASP, Luog. Polizia, b.1503, f. affari diversi Cefalù.   [36] Mack Smith, 'The Peasants' Revolt in Sicily', 198.

[37] Ibid. 207.

of fire'.[38] On 3 May Castelcicala noted that the shops on the via Toledo in Palermo had reopened, that the city appeared calm, and that the news from the other Sicilian provinces was also positive. However, an atmosphere of fear and anxiety still prevailed; 'there is a general sense of concern at new disasters which may yet befall us'. Even more ominously, Castelcicala warned that 'popular passions stirred up by factions wanting to sweep Sicily into anarchy have begun to bear their bitter fruit'. Armed bands continued to cause periodic disturbances and to attack government offices and officials.[39]

The successful landing of Garibaldi and his volunteers at Marsala and their defeat of Bourbon troops near Calatafimi completely destroyed the credibility of the Bourbon administration. Garibaldi encouraged peasants to join him by promising land to every Sicilian male who fought against the Bourbons. Garibaldi also sent Giuseppe la Masa, the leader of the *picciotti* in 1848, to organize peasant revolt in Trapani and Girgenti. Soon the *garibaldini* were joined by bands of peasant volunteers from villages all over Western Sicily. Garibaldi incorporated a number of *squadre* into his army as the so-called *Cacciatori dell'Etna*. These behaved as a kind of advance guard, which cut telegraph wires, disrupted the mail service, and generally undermined the enemy's position.[40]

By the beginning of June, less than a month after the landing at Marsala, the *garibaldini* had been able to place themselves at the head of a large peasant army which surrounded and invaded Palermo. In a few days of fighting Garibaldi gained control of the whole city from the Bourbons. On 6 June, and after mediation from the British navy to halt the bombardment of Palermo by Bourbon forces, the Bourbon generals commanding Palermo signed a capitulation and agreed to evacuate their troops. After the battle of Milazzo (on Sicily's north-east coast) in July, the Bourbon government decided to withdraw its army from the island altogether and prepare for the defence of the mainland. By August 1860 the only reminder of Bourbon rule in Sicily was its command of the military citadel in Messina.[41]

---

[38] ASP, Min. Affari Sicilia, Polizia, b. 1238.
[39] 3 May, 5 May, and 10 May 1860, ibid.
[40] For more details on these *squadre* and their movements towards Palermo, see Romano, *Momenti del Risorgimento in Sicilia*, 135–7, R. Del Carria, *Proletari senza rivoluzione* (Milan, 1966), 41–3, and Berti, *I democratici e l'iniziativa meridionale*, 747–8.
[41] For a full description of these military events, see Candeloro, *Storia dell'Italia moderna*, iv. 439–68.

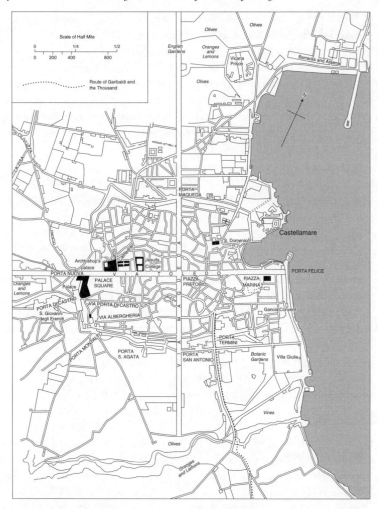

MAP 3. Palermo in 1860

According to Scirocco, Garibaldi became the new ruler of Sicily 'more as a result of his enemy's incapacity and demoralization than because of a superiority in arms and men'.[42] The collapse of provincial and communal administration during April greatly assisted Garibaldi's progress in May and June. After his arrival the situation in Palermo became rapidly so threatening that the government was obliged to order its troops into the city from the outlying districts. It was partly as a result of this that the activity of armed bands increased.[43] For much of this time the isolation of the government in Palermo was such that they had no idea where Garibaldi was, or even where his volunteers were gathering to invade Palermo. The ease with which he finally entered Palermo, taking Bourbon troops completely by surprise, is also a striking indication of the speed with which all public administration had collapsed. Castelcicala's despairing letter to Naples, written shortly before he was replaced by the *commissario straordinario*, General Lanza, on 18 May, indicates how far his control of events had slipped away:

After the invasion of Garibaldi's band of adventurers, the whole country rose up and gave itself with renewed violence to the insurrection, and all telegraphic communications were broken, the mail service was intercepted, and every communication with the interior of the island was cut so that the government did not know what was happening beyond the mountains which surrounded Palermo . . . the numerous bands which have appeared at every point have caused terror throughout the countryside . . . the public mood could not be worse and sympathy for the revolution prevails. I have no idea what conditions are in the provinces.[44]

There was chaos in Sicily's provinces. Only Siracusa and Caltanissetta were relatively quiet. In Girgenti, apart from the town itself which was held by a detachment of Bourbon troops, there was open insurrection, particularly in the district of Sciacca.[45] Many communes in the district of Mistretta (Messina), on the border with the province of Palermo, also rebelled against the crown. In some, feuding was reported between rival factions.[46] As Garibaldi advanced towards Palermo, both Messina and Catania erupted in revolt. The population began to flee Messina: an estimated 25,000 people fled on one occasion and 50,000 on another,

---

[42] Scirocco, *L'Italia del Risorgimento*, 404.
[43] See Castelcicala's letter of 13 May 1860, ASP, Min. Affari Sicilia, Polizia, b. 1238, and the telegram of 15 May from the intendant of Caltanissetta, ibid. b. 1239.
[44] 15 May 1860, ibid. b. 1238.
[45] 21 and 23 May 1860, from General Lanza, ibid.
[46] 18 May 1860, from the intendant of Messina, ibid.

leaving a garrison 'of about 3,000 troops not supposed to be well disposed to the government'.[47] Commerce ground to a halt and food supplies to the city ceased. The intendant of Messina reported that the police forces 'have been of no use at all, either because of problems in the make up of personnel or because they are intimidated by or caught up in the existing complex of events'.[48] Some of the worst outbreaks of violence took place in and around Catania, which declared itself openly for Garibaldi and where there were vicious reprisals on both sides.[49] On 19 May, the intendant of Catania reported that the outlying towns of Paternò, Adernò, and Misterbianco had all fallen to the rebels.[50]

III

Given these conditions, it was inevitable that the collapse of Bourbon government in Sicily should bring huge problems with it. Economic activity and commerce was seriously disrupted, and unemployment increased. Few among the rural *squadre* showed any sign of abandoning their activities. The presence of large numbers of escaped and released convicts added to existing security problems.[51] Peasant unrest over land increased, rather than decreased, with Garibaldi's occupation of Palermo. Most importantly, perhaps, for the future stability of government administration was the fact that, in many communes, Bourbon power collapsed long before the arrival of any *garibaldini*. With the success of the Sicilian revolution in 1860, the common enemy had been overcome. But the real problems of government were, arguably, just beginning.

Towards the end of May 1860, General Lanza wrote to Naples in an attempt to convince the Bourbon government (and perhaps himself) that the situation could still be salvaged. Garibaldi, he reported, was having serious problems with the Sicilian insurgents; everyone was surprised 'at their lack of willingness to fight, at their ill-disciplined

---

[47] 18 May 1860, Elliot to Russell reporting on intelligence from British ships in Sicily, PRO, FO 70/316. See also F. Brancato, 'L'amministrazione garibaldina e il plebiscito in Sicilia', in *Atti del XXXIX congresso di storia del Risorgimento in Italia: la Sicilia e l'unità d'Italia* (Salerno, 1961), 180–1, and Mack Smith, 'The Peasants' Revolt in Sicily', 204.

[48] 27 May 1860, ASP, Min. Affari Sicilia, Polizia, b.1239.

[49] 24 May 1860, from Lanza to the minister in Naples, ibid. b. 1238 and 29 May 1860, from the intendant of Catania to the same, ibid. b. 1239. The British vice-consul in Catania sent vivid eyewitness accounts of the violence: 30 May 1860 to Rickards in Messina, PRO, FO 70/317, and 7 June 1860 to Goodwin in Palermo, ibid.

[50] In report from Lanza of 24 May 1860, ASP, Min. Affari Sicilia, Polizia, b.1238.

[51] Mack Smith, 'The Peasants' Revolt in Sicily', 207.

and turbulent character, at their readiness to steal, stealing guns, munitions and equipment belonging to the Piedmontese'.[52] While Lanza was hardly a disinterested observer, and while his optimism was to prove ill-founded, it is nevertheless revealing that he focused on these particular problems. For Lanza, the lack of stable support for Garibaldi and the inability of Garibaldi's forces to control the countryside had led to a sense of 'cruel disillusionment' once they joined up with the Sicilian insurgents.

In reality, Garibaldi's success in the early summer of 1860 was far from secure. The collapse of the Bourbon administration before and during May 1860 had left a political vacuum which the *garibaldini* were able to take advantage of. The wave of popular support won for the *garibaldini* by their promise of land reform also ensured their rapid military success. In short, political collapse and popular unrest brought down the Bourbon government in 1860. However, this situation was to persist long after the Bourbon government had gone. The speed with which Garibaldi was able to oust the Bourbons from Sicily was an indication of much deeper problems, to which the impulsive expeditionary force from Northern Italy had few answers. Armed bands, impoverished peasants, and discontented property-owners in rural communes all helped Garibaldi to victory in 1860. Yet the aims of the peasants and property-owners fundamentally conflicted over the issue of land.[53] Whether either group would continue to support Garibaldi and guarantee his control over the countryside after the Bourbons had gone also remained to be seen.

Garibaldi's leadership was all the more precarious because his followers in Sicily disagreed amongst themselves. As we shall see in Chapter 3, the political opposition in Sicily—henceforth, the ruling political élite—had never been able to agree on a common programme. They were internally divided, had no obvious means of controlling the countryside, and had rarely been in a position to look beyond the end of rule from Naples. In the event, getting rid of the Bourbons in 1860 proved relatively easy. Solving the crisis which had led to their defeat was to prove another matter entirely.

---

[52] 25 May 1860, in ASP, Min. Affari Sicilia, Polizia, b. 1238.
[53] Mack Smith, 'The Peasants' Revolt in Sicily', 198–9.

3

Garibaldi's Dictatorship: The Reality of Government, May–November 1860

I

The decade before 1860 had been a difficult time for Italian democrats everywhere. After the defeat of the revolutionary governments in Italy during 1849, democrats lacked a regional base from which they might have been able to withstand the effects of political persecution and rebuild themselves as a movement. Initially, however, the revolutionary experiences of 1848–9 had seemed to enhance the reputation of Italian democrats and Italian nationalism, and to give enormous publicity to Mazzini's ideal of a democratic, republican Italy.[1] During 1848 and 1849 democrats had created republics in Rome and Venice, and had established a Republican-dominated government in Tuscany. The already famous revolutionary general, Giuseppe Garibaldi, became more famous still after his extraordinary, if ultimately unsuccessful, defence of the Roman Republic against French attempts to restore the Pope in 1849. The tragic defence of the Venetian Republic against the powerful Austrian army also confirmed the heroism and political commitment of Italian democrats.

The heroism of Italian democrats in 1848–9 was all the more striking by contrast to the performance of their main rivals in opposition circles, the moderate liberals. In much of revolutionary Italy during 1849, moderate liberals had allowed their fear of popular violence and social change to outweigh their belief in individual liberties and constitutionalism. From Piedmont to Palermo, they had ultimately preferred to remain loyal to the old regime than see a republican form of government come to power.

Yet, after 1849, Italian democrats were unable to capitalize on their advantage. By contrast, the status of moderate liberalism, which after 1852 enjoyed an increasingly stable political basis in Piedmont, went from strength to strength. Generally, the effects of exile and political

---

[1] C. M. Lovett, *The Democratic Movement in Italy* (Cambridge, Mass., 1982), 157–8.

isolation eroded the democrats' sense of purpose. 'Police harassment, economic deprivation and homesickness were the lot of nearly all democratic leaders after 1848,' Clara Lovett comments; '[g]radually these collective experiences sapped the vitality of the democratic movement to the point that its very survival was in doubt.'[2] A series of failed insurrections, from Mazzini's revolt in Milan in 1853 to Carlo Pisacane's tragic attempt to lead a peasant revolt in the South in 1857, also signalled a reversal in democratic fortunes. In Lombardy-Venetia, the Central Duchies, the Papal States, and the Two Sicilies, the police cracked down on the democratic movement, driving its leaders into exile and marginalizing its activities relative to the more 'respectable' moderate liberal movement.

The disastrous end to the attempted revolts of 1853 and 1857 encouraged many democrats to doubt the utility of the revolutionary conspiracies favoured by Giuseppe Mazzini as the means of organizing resistance to Italy's Restoration regimes. They also started to question his confidence in popular insurrection as the vehicle for overthrowing the forces of religious and monarchical reaction. In 1857 the Tuscan democrat Antonio Mordini wrote that, although the democratic movement still had strength in popular numbers, effective leadership was lacking. 'Wealth and intelligence', he feared, was actually deserting the democratic movement, 'and with wealth the material forces which are essential to hatch a conspiracy and to start a revolution'.[3]

In this way, the reversals of the 1850s also undermined the democrats' unity of purpose. Between 1849 and 1859 they proved unable to unite themselves into a single, coherent movement with a concrete programme which expressed their political ideas and aspirations. They had difficulty in establishing themselves as a credible political leadership and in appealing to the increasingly organized and vocal middle class, particularly in the economically dynamic regions of Central and Northern Italy. Finally, they could not resolve the two central questions raised by their defeat in 1849, namely, how to prepare the military defence of the revolution, and how to reconcile the liberal—and middle-class—ideal of property and social order with the democratic ideal of popular sovereignty and social justice.

One way in which some Italian democrats expressed their disillusionment was by aligning themselves with Cavour's moderate liberal

---

[2] *The Democratic Movement in Italy*, 165.
[3] Quoted in A. Scirocco, *I democratici italiani da Sapri a Porta Pia* (Naples, 1969), 15.

government in Piedmont. In 1857 Daniele Manin and Giorgio Pallavicino formed the Italian National Society, intended as a pressure-group organization to mobilize public opinion (especially public opinion in Piedmont) in favour of Italian unification. The National Society, particularly after it came under the leadership of the Sicilian democrat, Giuseppe La Farina, aligned itself ever more clearly with the moderate liberal 'solution' for Italy, and actively promoted the Piedmontese monarchy as the vehicle for uniting Italy.[4] A military planning group set up in Genoa under Agostino Bertani and Giacomo Medici also began to argue that the military success of the national revolution was dependent on Piedmontese support.[5] Even Mazzini adopted what was called a 'neutral flag' in 1856, that is to say, a policy of support for either republic or monarchy as long as national unification was the declared objective.[6] At the other extreme, however, socialists such as Pisacane criticized Mazzini's failure to distinguish himself fully from moderate liberalism; 'moderate solutions such as the constitutional regime in Piedmont,' in Pisacane's words, 'far from advancing the Risorgimento in Italy, actually retard its progress.'[7] It was precisely Mazzini's refusal to address social issues and espouse social revolution which, according to Pisacane and others, had led to their defeat in successive revolutions.

Among the 'Thousand' who joined Garibaldi's expedition to Sicily in 1860 and, even more, among those who gave material support to the expedition (the National Society, the Genoese military committee), there were many enthusiastic adherents to the Piedmontese cause. Even Francesco Crispi, who planned the expedition, and Garibaldi, who led it, were prepared to support Piedmont if it helped to unite Italy. Garibaldi had fallen out with Mazzini after the events of 1849; thereafter, he had established links with the Genoese military committee, and had even had some tentative contact with Cavour. Both he and Crispi were prepared to sacrifice other ideals, particularly their republicanism, if unity could be achieved.[8] In June 1860, Crispi wrote to Agostino Bertani that while 'our friends among the Republicans accuse

[4] See R. Grew, *A Sterner Plan for Italian Unity: The Italian National Society and the Risorgimento* (Princeton, 1963), 3–66, 111–90.

[5] On the Genoese military committee, see G. Candeloro, *Storia dell'Italia moderna*, iv: *dalla rivoluzione nazionale all'unità* (Milan, 1964), 100.

[6] G. Berti, *I democratici e l'iniziativa meridionale nel Risorgimento* (Milan, 1962), 664–5.

[7] C. Pisacane, *La rivoluzione in Italia* (Rome, 1968), 223.

[8] D. Mack Smith, *Cavour and Garibaldi: A Study in Political Conflict* (Cambridge, 1954; 2nd edn., 1985), 17.

us of forsaking the banner [and] Cavour's followers say we want a Republic . . . what we really want is Italy and we will have her!'.[9] The slogan adopted for the expedition of the 'Thousand'—*Italia e Vittorio Emanuele*—also suggests the extent to which many democrats had come to identify Italian unity with the Piedmontese monarchy. 'I love Italy above all else,' Crispi wrote to Cesare Correnti at the beginning of July, 'and as Italy is destined to come into existence through the house of Savoy, I accept this condition without *arrière pensée*.'[10]

Garibaldi's success in Sicily in May 1860 none the less represented a huge political opportunity for Italian democrats. It allowed them to seize back some of the initiative from Cavour and from Piedmont. Democrats held power in a region of Italy for the first time since 1849; indeed, for Mack Smith, 'this was almost the only time during the whole risorgimento that the radical democrats had a *pied à terre*, and not only that, but also an army, a momentum and something of a practical programme'.[11] Moreover, many committed democrats had long argued that the real potential for revolution lay in the South. Despite the setback of Pisacane's failure in Sapri, Sicilian revolutionaries such as Pilo and Corrao continued to argue that there was popular support for a revolution. In Sicily, they suggested, the combination of an unstable and weak state with widespread popular discontent—most notably peasant unrest over land—meant that a revolutionary conspiracy could bring about popular insurrection (or 'popular war').[12] For Pilo, the potential for a successful revolution in Sicily was also indicated by the relative lack of support for moderate liberalism among the middle-class élites.[13]

Against this, however, many democrats were not convinced of the wisdom of an expedition to Sicily at a time when the whole of Italy was in turmoil following the historic defeat of the Austrian Empire. Garibaldi himself was reluctant to lead it, writing to Rosolino Pilo as late as March 1860 that 'at the present moment I believe any revolutionary movement in any part of Italy whatsoever, would be ill-timed, and would have little chance of success'.[14] It was apparently only when Cavour

---

[9] Crispi, *The Memoirs of Francesco Crispi*, i: *The Thousand*, ed. T. Palmenghi-Crispi, trans. M. Prichard-Agnetti (3 vols.; London, 1912–14), 266.

[10] Ibid. 5 July 1860, 305.   [11] *Cavour and Garibaldi*, 18.

[12] G. Giarrizzo, 'Il "popolo" di Garibaldi', in G. Cingari (ed.), *Garibaldi e il socialismo* (Rome and Bari, 1984), 21. For a more detailed discussion, see P. Ginsborg, 'Risorgimento rivoluzionario: mito e realtà di una guerra di popolo', *Storia e Dossier*, 47 (1991), 61–97.

[13] Berti, *I democratici e l'iniziativa meridionale*, 539–60, 600–48.

[14] 15 March 1860, in Crispi, *Memoirs*, i. 134.

announced the cession of Nice (Garibaldi's birthplace) to the French in return for Piedmont's annexation of the Central Italian duchies that he changed his mind. Thus, it was anger against Cavour rather than a set of detailed policy aims which led Garibaldi to head the expedition to Sicily.

Even before their arrival in Sicily, in other words, there were conflicts among Italian democrats about what they could and would achieve there. Added to this was the intense factionalism and political rivalry which had long characterized oppositional politics in Sicily itself. The democratic movement in Sicily was always in a minority compared to the larger and more prestigious autonomist party and, ever since 1820, demands for regional autonomy, agitation for democratic revolution, municipal jealousies, and struggles over land ownership had jostled uneasily against each other within opposition circles in Sicily. Perhaps the most important points of disagreement were over popular insurrection and the land question, issues which, as we saw in Chapter 2, were at the centre of the revolution against the Bourbons in 1860. In 1849 the Cordova land reform, introduced in an attempt to resolve the problem of ecclesiastical land, had destroyed the unity of the provisional government in Palermo and led to bitter tensions between autonomists and democrats.[15] Popular insurrection continued to be the 'watershed' issue dividing autonomists and democrats between 1849 and 1859.[16] For many democrats—Pasquale Calvi, Rosolino Pilo—the failure of 1848–9 was due to the failure to give direction to peasant revolt. Popular insurrection was the key to revolutionary success.[17] By contrast, autonomists (Ruggiero Settimo, the Marchese di Torrearsa, Emerico Amari), whose political sympathies were far closer to Cavour's moderate liberalism than to Mazzinian republicanism, saw popular insurrection as a threat and an obstacle to their political aspirations.

These divisions in the Sicilian opposition movement also had a regional basis: traditionally, democrats had a more significant foothold in Messina and, increasingly, throughout Eastern Sicily (in Catania), while the more aristocratic autonomists were much more powerful in Palermo.[18] After the failure of the 1848–9 revolution, the experience of

[15] G. Cingari, 'Gli ultimi Borboni: dalla restaurazione all'unità', in *Storia della Sicilia*, 8 (Naples, 1977), 57–9.

[16] A. Recupero, 'La Sicilia all'opposizione, 1848–1874', in M. Aymard and G. Giarrizzo (eds.), *La Sicilia* (Turin, 1987), 43.

[17] Ibid. 43–53; on Calvi, see G. Giarrizzo, 'La Sicilia dal Cinquecento all'unità d'Italia', in V. d'Alessandro and G. Giarrizzo, *La Sicilia dal vespro all'unità d'Italia* (Turin, 1989), 769–73.   [18] Ibid. 676–8, Cingari, 'Gli ultimi Borboni', 69.

political exile further accentuated the tendency towards ideological and geographical dispersal. Of the three currents of Sicilian exiles after 1849—radical democrats (Rosolino Pilo, Saverio Friscia), moderate democrats (Francesco Crispi), and moderate liberals (autonomists like Torrearsa)—the moderate liberals tended to be based in Turin. Sicilian democrats, by contrast, moved between Turin, Genoa, Marseilles, Malta, Paris, and London.[19]

In many respects the divisions in the Sicilian opposition had a positive effect, in that they made for vibrant political debate and the intermingling of different traditions and influences.[20] On a practical level, however, the persistence of such political diversity undermined the struggle against the Bourbons. Romeo argues that in the 1850s the Sicilian opposition was unable to overcome the contradictions which had led to their defeat in 1849. As a result, Sicilian autonomists such as Torrearsa, Trabia, and Cusa abandoned their attempt to find 'an autonomous solution to the Sicilian problem'; increasingly they promoted Piedmontese leadership in a united Italian kingdom as the only means of undoing the union with Naples.[21] Sicilian democrats, by contrast, sought a repeat of the popular insurrection of 1848 but without the errors—without, in other words, succumbing to the municipal and political rivalries which they felt had destroyed the revolution.[22] Yet the Sicilian democratic movement was itself weakened by the internal disagreements characteristic of the democratic movement nationally; and it was still further divided by a series of personal quarrels, rivalry, and ill-feeling.

Some Sicilian democrats, notably Giuseppe la Farina, abandoned their republicanism after 1849 and became staunch supporters of the Piedmontese 'solution'. Others (Michele Amari) increasingly supported Sicilian autonomy. Even revolutionary activists were unable to agree. As we have seen, Crispi was in favour of a united Italy 'above all else', while Pilo remained a loyal Mazzinian. Both were staunchly anti-socialist and unitarian. They clashed with those like Saverio Friscia, Pasquale Calvi, and Giovanni Interdonato, who were influenced by Proudhonist socialism and were in favour of a decentralized, federal Italy.[23] Thus,

[19] P. Alatri, *Lotte politiche in Sicilia sotto il governo della Destra, 1866–1874* (Turin, 1954), 21, Cingari, 'Gli ultimi Borboni', 70. [20] Ibid. 41–6.
[21] R. Romeo, *Il Risorgimento in Sicilia* (Bari, 1950), 305–45, 355–6. For an analysis of how the experience of exile in Piedmont influenced the autonomists, see G. Ciampi, *I liberali moderati siciliani in esilio nel decennio di preparazione* (Rome, 1979).
[22] Recupero, 'La Sicilia all'opposizione', 52.
[23] Cingari, 'Gli ultimi Borboni', 70–1; and on the divisions within radical democrats see S. F. Romano, *Momenti del Risorgimento in Sicilia* (Messina, 1952), 131–355.

revolutionaries like Pilo and Friscia only came together on the basis of a common republicanism and of their common opposition to the other 'tendencies'.[24]

Before 1860 neither moderates nor democrats in Sicily had been able to establish an alliance with their counterparts in Naples against the Bourbon monarchy. Indeed, from 1820 the demand for Sicilian autonomy was as unpopular with Neapolitan liberals as it was with the Bourbons themselves. Hardly surprisingly, therefore, the issue of Sicily's relationship with the rest of Italy caused enormous problems in 1860. Although, given the circumstances prevailing in 1860, almost everybody accepted the necessity of some kind of union with Piedmont, there was little agreement as to exactly when this union should take place and what form it would take. A pro-Piedmontese lobby, led by La Farina and Filippo Cordova, called for a plebiscite to vote on the immediate and unconditional annexation of Sicily by Piedmont. Sharply opposed to them was the group led by Crispi (and supported by Garibaldi) who wanted to delay annexation until Garibaldi had reached Naples and even, perhaps, until the 'liberation' of Rome had been achieved. A third group of autonomists (including Michele Amari and Torrearsa) opposed both the annexationists and the nationalists, demanding the establishment of an elective assembly in Sicily which would negotiate terms with the Piedmontese.[25] Amari also saw himself working as a mediator between Cavour's and Crispi's followers in order to safeguard Sicily's future. Autonomists had entered the government, he told the Englishman William Cartwright, 'to prevent the clash of these two opinions'.[26] Only the left-wing democrats were left out of this coalition of forces in favour of some kind of alliance with Piedmont. Saverio Friscia accused the government of wanting to 'extinguish the revolution', but he was on the left of the party, and was one of the very few democrats publicly to make a stand against the Piedmontese 'solution'.[27]

On the whole, therefore, Italian democrats had not agreed on why they were going to Sicily in 1860. There was even less consensus as to what they would do once they were there. Most of Garibaldi's volunteers were from Northern Italy; few among them were familiar with

---

[24] G. C. Marino, *Saverio Friscia: socialista libertario* (Palermo, 1986), 84.

[25] Mack Smith, *Cavour and Garibaldi*, 174–5.

[26] 13 July 1860, in M. Amari, *Carteggio di Michele Amari*, ed. A. d'Ancona (Turin, 1896), ii. 106.

[27] F. Brancato, 'L'amministrazione garibaldina e il plebiscito in Sicilia', in *Atti del xxxix congresso di storia del Risorgimento in Italia: la Sicilia e l'unità d' Italia* (Milan, 1962), 192.

Sicily. Many were probably swept away by a wave of nationalist enthusiasm following the war of 1859 and its aftermath, and saw in the
expedition a chance to do 'something' for the Italian cause.[28] Crispi
and Garibaldi saw the liberation of Sicily as the springboard for the
realization of grander plans, which included the conquest of Rome.
Some Sicilians, most obviously La Farina and Cordova, aimed primarily
to protect the interests of Cavour and Piedmont. Since the Sicilian
democrats in the new government disagreed among themselves, they
were unable to offer a united political front and direction. Almost
nobody, as far as the evidence reveals, thought at all about the immense
practical difficulties of filling the political and social vacuum left by the
collapse of Bourbon government in Sicily.

II

Following the defeat of Bourbon troops by the volunteers at Calatafimi in
May 1860 Garibaldi assumed the title of dictator of Sicily. However, the
title 'dictator' is rather misleading. Each successive government in
Palermo was a coalition and included moderate liberals and autonomists.
Democrats were always in a minority.[29] In all, there were three separate
periods of 'dictatorship' during 1860, the first of which was direct rule
by Garibaldi himself and lasted until July. Garibaldi was always more
interested in pursuing the war against the Bourbons and, in July, he
resumed this campaign and crossed over to the mainland. Agostino
Depretis became prodictator in Garibaldi's place. After Depretis's resignation in mid-September, Antonio Mordini was appointed prodictator, a post which he occupied until December (but which effectively
ended with the October vote for union with Northern Italy).

The Sicilian government of 1860, like its predecessors in 1820 and
1848–9, rested on a fragile consensus, with conflicts and personal
rivalries frequently paralysing its work. There was a marked contrast
in style and aims between the two prodictators. Depretis was a
Piedmontese Leftist and a supporter of the political alliance (*connubio*)
between the centre-Left and centre-Right in Piedmont; as such, he
was initially welcomed as an intermediary between the democrats and
Piedmontese in Sicily.[30] It soon became apparent, however, that

---

[28] Giarrizzo, 'Il "popolo" di Garibaldi', 21.

[29] Mack Smith, *Cavour and Garibaldi*, 21.

[30] Ibid. 105–7; C. Maraldi, 'La rivoluzione siciliana del 1860 e l'opera politico-amministrativa di Agostino Depretis', *Rassegna Storica del Risorgimento*, 19 (1932), 489.

Depretis had established strong links with Cavour and sought simply to prepare Sicily for annexation to Piedmont. As a result, his actions increasingly aroused the suspicions of the democrats.[31] By the middle of August, relations between Crispi and Depretis had deteriorated sharply, while Mazzinians like Giorgio Asproni had begun to agitate publicly against Depretis.[32]

By all accounts, moreover, Depretis felt overwhelmed by the administrative chaos which he found in Sicily, and by the scale of the task which faced him. Although initially optimistic about his ability to deal with these problems,[33] he soon became convinced that the situation could not be resolved without annexation. The extent of popular unrest, the lack of security forces, and a deteriorating financial situation in Sicily further persuaded him of the need for prompt annexation by Piedmont.[34]

Mordini had very different ideas and aims. Under Depretis, and with attention shifting anyway towards the war on the mainland, government interest in solving the problems in Sicily seemed to decline. Under Mordini, however, renewed efforts were made to develop a democratic policy for Sicily. Although Mordini, a Tuscan democrat, had supported Tuscany's union with Piedmont in March 1860, he was not in favour of immediate or unconditional annexation of Sicily by Piedmont. According to Mack Smith, Mordini combined 'the loyal monarchist and the radical, the convinced annexationist and the non-Piedmontese'. Yet he was not popular in Turin, and Cavour convinced himself Mordini was a Mazzinian.[35] Mordini aimed to show that an effective administration could restore order, without having to rely on the Piedmontese or annexation, simply by broadening Sicilian support for a democratic government. He attempted to make popular enthusiasm for Garibaldi and a new programme of reform the basis for his rule, and thereby to demonstrate that a democratic system of government was as viable as a more authoritarian one.[36]

Although Mordini eventually gave up the attempt to prevent unconditional annexation, his administration did win praise for efficiency,

---

[31] Mack Smith, *Cavour and Garibaldi*, 108–9, 166.

[32] 15 Aug. and 21 Aug. 1860, G. Asproni, *Diario politico 1855–1876* (7 vols.; Milan, 1974–91), ii. 510–11, 516–17.

[33] See his letter to Bertani of 24 July 1860, in Istituto per la Storia del Risorgimento, Milano (henceforth, ISRM), Carte Bertani, cartella 17, elenco 2, plico xxvi bis, 6.

[34] He wrote to Garibaldi on 1 Sept. that the only solution to these difficulties was annexation; ibid. cartella 10, elenco 2, plico xi, 2.   [35] *Cavour and Garibaldi*, 263.

[36] Ibid. 274.

honesty, and openness during its short life.[37] However, some democrats were more muted in their praise of Mordini. Gregorio Ugdulena wrote to Crispi on 25 October that although Mordini had showed himself an expert in the art of government, he had had too much to do with the 'old regime' and showed himself too willing to conciliate.[38] Asproni was more forthright: Mordini was 'a sincere liberal', but timid and hesitant.[39] Mordini himself appears to have been satisfied with his achievements. To his mother he wrote from Naples on 5 December 1860 that 'I left Sicily in a truly good condition because my government operated in a regular fashion, as though we were living in normal conditions'.[40] Unlike Depretis, Mordini possessed a detailed knowledge of the Sicilian countryside, and had established links with local notables which he used when he became prodictator.[41] He was, as a result, far more sensitive to the need to work with rural élites than Depretis, whose attention was fixed far to the north of Palermo and who seldom left Palermo during his prodictatorship.[42]

The effect of Mordini's policies are, however, difficult to assess since he was prodictator for a relatively short time, and at a time when annexation to Piedmont was looking increasingly likely. Although the pro-annexationists had suffered a series of early defeats, most notably with the expulsion of Giuseppe La Farina by Garibaldi in July, by September they had begun to win the day. The decision to hold a plebiscite on the question of annexation (in October 1860), which resulted in an overwhelming vote for union with Piedmont, represented a victory for the annexationist group and, ultimately, for the Piedmontese government and for Cavour. These developments considerably constrained Mordini's freedom of action in Sicily. Furthermore, although Depretis and Mordini held the title of prodictator, for much of the summer and early autumn the real power in the government was in fact Francesco Crispi. Crispi served in all three governments and was involved in all important administrative and legislative decisions. The

---

[37] Mordini wrote a series of letters to Bertani in September which outline his hopes and the progress he is making. ISRM, Bertani, cartella 11, elenco 2, plico xii, n. 83: 1, 4, 5.

[38] Archivio Centrale dello Stato, Roma (henceforth, ACSR), Carte Crispi (Archivio dello Stato, Palermo), fasicolo 54, xlviii.

[39] 26 Aug. and 19 Nov. 1860, *Diario politico*, ii. 561, 574.

[40] M. Rosi, *Il Risorgimento italiano e l'azione d'un patriota cospiratore e soldato* (Rome, 1906), 429.

[41] Prior to his appointment as prodictator, Mordini had been president of the military court in Sicily and was a frequent visitor to the Sicilian interior.

[42] Brancato, 'L'amministrazione garibaldina', 19, 32.

day-to-day running of the government was usually left to him. As Garibaldi's secretary of state, Crispi was, according to Brancato, 'the real inspiration behind his policies'. At least once Crispi referred to Garibaldi's decrees as 'my decrees'.[43] Before he quarrelled with Depretis, Crispi influenced almost all of Depretis's political actions. Even while away in Naples during September, Crispi sent detailed instructions to the new prodictator, Mordini, about how to deal with the political situation in Palermo.[44]

Crispi's commanding position had a visible impact upon government policy in Sicily. He was, by all accounts, a difficult man to work with, who quarrelled with almost everyone. Autonomists were wary of him, suspecting him of having secret agendas of his own. His relations with the annexationists and former democrats Cordova and La Farina were hostile. Even Mazzinian friends were sometimes alarmed by his behaviour. The Mazzinian Giorgio Asproni has left a vivid account in his diary of a meeting with Crispi in August 1860, where Crispi bad-mouthed his opponents within the revolutionary movement ('the Sicilian aristocracy is defunct . . . Pignatelli is a wretched *capo* of thieves . . .. La Porta protects ruffians') and terrified Asproni by letting a gun, which he always carried with him for personal protection, go off by mistake.[45] All of this meant that a lot of the government's (and Crispi's) energies were taken up with personal and political battles, diverting attention away from the formulation of official policy.

Furthermore, since the wider imperatives of the nationalist initiative were what mattered to Crispi, the wider imperatives of the nationalist struggle came to determine the Sicilian government's domestic policy. For Crispi, the government's main purpose was to ensure effective and efficient control of the struggle against the Bourbons. All of the government's aims related ultimately to this end. Crispi sought to unite and organize the Sicilian population behind the revolution, to establish a system for the maintenance of law and order so as to win the support of the propertied élites, and, finally, to reorganize the administration of Sicily. These were, it should be stressed, short-term policies intended to facilitate the preparation for war on the mainland.[46] Crispi's main long-term policy for Sicily was to make it part of an Italian nation-state.

[43] Brancato, 'L'amministrazione garibaldina', 9–10.
[44] See his letters to Mordini of 20 Sept. and 29 Sept. 1860 in Archivio Mordini, Barga (henceforth, AMB), Filza 17, F. B., nn. 1 and 2.
[45] Asproni, *Diario Politico*, ii. 503.
[46] Brancato, 'L'amminstrazione garibaldina', 9.

The government managed, nevertheless, to establish an unprecedented popular following in Sicily. Garibaldi presented himself as a popular saviour and liberator, and used his immense personal charisma to encourage enthusiasm for the revolution. One British observer, Commander Forbes, described the communication between Garibaldi and the mass of the population as 'perfectly electrifying', while Michele Amari observed that 'the common people . . . worship Garibaldi as a mythical hero'.[47] The government also took immediate and concrete steps to win the support of the Sicilian peasantry and to give direction to the existing peasant revolt. On 17 May, a decree announced the abolition of the hated *macinato* or grist tax. This was followed by a decree on 2 June which announced the division of Crown land among the peasantry. Special provision was made for those who fought with Garibaldi. This initial decree was followed by a later, and more sweeping, measure of land reform introduced by Mordini in October. Mordini's decree involved the transfer of some 230,000 hectares of Church and Crown land into perpetual leases (*enfiteusi*) for smallholders.[48] Other reforms intended to win the favour of the Sicilian poor included the abolition of feudal customs and titles: the title of 'excellency' and the customary hand-kissing of noblemen by peasants were both outlawed. On a practical note, the Piedmontese Casati law, which established the principle of compulsory primary education, was also introduced, along with the Piedmontese system of foundling homes (*asili per infanzia*).

Renda argues that the decree of 2 June relating to Crown land was part of a broader attempt to give direction to the revolution in the countryside.[49] One of the first acts of the new government was to bring in compulsory military service (*leva*) in order both to mobilize the population against the Bourbons and to safeguard internal order. On the same day that Garibaldi became dictator of Sicily (14 May), a decree was issued setting up a militia composed of all able-bodied Sicilian males between the ages of 17 and 50. The militia was divided into three categories; the first (those aged 17 to 30) were required for active service in the army, the second for policing duties ('to uphold public

[47] Forbes's comment is quoted in Mack Smith, *Cavour and Garibaldi*, 21; Amari's in *Carteggio Amari*, ii. 134.

[48] G. Candeloro, *Storia dell'Italia moderna*, v: *la costruzione dello stato unitario* (Milan, 1968), 321.

[49] F. Renda, 'Garibaldi e la questione contadina in Sicilia nel 1860', in Cingari (ed.), *Garibaldi e il socialismo*, 40–3.

order') in the various provincial districts, and the third for policing in individual communes.[50] Crucially, the introduction of the *leva* enabled the government to suppress the *squadre*. Although Garibaldi and Crispi had initially encouraged such armed irregulars to participate in the fight against the Bourbons, once the Bourbons were in retreat Crispi saw the *squadre* as a direct threat to law and order, who needed urgently to be disbanded and replaced by a regular force.[51]

A recurring fear of many democrats in 1860 was of a conservative backlash against peasant revolution of the kind which had benefited the Bourbons in 1820 and 1848.[52] Perhaps particularly for Crispi, the lessons of 1848–9 were not to be forgotten. From May onwards, the government made considerable efforts to safeguard the interests of the propertied élites and, most of all, to protect their property. A determination to control crime and disorder was evident from the outset. On 18 May a military court (*consiglio di guerra*) was set up to try civilians. This was followed by a decree of 28 May which established the death penalty for theft, looting, and murder. On 9 June, certain offences (such as kidnapping) were declared punishable by summary execution.[53] Crispi also sent a circular to district governors on 5 June, reminding them that 'police superintendents must have no eye for anything except defending property, defending individuals and defending the inviolability of the home'.[54]

Besides adopting a strong line on the defence of law and order, the government introduced a number of reforms aimed specifically at the urban middle classes. Most involved economic or infrastructural improvements. Responding to a long-standing grievance among Sicilian merchants, the Secretary of State for Public Works, Giovanni Raffaele, drew up plans for the construction of a railway between Palermo and Messina, with branch lines to Caltanissetta and Catania.[55] Various restrictions on the free operation of the labour market were removed,

---

[50] Brancato, 'L'amministrazione garibaldina', 9.   [51] Ibid. 10–11.

[52] Scirocco, *I democratici italiani*, 123.

[53] *Raccolti degli atti del governo dittatoriale e prodittatoriale in Sicilia* (Palermo, 1861), 12, 19, 38–40.

[54] Quoted in D. Mack Smith, 'The Peasants' Revolt in Sicily: 1860', in *Victor Emmanuel, Cavour and the Risorgimento* (London, 1971), 220.

[55] R. Giuffrida, 'La dittatura di Garibaldi ed il problema ferroviario in Sicilia', in *La Sicilia e l'unità d'Italia* (Palermo, 1960), and the same author's remarks in *Politica ed economia nella Sicilia dell'Ottocento* (Palermo, 1980), 240–2. See also Z. Ciufoletti, 'Affarismo e lotta politica nell'impresa dei Mille: Garibaldi e le ferrovie meridionali', in Cingari (ed.), *Garibaldi e il socialismo*.

with the final abolition of the Palermo *maestranze* (guilds). A detailed programme was also introduced to improve and restructure the urban environment in Palermo, and both universities at Palermo and Catania were given extra funding for scientific research.[56] Finally, the Jesuits, one of the most potent symbols of the cultural and religious despotism of the old regime, were expelled from Sicily by decree on 16 June.

The reforms introduced by the dictatorship during 1860 expressed its commitment to broad democratic ideals and to establishing a popular and élite following on the basis of a common national identity. Yet most of the reforms which were introduced in 1860, however well-intentioned, did little more than scratch the surface of deep-rooted problems. Even Mordini's land reform, arguably the most radical measure undertaken by the dictatorship, was more impressive in appearance than in reality. The credit facilities necessary to make the reform beneficial to peasants were never made available (an omission which the economist Carlo Cattaneo described as 'giving away bottles without any wine in them').[57] What the dictatorship lacked was either the resources or the time to bring in a detailed agrarian programme. By the summer, moreover, the democrats had begun to lose the political initiative to Cavour.[58]

There were also inherent limitations in the democrats' approach to reform. Since the majority of them, including Crispi, sought to discourage social conflict, they feared the consequences of too radical a redistribution of land or wealth. Instead, they attempted to reconcile the aspirations of the Sicilian peasantry with the aims of the Sicilian élites. Unfortunately, this policy satisfied no-one. The peasants became increasingly frustrated at the government's inability to enforce reform, while the élites became increasingly fearful at the rising tide of peasant unrest and the failure to control the *squadre*. In truth, the government had little concrete basis on which to appeal to the landed élites in Sicily. The appeal to nationalism satisfied only a small group of urban professionals and (perhaps ironically) the more cosmopolitan nobility, both of whom had begun to identify Italian nationalism with their sense of *sicilianismo*. Among landed élites in the countryside, however, the government's programme held much less interest. The support of landowners for the *garibaldini* in May 1860 had been based largely on the government's promise to maintain law and order and to protect

---

[56] C. di Seta and L. de Mauro, *Palermo* (Bari, 1981), 156.
[57] G. Cerrito, 'La questione della liquidazione dell'asse ecclesiastico in Sicilia', *Rassegna Storica del Risorgimento*, 43 (1956), 271.
[58] Renda, 'Garibaldi e la questione contadina in Sicilia', 47–9.

property. The persistence of peasant unrest over land, fuelled in part by the democrats' promise of land reform, rapidly undermined their support.

The lack of a solid basis of support in the countryside meant that the final aim of the dictatorship—that of 'normalizing' the administration of Sicily and instituting 'good government'—was increasingly seen as the crucial means of gaining control of the countryside (particularly bearing in mind the disastrous experiences of 1848). This policy was pursued relentlessly by Crispi from May onwards.[59] It posed itself all the more urgently in 1860 because the revolution against the Bourbons had led to such a complete breakdown in the island's administration. The dictatorship was thus faced with the need to create, *ex nuovo*, an effective machinery of government.

After the defeat of Bourbon troops at Calatafimi on 17 May, Crispi issued a decree which provided for the nomination of governors in all twenty-four districts of Sicily. The governors were charged with the organization of an administrative system for public security in the major cities, districts, and communes of Sicily, and with appointing the personnel in charge of communal administration. As part of an attempt to ensure political loyalty, the decree also stated that the revolutionary councils of 1848 should be reconstituted. Those who had supported the Bourbon restoration of 1849 were to be replaced.[60] Following the armistice with the Bourbons in June, a civilian government with six ministries (War and Navy, Interior and Finance, Justice, Education and Culture, Foreign Affairs and Commerce, and Public Works and Finance) was set up in Palermo.[61]

Subsequently, one of the most striking features of the organization of government under the dictatorship was the extent to which it was modelled on the Piedmontese system. Under Depretis, and with Crispi's encouragement, the process of administrative 'normalization' became one of 'Piedmontization'. In under a month, the Piedmontese constitution (*statuto albertino*) was extended to Sicily (3 August), along with the Piedmontese monetary system (17 August), the Piedmontese copyright laws (18 August), the Piedmontese system of provincial and communal administration (26 August), the Piedmontese military code (28 August), and the Piedmontese public security law of 1859 (30 August).[62] Even Mordini, who attempted to delay annexation by sum-

---

[59] A. Albanese, 'Premessa per uno studio storico-giuridico sulla legislatura della dittatura e della prodittatura in Sicilia', in: *Congresso internazionale del Risorgimento, la Sicilia e l'unità d'Italia* 614.   [60] Brancato, 'L'amministrazione garibaldina', 10.
[61] Ibid. 14.   [62] *Atti del governo dittatoriale e prodittatoriale*, 171–318.

moning an assembly (*consiglio di stato*) to negotiate political terms with Piedmont,[63] made no attempt to reverse the 'piedmontization' of the administrative system.

This process of 'piedmontization' reflected the democrats' commitment to Italian unity under Piedmontese leadership; but it also reflected the internal problems of Sicilian government. 'Piedmontization' was in part a response to the prevailing administrative chaos; it was seen as a solution to the administrative difficulties encountered by the government. By introducing Piedmontese legislation to Sicily, democrats introduced a system which seemed already to have proven its effectiveness and worth in Piedmont. Unfortunately, it was a system which also bore a strong resemblance to the one adopted by the Bourbon monarchy after 1815. Thus, by introducing Piedmontese legislation to Sicily, democrats were actually exposing themselves to the same administrative difficulties which had undermined the previous regime.

To succeed in 'normalizing' government in 1860, the democrats had to do more than simply calm the immediate revolutionary crisis. They had also to deal with the causes of this crisis: they had to reconstruct a whole system of political authority, they had to attract the support of rural élites, they had to solve the land question, and they had to find a solution to the conflicts within the communes. There was, in practice, very little reason for government optimism. The dictatorship in 1860 was preoccupied with other issues, and had little perception of the problems affecting rural areas. The policy-making process was itself beset by internal wranglings. Finally, as we shall see in the next section, during the summer of 1860 the revolutionary crisis intensified as peasant disorder became more widespread and there was a rapid increase in violent crime. In this situation it is not surprising that another striking feature of the organization of government in Sicily in 1860 was that it hardly worked at all.

III

It rapidly became apparent, during the summer of 1860, that governing Sicily was far more of a problem than the *garibaldini* had ever imagined. First, the partition of land provoked a series of dramatic conflicts between peasants and landowners, most infamously in the violent uprisings which took place in Bronte, Biancavilla, Montemaggiore, and elsewhere during

---

[63] For a discussion of Mordini's motives, see Mack Smith, *Cavour and Garibaldi*, 293–306.

July and August. Although these disturbances formed part of a broader pattern of community conflict, peasants had immediate grievances of their own. In many communes, where the seizure of power on behalf of Garibaldi took place before his arrival, the promised partition of land did not take place, or did not take place soon enough for the peasants.[64] Considerable doubt also grew up among the peasantry about the status of agrarian contracts and credit facilities after the revolution. In Spaccaforno, for example, peasants refused to work the land; elsewhere land was occupied on the basis that it had been 'usurped' by the *civili*.[65]

The attempt to introduce conscription also ran into serious problems. Under the Bourbons, exemption from conscription had been a special privilege reserved for Sicilians. In 1860 officials soon began to complain of the 'disillusionment' of local inhabitants over conscription.[66] Governor Scelsi of Girgenti claimed that the decree was generally 'considered impracticable' and warned Crispi 'that the edict concerning conscription has awakened dissatisfaction'.[67] According to one police officer, opposition to conscription was being used by anti-liberal agitators to encourage opposition to Garibaldi.[68] Conscription was also blamed for an increase in disorder. The British vice-consul in Catania reported on 15 June that the printed placards announcing conscription had 'been torn from the walls'.[69] More ominously, the governor of Caltagirone warned in July of the popular anger which would result from the decree. By taking peasants away from their home and hearth, he wrote, the decree would change them from 'sheep' into 'lions'.[70]

[64] Renzo del Carria makes a distinction between communes liberated by Garibaldi and those liberated on his behalf by internal forces, although he probably over-estimates the element of class conflict in the communes: *Proletari senza rivoluzione* (Milan, 1966), 47–9.

[65] Numerous reports to the government of Palermo refer to peasant land occupations and impromptu strikes throughout Sicily. See e.g. the 'rapporto del governo del distretto di Acireale sopra lo avvenuto in Castiglione sino al 14 agosto 1860' in ASP, Luog. Polizia, b. 1549, f. reati avvenimenti Acireale, and the report from the *questore* of Corleone, 6 September 1860, in ASP, Luog. Polizia, b. 1547.

[66] From the mayor of Spaccaforno, 25 July 1860, in ASP, Ministero e Real Segretario di Stato presso il Luogotenente Generale, Interno (henceforth, Luog. Interno), b. 1615, f. leva.

[67] Letters of 12 and 13 June 1860, from Giacinto Scelsi to Crispi, in Crispi, *Memoirs*, i. 226–7.

[68] Delegate Vincenzo Bonanno wrote to Crispi on 13 June about the pro-Bourbon activities of Stefano Scumardi in Casteltermini, in ACSR, Crispi (ASP), f. 95/7, and similar activities were reported in Nicosia by the Governor on 16 June, in ASP, Luog. Polizia, b. 1560, f. Palermo.   [69] PRO, FO 70/317.

[70] 7 July 1860, ASP, Luog. Polizia, f. reati avvenimenti Caltagirone.

During the summer there was a marked increase in violence and popular disorder. Popular disturbances over land and conscription persisted. Violent crime—armed robbery, kidnapping, extortion, murder—was said to be on the increase. At the end of August the British wine-merchant, Benjamin Ingham, complained to the British consul, John Goodwin, that crime was so widespread in the Trapani area that rents were not being paid and the harvest could not proceed.[71] Armed gangs seem to have been responsible for this increase in crime. The *squadre* involved in the fight against the Bourbons refused to return to civilian life, while the huge numbers of criminals 'liberated' from prison during the confused events between April and June formed new gangs of their own.[72]

Government records from June onwards show that the authorities in Palermo and elsewhere were inundated with complaints about public security. According to the Governor of Mazara an armed gang had come to dominate the commune of Salemi, pursuing personal vendettas and intimidating 'honest citizens'.[73] The governor of Alcamo described 'kidnapping, destruction, arson, looting, robbery and homicide' as an everyday occurrence in the town.[74] The most notorious of these armed gangs was led by the bandit Santo (or Sante) Meli; having been thrown out of service in Garibaldi's army by La Masa in May, they conducted something of a reign of terror in the area between Corleone and Santa Margherita between June and August.[75]

As serious as the sharp deterioration in law and order was the government's apparent inability to do anything about it. The 'normalization' of government remained an aspiration rather than a reality. Relative calm was restored to the major towns where (Messina apart) the urban élites seemed to welcome Garibaldi: 'the present tone of public opinion contrasted with that of former times, strikes the observer with a lively pleasure', the British Consul John Goodwin wrote of

---

[71] 27 August 1860, in PRO, FO 165/134.

[72] Referred to in letter of 25 September 1860 from Girgenti, Saverio Imborrone (president of the *commissione speciale*) to Mordini, AMB, filza 18, f. 1, n. 1.

[73] 27 June 1860, ASP, Luog. Polizia, b. 1510, f. personale del distretto di Mazara, and ibid. b. 1552, f. reati avvenimenti Mazara.

[74] 20 August 1860, ibid. b. 1510, f. personale del distretto di Alcamo.

[75] 'Riassunto processo Sante Meli: 1860', in AMB, filza 16, f. Q, n. 1. On their activities in August, see the letter of 5 Aug. from the Governor of Girgenti's secretary to the Secretary of State for public security in ASP, Luog. Polizia, b. 1550, f. reati avvenuti in Girgenti. See also Berti, *I democratici e l'iniziativa meridionale*, 748.

Palermo in his journal of 9–10 June.[76] Large parts of the countryside, however, remained beyond the control of the government.

One practical obstacle to setting up an effective administration in the countryside was financial. The financial demands on the resources of the dictatorship were enormous. According to one report

the Sicilian government has to provide an army with guns and weaponry and a navy . . . it has to prepare a reserve of material as well as men, it has to organize the whole force of the country in order to strengthen and safeguard this great enterprise.[77]

Money was also needed to finance reform, in particular the programme of public works, and to provide for the organization of government and public security. Unfortunately, the abolition of the *macino* tax, however essential to win the support of the peasantry for the revolution, devastated government finances. No new taxes were introduced to take the place of the *macinato* which, before the revolution, had been the largest source of government revenue in Sicily.[78] 'The truth,' according to Angelo Bargoni, 'is that there is an incredible lack of funds.'[79] Although, during July and August, the possibility of either reintroducing the *macinato* or levying new taxes on wine and foodstuffs was discussed in various communes, nothing ever came of these discussions.[80]

Efforts to raise money for the nationalist initiative by public subscription were also unproductive. Support for the new government seemed, in this respect, little more than skin deep. Goodwin wrote in his journal on 8 July that 'the reception of Garibaldi in Palermo has been everything the heart could wish, in so far as cheers go, but at "cheers" it stops short. Very little money has been given.' 'Manifestos and addresses', he added on 19 July, 'make a grand show in the papers but the money and materials are wanting.'[81] It was also very difficult to enforce the payment of taxes which were already in force. In many

---

[76] PRO, FO 165/134. See also Mack Smith, 'The Peasants' Revolt in Sicily', 207.

[77] ACSR, Archivio Depretis, iv, b. 1, f. 1.

[78] See Goodwin's journal of 18 June, in PRO, FO 165/134. That the situation had not improved by August was confirmed in a long and detailed financial report to Depretis, in ACSR, Archivio Depretis, iv. b. 1, f. 1.

[79] 27 Aug. 1860, in *Memorie di Angelo Bargoni, 1829–1901*, ed. A. Bargoni (Milan, 1911), 142.

[80] The proposals for new taxation are in ASP, Luog. Interno, b. 1583, 1584, 1585.

[81] PRO, FO 165/134.

communes, people simply refused to pay taxes, apparently believing, in the Governor of Corleone's words, that 'freedom brought with it exemption from every form of taxation'.[82]

At the root of the administrative difficulties facing the government was the existing chaos and conflict in the countryside. Although the new system of provincial and communal administration set up in May retained the territorial divisions and responsibilities of the Bourbon period, new governors were appointed to all twenty-four administrative districts in Sicily. The new governors were put in charge of the transfer of power in the communes and of the organization of local government; they were to be the linchpin of communications between the dictatorship in Palermo and the rural communes. For the most part, Crispi appointed local men as governors, hoping that their local influence would assist the government in controlling the countryside.[83] In some cases, however, this decision had the reverse effect, as governors used their powers to pursue independent policies of their own rather than obeying instructions from Palermo.

Having failed, for example, to replace all the employees in his district and bring liberals into local councils, the governor of Girgenti defended his (in)action on the grounds that these employees were 'honest men and fathers', while liberals were both subversive agitators and completely inexperienced.[84] According to various reports, the governors of Bivona, Caltagirone, Siracusa, and Catania also failed to proceed against Bourbon officials.[85] Others simply did nothing at all. 'It is said,' one correspondent wrote to Crispi, 'that there is a governor in Termini but in this capacity he doesn't exist. He is extremely ignorant of everything

---

[82] To the Secretary of State for Public Security, 9 Aug. 1860 in ASP, Luog. Polizia, b. 1547. [83] Mack Smith, *Cavour and Garibaldi*, 269–70.
[84] 7 June 1860, in ASP, Luog. Interno, b. 1585, f. 4, amministrazione pei comuni della provincia di Girgenti.
[85] On the governor of Bivona: there are letters of 24 and 30 June to Crispi from Pietro Mancuso, in ACSR, Carte Crispi (ASP), f. 95/3, of 13 Sept., from the Secretary of State for Finance, in ASP, Luog. Polizia, b. 1517, f. Girgenti (a similar letter from him written on the same day is in ASP, Luog. Interno, b. 1585, f. 4 amministrazione pei comuni di Girgenti), and of 29 October from the governor of Girgenti, in ISR, b. 221, f. 31, n. 4. On the governor of Caltagirone: there is a letter of 20 June from Vincenso Cordova to Crispi, in ACSR, Carte Crispi (ASP), f. 95/4. On the governor of Siracusa: see the complaint about his activities in Lentini, dated 3 July, in ASP, Luog. Polizia, b. 1517, f. affari diversi Modica. On the governor of Catania: there is a report written on 12 June addressed to Garibaldi in ACSR, Carte Crispi (ASP), f. 95/9, and a letter of 4 Aug. from the governor of Nicosia in ASP, Luog. Polizia, b. 1549, f. reati avvenimenti Nicosia.

and is hugely lazy.'[86] The governor of Acireale was, in the words of another of Crispi's correspondents, 'imbecile, irrational, useless'.[87]

Some governors used their considerable powers to pursue personal goals. In October, the governor of Trapani accused the governor of Alcamo of involvement with local crime.[88] According to one report sent to Crispi, Alcamo had long been dominated by the three Sant'Anna brothers (Barone Don Benedetto, Don Giuseppe, and Don Stefano). Don Giuseppe had been mayor of Alcamo before the revolution, and had allegedly used the revolution as an opportunity to loot the coffers of the local administration. Don Stefano, who was wounded at Calatafimi fighting for Garibaldi and was subsequently appointed governor of the district, used all the power of the governor's office to pursue 'private vendettas' and to blackmail former Bourbons. His brother, Barone Don Benedetto, the incumbent in October 1860, also cared little for official duties and used his office for personal enrichment.[89]

The Governor of Caltanissetta, Baron Francesco Morillo di Trabonella, caused the Palermo government particular difficulties. 'Trabonella' (as he was generally known) was a 'new man', in many respects typical of mid-nineteenth-century Sicily. He had acquired most of his considerable wealth during his own lifetime, and owned many of the district's sulphur mines.[90] It was Trabonella who, once Garibaldi's victory seemed assured at the end of May, had led the revolution in Caltanissetta against the Bourbons.[91] Early reports from Caltanissetta spoke in praise of Baron Morillo di Trabonella.[92] By September, however, this praise had turned to concern about his loyalties. A furious row developed between Trabonella and the head of Caltanissetta's civic council and national guard, Lanzirotti, where Lanzirotti accused Trabonella of favouring Bourbon supporters and frustrating

[86] 13 Aug. 1860, in ACSR, Carte Crispi (ASP), f. 95/24. A later report, written on 21 Sept. by the *commissario straordinario* (presumably sent to investigate these allegations), states that both the governor and his officials lacked skill, energy, and purpose. ASP, Luog. Polizia, b. 1548, f. reati avvenimenti Termini.

[87] 27 Aug. 1860, ACSR, Carte Crispi (ASP), f. 54/lxvi.

[88] 21 Oct. 1860, ASP, Luog. Polizia, b. 1517, f. Trapani.

[89] The report is in ACSR, Carte Crispi (ASP), f. 95/2.

[90] My thanks to Dott. Torrisi of the Archivio di Stato in Caltanissetta for this information about Baron Morillo di Trabonella.

[91] *Il Giornale di Sicilia*, 8 June 1860.

[92] 10 July 1860, from the military commander of Caltanissetta, Ignazio Colonna, to Crispi, in ACSR, Carte Crispi (ASP), f. 95/5.

the liberals.[93] A suggestion to transfer Trabonella to Messina met with a large popular demonstration in his favour, apparently orchestrated by Trabonella himself.[94]

This kind of behaviour by governors gravely compromised every principle of bureaucratic rationality and centralized control. Official reports sent by governors were often of questionable use to the government. Personal quarrels and factionalism also distorted the flow of information from the administrative districts to the government in Palermo. All this severely limited the practical influence which the Palermo government had over local politics. On at least one occasion Trabonella was able to use his influence at the telegraph office to delay official reports which were critical of him, so that his version of events would arrive in Palermo first. The military commander of Caltanissetta, Ignazio Colonna, who had praised Trabonella in July but had subsequently made himself unpopular for breaking up the demonstration in Trabonella's favour, saw himself confounded by the governor in precisely this way.[95] Equally, it comes as no surprise to the reader to learn, at the end of a long political report by Trabonella, that his adversary, Lanzirotti, has resigned his post.[96] Trabonella, on the other hand, survived to acquire yet more power under the Piedmontese.[97]

In practice, therefore, the Palermo government knew little about what its provincial governors were up to. The political loyalties of men like Trabonella or Benedetto Sant'Anna seem to have been a source of considerable confusion to the government. Trabonella was described as a liberal in May, a Bourbon in August, and a *cavouriano* in September.[98] It is tempting to conclude that what really mattered to Baron Morillo di Trabonella was control of Caltanissetta and its wealth.

---

[93] 6 Sept. 1860, Lanzirotti to the prodictator, ASP, Luog. Polizia, b. 1552, f. reati avvenimenti Caltanissetta.

[94] 5 Sept. 1860, from Antonio Ribaudo to Crispi, in ACSR, Carte Crispi (ASP), f. 95/5.

[95] See his letter of 13 Sept. 1860 and other correspondence in ASP, Luog. Interno, b. 1602, f. affari diversi Caltanissetta.

[96] Ibid. This report included Trabonella's account of the popular demonstration, dated 6 Sept. and addressed to the prodictator.

[97] On which, see below, pp. 141–2, 144. His feud with Lanzirotti also continued: see his telegram of 13 Oct. to Mordini, AMB, filza 16, f. f, n. 12.

[98] The latter accusation is made by Antonio Ribaudo in a 7 Sept. letter to Crispi: ACSR, Carte Crispi (ASP), f. 95/5.

The obstacles to 'normalizing' government went beyond the deviant behaviour of Crispi's governors. Even the most energetic and committed governors had difficulty organizing local councils. Francesco Perroni Paladini, a loyal follower of Crispi's and a leading light of the democratic movement in Sicily, sent detailed reports recounting the various problems he faced in the district of Castroreale.[99] In June, shortly after his arrival as governor, he wrote to Palermo that he could find no sign of regular administration in the various communes; 'we are' he feared, 'in danger of falling into total anarchy'.[100] He subsequently embarked on a tour of the district with the aim of organizing local councils (*consigli civici*). Lack of suitable candidates sometimes frustrated his efforts. In Mojo, a commune of 300 to 400 inhabitants, he was obliged to set up a council of illiterate peasants, since only two or three people there could read and write. Elsewhere he found that Crispi's decision to order all the revolutionary councils formed during 1848 to reconvene had caused particular chaos and resentment. There were tensions in Casalnuovo between peasants and landowners over access to the water supply, and in Tripi over the usurpation of common land.[101]

The problems which Perroni Paladini faced in Castroreale were common to other parts of Sicily. Since the seizure of power on behalf of Garibaldi had taken place in many communes without the assistance of the *garibaldini*, they tended to follow an independent logic of their own during the revolution of 1860. One official in the governor of Girgenti's office described this situation in vivid terms. In Girgenti district at the time of revolution, there were, he wrote 'communes . . . which wanted to think of themselves as independent and entirely in control of themselves . . . [and which] in the name of liberty committed acts of the most total anarchy and the most unbridled licence'.[102] In other districts there was simply no 'revolution' at all. According to one report sent to Crispi, all that had happened as a result of Garibaldi's victory was that the 'party of property owners (that is, the party of the ex-government)' had changed sides in order to hold on to power. As a

---

[99] For more details on Perroni Paladini's career, see F. Brancato, *Francesco Perroni Paladini* (Palermo, 1962).

[100] 4 June 1860. The report is addressed to Gaetano La Loggia, President of the Committee on Interior Affairs in ACSR, Carte Crispi (ASP), f. 95/8.

[101] Perroni Paladini sent a long report to the prodictator on what he had done in the district on 20 Aug. 1860, in ASP, Luog. Interno, b. 1615, f. leva.

[102] 28 Nov. 1860, ASP, Luog. Interno, b. 1761, f. Girgenti.

result, the report went on, those who had been 'mayors, electors, decurions, *capi-urbani*, *sottocapi* and even known spies' under the Bourbons were now presidents or members of local councils and commanders of National Guards under the democrats.[103] In these cases, when governors arrived in communes to supervise the formation of local councils, they found them already reorganized under the control of former Bourbons.[104]

The town of Lercara Friddi, for example, had long been dominated by the Nicolosi family before 1860, and nothing changed after the revolution. Niccolò Nicolosi, a powerful magistrate known in Lercara for his association with the Bourbons and persecution of liberals, died (rather luckily for the family) in 1860; whereupon the next generation—Niccolò's sons Francesco, Giovanni, Vincenzo, and Luigi, along with their cousin, Calcedonio—simply seized control of the commune in the name of Garibaldi.[105] Yet the extent of their enthusiasm for Garibaldi and the revolution was dubious. By October, government officials had already started to voice their concern about the domination of Lercara by *borbonici*.[106] How much the Nicolosi family dominated Lercara, and how little the revolution did to alter their domination, is indicated in Table 1, which shows members of Lercara's National Guard and which was sent from the district of Termini's office to Palermo.

Those in control of Sicilian communes before and/or after the revolution of 1860 were not readily prepared to relinquish power to anyone. They were certainly not prepared automatically to bow to the authority of the new government in Palermo. Control of the commune seems to have mattered a great deal more to local élites than who was in power in Palermo. Some reports suggested that the change of government just involved a change of names. Under the Bourbons, governor Perroni Paladini wrote to Palermo, factions would accuse

---

[103] 'Relazione di Vincenzo Cacioppo sulla sicurezza pubblica in Sicilia', ACSR, Carte Crispi (ASP), f. 94.

[104] Raffaele de Benedetto wrote to Crispi on 5 June from Torretta that when the governor arrived to organize the local council, the old *borbonici* managed to regain control of the commune. Ibid. f. 95/25.

[105] R. Mangiameli, 'Banditi e mafiosi dopo l'unità', *Meridiana*, 7–8 (1990), 82–8.

[106] See the correspondence between the intendant of Termini and the Minister for Public Security: 25 and 26 Oct. 1860, ASP, Luog. Polizia, b. 1548, f. reati avvenimenti Termini.

TABLE 1   Members of Lercara's National Guard

Name	Rank	Remarks
Don Antonio Orlando	Inspector of national guards	Ex-Inspector of the militia under the old government
Giacchino Orlando	Captain	Nephew and lieutenant to Antonio
Giacchino Barsalone	Captain	Nephew of Antonio and future father-in-law of Giovanni Nicolosi
D. Francesco Nicolosi	Major	Brother of Giovanni
D. Giovanni Nicolosi	Captain	Future son-in-law of Barsalone and thus nephew of Orlando
Francesco Garafalo	Captain	Husband of a nephew of the same Orlando
Don Vincenzo Nicolosi	Receiver of taxes and book-keeper for the *Fidecommesseria Palagonia* (now belonging to the nation)	Brother of the same Nicolosi
Don Vincenzo Furitano e Nicolosi	President of the municipality	Cousin of the same Nicolosi
Don Domenico Nicolosi	Delegate	Cousin
Don Domenico Miceli	Major	Husband of the Nicolosi's cousin, Donna Anna Nicolosi
Sacerdote Don Marino Nicolosi	President of the civic council	Uncle of same Nicolosi
Don Calcedonio Consales	Captain	Cousin of same Nicolosi
Don Gioacchino Consales	Captain	Father of Calcedonio, Uncle of Nicolosi
Don Antonio Mavaro	Member of the civic council	Brother-in-law of Nicolosi
Don Pasquale Ansalone	Advisor to the guard	Standard-bearer under the Bourbons[107]

[107] See the correspondence between the intendant of Termini and the Minister for Public Security: 25 and 26 Oct. 1860, ASP, Luog. Polizia, b. 1548, f. reati avvenimenti Termini. See also Mangiameli, 'Banditi e mafiosi dopo l'unità', table 1.

each other of being 'liberals'; now 'Bourbon' was the usual term of abuse.[108]

Hardly surprisingly, the rivalry between élites for control of a commune also compromised the principle of regular administrative government. In many cases the factionalism of rural communes was so intense, and often so violent, that it was impossible to organize any kind of local government at all. Few government officials were immune to its effects. Even Perroni Paladini encountered personal animosity when his efforts to set up a council in Francavilla were frustrated by the activities of the Pellegrino family, long-time adversaries of Perroni Paladini. In a separate incident, Luigi Pellegrino accused Perroni Paladini's family of having been supporters of the Bourbons.[109]

Locally based and personal conflicts of this nature were usually focused on control of the *consiglio civico*. Frequently, they also involved the encouragement of peasant discontent. This rivalry produced more than its share of violence and crime. The infamous conflict in the village of Bronte, for instance, combined peasant unrest over land with élite rivalry. One side, led by the lawyer Niccolò Lombardo, was enraged by its exclusion from local government after the revolution by those who had held power before 1860. Lombardo encouraged peasant discontent over land as a means of threatening and undermining those in power. Unfortunately for Lombardo and his followers, they were ultimately unable to control the peasant violence which they had helped to unleash.[110] In Lercara Friddi too, the dominant position of the Nicolosi brothers was constantly under threat from rival factions and popular discontent. A long-standing feud between the Nicolosi family and the Sartorio family (in control of Lercara during the eighteenth century)— an 'enmity between them due to old hatreds and old family resentments'—frustrated the repeated attempts to reorganize and regularize communal administration.[111] There were also continual rumblings of

---

[108] 20 Sept. 1860, to the prodictator, in Istituto per la Storia del Risorgimento, Roma (henceforth, ISR), b. 221, f. 23, n. 9.

[109] Brancato, *Francesco Perroni Paladini*, 25, 41.

[110] There is a large literature on the revolt at Bronte. See, in paticular, B. Radice, 'Nino Bixio a Bronte', *Archivio Storico per la Sicilia Orientale*, 7 (1910), 252–94; Mack Smith, 'The Peasants' Revolt in Sicily'; and Romano, *Momenti del Risorgimento in Sicilia*, 214–17. Giovanni Verga wrote a famous short story about the revolt at Bronte, 'Libertà', in G. Verga, *Tutte le novelle*, i (1942; Milan, 1983 edn.); see also L. Sciascia, 'Verga e la libertà', in *La corda pazza* (Turin, 1970). A number of documents relating to the trial of those involved have been published by E. Bertini, *Rapporto sui fatti di Bronte del 1860* (Palermo, 1985).

[111] From the *commissario straordinario* in Lercara, 21 Sept. 1860. ASP, Luog. Polizia, b. 1548, f. reati avvenimenti Termini. Also in ACSR, Carte Crispi (ASP), f. 95/4.

popular discontent over the rapid expansion of sulphur-mining which, controlled by the Nicolosi family, had drastically curtailed the amount of land available for pasturage.[112]

The government service which was most profoundly affected by all these problems was the provision of law and order. Lack of money and of adequate sources of supply meant that there were significant delays in providing National Guards with firearms and/or uniforms.[113] Without uniforms, the guardsmen were indistinguishable from ordinary peasants or, more worryingly, bandits.[114] Moreover, since local councils were responsible for organizing the divisions and officers of the local National Guard to act as a police force, National Guards tended to reflect the power structure and the tensions within communes. The governor of Girgenti wrote that the organization of National Guards in his district was made on the basis of either factional divisions, personal influence, or *a capriccio*.[115] Various reports refer to the National Guards being 'divided into parties', 'driven by a factional spirit', poorly organized, or not organized at all.[116] In Lercara, where the National Guard was dominated by the Nicolosi family, they failed to perform any of the duties assigned to them.[117]

Local notables also tended to view the new police forces as an extension of their personal power. National Guards were often used more as an instrument of local influence than of the law. In Licata (Girgenti) and Cimina (Termini), it was alleged that they were made up of 'mercenaries' or 'hired men' (*prezzolati*).[118] Only a very fine line divided those who upheld the law from those who opposed or were outside it. Complaints abounded about the presence of 'bad' (*cattivi*) or 'impure' elements in the National Guards. The National Guard in

[112] Mangiameli, 'Banditi e mafiosi dopo l'unità', 82–3.
[113] Complaints about lack of firearms in 1860 fill the police archives in Palermo. See, in particular, ASP, Luog. Polizia, b. 1510, f. personale del distretto di Bivona; b. 1516, f. affari diversi Cefalù; b. 1517, f. Noto, f. Trapani, f. affari diversi Sciacca.
[114] This complaint is made by the *delegato di pubblica sicurezza* in Gangi, 19 Sept. 1860, ASP, Luog. Polizia, b. 1516, f. Messina.
[115] 28 Nov. 1860, ASP, Luog. Interno, b. 1761, f. Girgenti.
[116] See the reports from Terranova (16 Aug., ASP, Luog. Polizia, b. 1552, f. reati, avvenimenti Terranova) and Modica (Nov., ASP, Luog. Polizia, f. 1517, f. affari diversi Modica).
[117] Letter of 16 Sept. from the lieutenant-colonel in Lercara, ASP, Luog. Polizia, b. 1548, f. reati avvenimenti Termini.
[118] On Licata, see the governor of Girgenti's report, 26 June 1860, ASP, Luog. Polizia, b. 1550, f. reati avvenimenti Girgenti; on Cimina, see the governor of Termini's report, 7 Sept. 1860, ASP, Luog. Polizia, b. 1548, f. reati avvenimenti Termini.

Comitini, according to the governor of Girgenti, 'instead of safeguarding order and the security of persons and property, disturbs it'.[119] Most of the militia in Caltagirone were said to be 'murderers capable of the worst disorder'.[120] Even in a major town such as Trapani, the National Guard did not maintain order because it was 'commanded by those who collude with murderers'.[121]

Faced with these kinds of obstacles, the Palermo government could introduce as much new legislation and pass as many decrees as it liked; but it would almost invariably lack the ability to implement them. At the beginning of August, Michele Amari lamented the existence of a situation where laws passed to prevent disorder were useless because nobody would carry them out—'with a few exceptions, the district governors have not acquitted themselves well; the National Guard, either because of the governors' inaction or because of local divisions, is not powerful enough to fight violence and robbery'.[122] Amari's complaints were echoed in the report of a police officer (*delegato di pubblica sicurezza*) in Burgio to the prodictator. Without a militia capable of upholding the law, he wrote, 'vigorous laws, capital punishment, special tribunals are dead letters . . . [they are] laws which have been, and will remain, unexecuted, which have not produced, and will not produce, any effect'.[123]

Increasingly, as the summer wore on, the government responded to these difficulties by relying on the use of exceptional measures. From an early stage the dictatorship had used military justice as a means of dealing with the crimes committed by ordinary citizens. 'Mobile columns' of volunteer troops were organized in order to repress outbreaks of disorder in the interior. Additionally, a service of *carabinieri*, made up of both Sicilians and non-Sicilians, was set up for the 'surveillance of public security and of the behaviour of the mounted militia [*militi a cavallo*]'.[124] Some governors were also given emergency powers to enable them to deal more promptly with outbreaks of unrest.[125]

In August and September, as the problems of banditry and peasant violence over land worsened, more so-called 'energetic' measures were

---

[119] 21 June 1860, ASP, Luog. Polizia, b. 1510, f. Girgenti.
[120] From Luigi Patrizio to Crispi, 6 Aug. 1860 in ACSR, Carte Crispi (ASP), f. 95/4.
[121] 1 Nov. 1860, the allegation is made in a petition to the secretary for public security, ASP, Luog. Polizia, b. 1510, f. Trapani.
[122] 3 Aug. 1860, *Carteggio Amari*, ii. 110–11.
[123] 18 Aug. 1860, ASP, Luog. Polizia, b. 1550, f. reati avvenimenti Bivona.
[124] From the council meeting of 23 July 1860, in ASP, Miscellanea, ii. n. 71.
[125] Ibid. Council meeting of 24 July 1860.

introduced, largely through the initiatives of Crispi and Depretis. In many communes where the Governor had been unable to organize local councils, a temporary commissioner (*commissario straordinario*) was sent to do the job, usually with military assistance. Severe action was also ordered against Sicilians who deserted the army;[126] and increasing numbers of mobile columns were sent into the interior.[127] Their purpose was to enforce payment of taxes,[128] and to control the mounting tide of violent peasant unrest. Thus, the peasant revolts at Bronte were dealt with as promptly as the government's meagre resources and poor communications would allow. As soon as news reached Palermo of the revolt at Bronte, Crispi ordered the Garibaldian General, Nino Bixio, into the area to restore order. Bixio surrounded the town, imposed a curfew, and proceeded to arrest hundreds of suspected insurgents. Five of the Bronte insurgents were executed after a summary trial; nearby, after similar incidents, six insurgents were condemned to death in Montemaggiore, nine in Biancavilla, and thirteen in Alcara li Fusì.[129]

IV

Once the Bourbon government had been successfully overthrown in Palermo in June 1860, Garibaldi's dictatorship attempted to unite the Sicilian population behind the nationalist initiative. The government introduced popular reforms, attempted to control disorder, and set about 'normalizing' government by introducing a new administrative system. It faced almost insurmountable obstacles. The government lacked adequate financial resources, and was hampered by the absence of reliable communications outside Palermo. The mass of the population misunderstood the government's message about land and the possibilities of revolution. Rural élites were, at best, unenthusiastic about government policies; at worst they were actively hostile. In the mean time, conditions of law and order further deteriorated in the countryside. Thus, although Garibaldi's army was able to benefit

---

[126] These measures were ordered in a circular sent by Depretis on 1 Aug. 'ai governatori, ai commandanti militari delle provincie, alle autorità municipali e di pubblica sicurezza'. ACSR, Archivio Depretis, i. b.2, f. 8/4.

[127] 7 Aug. 1860, reported in a letter from the Secretary of State for War to the Secretary of State for the Interior, ASP, Luog. Polizia, b. 1546.

[128] The Minister of War gives this as a reason in his report of 7 Aug., ibid. See also a letter written on the same day from the commander of the mobile column in Bivona to the intendant of Bivona, in ASP, Luog. Polizia, b. 1550, f. reati avvenimenti Bivona.

[129] Romano, *Momenti del Risorgimento in Sicilia*, 223; Mack Smith, 'The Peasants' Revolt in Sicily', 214–15.

from the collapse of the Bourbon administration in Sicily to seize power for the democrats, the new government inherited many of the problems which had brought this collapse about.

The lack of an organized basis of support outside the major towns was one of the most serious problems facing the government. Crispi wrote that the lack of security forces meant the government was obliged to rule 'by love not force', and Mack Smith notes that this worked quite well in Palermo.[130] It did not work in the countryside because of the ambivalent attitude which the rural élites adopted towards the new government. Ironically, the lack of law and order in the countryside meant that the government's authority over local elites was further compromised. Attempts to establish reliable communications between central power in Palermo and local government were also disrupted by the unstable situation in the communes.

The government's policy of satisfying peasant demands for land lost momentum as the war shifted to the mainland and peasant frustration exploded into violent conflict. The repression at Bronte shows that, despite its revolutionary rhetoric, the government had decided to support rural élites and to give priority to establishing law and order. Those in power in Palermo must also have felt obliged to respond to the incessant demands from many officials in rural areas for firm action to control violent crime.[131] The problem was that, since local government had frequently collapsed in rural communes, many of the public order policies favoured by the Palermo government were actually unenforceable. Attempts were made to organize local councils and to provide a system for the administration of law and order in the countryside, but far too many of these attempts were defeated by the violence and lawlessness prevailing within the communes. As a result, it was often impossible to organize any kind of civilian administration at all, still less to set up a National Guard. In cases where a civilian local government or National Guard was organized, they often became enmeshed in the struggle between local élites.

Ironically, nothing shows more clearly how far the situation in the rural communes could elude central government control than the use of military force. In areas where government influence was at its weakest, military force was a particularly blunt instrument of control. Often the

---

[130] Romano, *Momenti del Risorgimento in Sicilia*, 207.

[131] For example, the repeated requests from Mazara (ACSR, Carte Crispi, ASP, f. 95/4; ASP, Luog. Polizia, b. 1517, f. Mazara; ibid. b.1552, f. reati avvenimenti Mazara) and from Corleone (ASP, Luog. Polizia, b. 1516, f. affari diversi, Corleone; ibid. b. 1547).

sheer lack of reliable sources of information meant that it was difficult to tell 'liberals' from 'Bourbons' (or those who were 'troublemakers' from those described as 'honest'). The military was effectively at the mercy of local power-holders; the military could only arrest and bring to justice those identified to them as Bourbons or troublemakers. None of this brought the government any closer to establishing a reliable basis of support in the countryside; in many cases the use of military force helped those most hostile to the new government to stay in power.

The use of force to uphold government authority also did little to resolve the persistent crisis of legitimacy. The reliance on the military was actually a sign of weakness and a recognition of failure. Among government ministers, only the prodictator Mordini seems to have been aware that the use of coercion emphasized the government's isolation, and that by using military force it was admitting its inability to rule through consent using 'normal' measures. In the long term, troops alone could not control the countryside. They could be used to quell disorder or to round up persistent criminals, but they were of much less use as a permanent form of control. A special commissioner could organize a council in a single commune with the help of troops; yet, without some local support for his work, he could never begin to hope to control a whole district on a continuous basis.[132]

Having chosen to rely upon the maintenance of order to win the support of landed élites, Garibaldi's government found itself utterly discredited by its inability to do so. In the course of the summer the government began to receive increasing numbers of requests from rural areas for Piedmontese troops (particularly, at this stage, for *carabinieri*). Their own officials began to argue that the Piedmontese were a more competent and a more reliable force.[133] So, just as the *garibaldini* had benefited from the collapse of the Bourbon government so, in turn, did the Piedmontese liberals benefit from the crisis which faced Garibaldi's dictatorship. Arguably, it was more than the weaknesses within the democratic leadership which explains their defeat at the end of 1860 over the issue of annexation to Piedmont. Cavour was also able to profit

---

[132] These difficulties are described in a letter complaining about the behaviour of the *commissario straordinario* in the district of Termini in ASP, Luog. Polizia, b. 1548, f. reati avventimenti Termini. The commissioner, named Galvagno, had allegedly given all the administrative posts in Lercara to the Nicolosi family.

[133] The governor of Mazara to the secretary of state for the interior, 27 June 1860, ASP, Luog. Polizia, b. 1510, f. Mazara. From the governor of Patti to the prodictator, 19 Sept. 1860, ISR, b. 221, f. 23, n. 8.

throughout 1860 from the dictatorship's persistent failure to control the situation in the countryside. The Piedmontese were welcomed by Sicilians, in part because they claimed to be able to bring order to the Sicilian countryside. It remained to be seen whether they would ever manage to live up to this promise.

4

From Moderate Liberalism to Destra Storica: *The Impact of Unification*

I

In contrast to the experiences of both Italian democrats and Italian conservatives, the decade before 1860 had been a time of great success for moderate liberals in Piedmont. After the failure of the 1848–9 revolutions Piedmont followed a different political path from the rest of Italy. In the Two Sicilies the constitutional reforms introduced during the 1848 revolution were revoked or otherwise allowed to lapse; in the Papal States and Central Duchies the constitutions were repressed by force. It was only in Piedmont that the liberal constitution of 1848 (the *statuto albertino* granted by the king, Carlo Alberto) survived the defeats of 1849. Moreover, political life in Piedmont during the 1850s seemed a far cry from the declining legitimacy, diplomatic isolation, and economic stagnation which characterized the Two Sicilies and much of Central Italy after 1849.[1]

After 1849 Piedmontese government differed from those elsewhere in Italy by being able to establish a stable 'middle way' between the two extremes of reaction and revolution. It did so on the basis of the constitution of 1848 and of the limited representative government allowed by it. The Piedmontese constitution represented a compromise between the royal prerogative and liberal principles.[2] It stated that legislative power was to be exercised jointly by the king and by parliament, and that this parliament was to consist of two chambers—a chamber of deputies whose members were to be elected, and a senate whose members were to be nominated by the king. The suffrage was

[1] For a brief and useful comparison between the 'reactionary states and liberal Piedmont' and a short summary of the liberal reforms of this period, see A. Scirocco, *L'Italia del Risorgimento* (Bologna, 1990), 315–66.

[2] On the *statuto albertino* see N. Nada, *Dallo stato assoluto allo stato costituzionale: storia del regno di Carlo Alberto dal 1831 al 1848* (Turin, 1980), 166–9. See also G. Maranini, *Storia del potere in Italia dal 1848 al 1967* (Florence, 1967), ch. 3, 'Lo statuto albertino', and E. Flora, 'Lo statuto albertino: l'avvento del regime parlamentare nel regno di Sardegna', *Rassegna Storica del Risorgimento*, 45 (1958), 26–38.

based on taxes, and itself represented a 'middle way' between two systems; one in sixty-two inhabitants had the vote in Piedmont, which was narrower than the suffrage in Britain after the Great Reform Act, but wider than that of the July monarchy in France.[3] This balance was maintained throughout the constitution; it established the principle of judicial independence, and guaranteed civil liberties such as the equality of all citizens before the law and the right of association. It stated that property was inviolable; nobody's property could be searched or confiscated, and nobody could be arrested or tried without due legal procedure. At the same time, the king was confirmed as the sole executive power and the commander of all military forces. To the king alone was given the right to declare war and conclude treaties. Finally, one aspect of the old alliance of 'throne and altar' was maintained: Catholicism was established as the state religion.

During the 1850s, and particularly after 1852, when the leading moderate liberal, Camillo Cavour, became Prime Minister, the liberal aspects of the constitution were consolidated. In a series of reforms starting with the Siccardi laws, both the judiciary and the bureaucracy were liberalized, and the political power of the nobility and the Church was reduced by parliament.[4] Cavour pushed these reforms through using the power of parliament to overcome the resistance of Church and monarch and, in so doing, he established the principle of parliamentary independence. Henceforth, no government in Piedmont was able to survive without the support of parliament. The Piedmontese parliament acquired a political legitimacy of its own.

The reforms introduced by the moderate liberal government during the 1850s in Piedmont were not confined to politics. New welfare measures were introduced, notably the provision of public education for children and a system of teacher training colleges.[5] Under Cavour the government pursued an increasingly liberal economic policy. Tariff barriers were swept aside, and free trade agreements signed with most European powers.[6] An extensive programme of road and railway building was also embarked upon: in 1859 some 1,110 kilometres of rail had been built or was under

---

[3] R. Romeo, *Dal Piemonte sabaudo all'Italia liberale* (Turin, 1963), 309.

[4] M. d'Addio, *Politica e magistratura, 1848–1870* (Milan, 1966), 8–41.

[5] On the educational policy of the moderate liberals and, in particular, the Casati law of 1859 which aimed to set up a state system of education, see D. Bertoni Jovine, 'La legge Casati', in *Problemi dell'unità d'Italia: atti del ii convegno di studi gramsciani* (Rome, 1962).

[6] Romeo notes that Piedmont's volume of trade doubled over the decade: *Dal Piemonte sabaudo all'Italia liberale*, 138.

construction in Piedmont, representing around 45 per cent of all railways in Italy. The scale of the achievement is all the more impressive in that Piedmont had only 8 km of track in 1849.[7] Commercial activity flourished. In 1850, a stock exchange was opened in Turin and another opened in Genoa in 1855. By 1860 there were 377 commercial and industrial credit institutions in Piedmont, compared to 56 in the whole of the Two Sicilies, 56 in Lombardy, and 73 in Tuscany.[8]

Perhaps the most remarkable aspect of all these achievements was that they were accomplished peacefully and with the agreement (however grudging on occasion) of the king, Vittorio Emanuele II. This in itself enhanced the successes achieved by moderate liberalism. In 1851 Massimo d'Azeglio, Cavour's predecessor as Piedmontese prime minister, wrote to his fellow moderate liberal Marco Minghetti, 'If you could see Turin you would not recognise it.' He went on:

I have never seen so much activity. There are ten theatres which are always full and endless balls. All the shops and small businesses are doing a trade which is beyond their wildest dreams.[9]

Even allowing for an element of exaggeration from a man proud of his achievements, this is still a striking statement of confidence and optimism at a time of repression and reaction in the rest of Italy.

The success of this compromise between revolution and reaction was due to a combination of favourable circumstances. First, Piedmont possessed one clear advantage over the other Italian states: guaranteed political independence from Austria and France (established at the Congress of Vienna in 1815). This meant that nationalism in Piedmont could be identified with the existing regime and with the Savoy monarchy. Whereas, in the Two Sicilies, nationalism had become a threat to the sovereignty, legitimacy, and political stability of the established regime, nationalism in Piedmont became, in the right hands, a source of political stability and a means of creating a new kind of consensus between ruler and ruled. Indeed, in Piedmont, the growth of nationalism—particularly as anti-Austrianism—actually increased loyalty to the state and to the

---

[7] G. Candeloro, *Storia dell'Italia moderna*, iv: *dalla rivoluzione nazionale all'unità* (Milan, 1964), 203–6. The difference which this decade made to the distribution and overall mileage of railway lines is shown by a map of Italian railways in 1848 and in 1861 in Scirocco, *L'Italia del Risorgimento*, 238, 240.

[8] D. Demarco, 'L'economia degli stati italiani prima dell'unità', *Rassegna Storica del Risorgimento*, 44 (1957), 244.

[9] 23 Feb. 1851. M. Minghetti, *I miei ricordi* (3 vols. Turin, 1888–90), iii. 319.

dynasty. As Broers, describing the period 1814–21, puts it: 'the fear of annexation to Austria rallied almost all Piedmontese to the dynasty'.[10] Opposition to Austrian interference continued to direct support towards the Savoy monarchy even when the threat of invasion receded. From the 1840s onwards, anti-Austrianism also became one means of reconciling moderate liberals to the existing regime.

The advantages of the greater political consensus in Piedmont were evident in 1849 when, despite strong disagreements between parliament and the monarch, there was still a sufficient willingness on both sides to compromise.[11] In addition, Piedmont enjoyed a considerable degree of administrative efficiency: what Scirocco calls 'the capacity of the state to guarantee internal order' was also demonstrated by the events of 1849.[12] This was largely the result of the reforms introduced by Carlo Alberto in the 1830s and 1840s. In this period, Piedmont's antiquated administration was replaced by the hierarchical Napoleonic model of provincial and communal administration, a system of elective communal and provincial councils was set up, and new penal and civil codes were introduced. Unlike the similar reforms introduced by de' Medici in the Two Sicilies, the centralizing 'administrative monarchy' put in place by Carlo Alberto was an enduring source of stability for the regime; indeed, his economic reforms won the approval of moderate liberals. Piedmont's rulers always managed to maintain a firm grip on the reins of power, offering 'good order'—protection along the country's borders, the eradication of banditry, the control of smuggling, and so on. Thus, in contrast to the Bourbon state in Sicily, it won the confidence of rural élites and was able to control the countryside.[13]

Particularly in the irrigated rice-plains, rural workers endured terrible poverty, bad housing, deplorable hygenic conditions, and a short life expectancy.[14] Recent research also suggests that the peasant diet in the North was greatly inferior to that of the South.[15] Nevertheless, the types of rural disorder prevalent in the South had been more or less eradicated in Piedmont by the end of the eighteenth century: many

---

[10] M. Broers, 'Policing Piedmont: The "Well-Ordered Police State" in the Age of Revolution, 1789–1821', *Criminal Justice History*, 15 (1994), 48.
[11] Scirocco, *L'Italia del Risorgimento*, 338–44.   [12] Ibid. 343.
[13] Broers, 'Policing Piedmont', 50–3.
[14] R. Romeo, *Cavour e il suo tempo* (3 vols.; Bari, 1969–84), ii. 24.
[15] G. Pescosolido, 'L'economia e la vita materiale' in G. Sabatucci and V. Vidotto (eds.), *Storia d'Italia*, i: *le premesse dell'unità* (Rome, Bari, 1994), 29–31.

parts of Piedmont even seemed to enjoy what Romeo calls a 'fundamental social stability'. The control of the countryside gave the Piedmontese moderates an enormous advantage over their Southern counterparts; indeed, Romeo argues that this was a 'decisive reason' for their 'final supremacy' over Southern liberals.[16] One crucial difference between Piedmont and Sicily was that the majority of Piedmontese landowners lived on their estates and took an active interest in their upkeep and improvement. The division of landed estates which had taken place during the French revolutionary wars and subsequent Restoration produced a new class of agriculturalists in Piedmont. Many went on to transform production techniques in the irrigated plains of Vercelli, Novara, and Alessandria, giving impetus to a process of rapid economic expansion which was unrivalled in Italy outside Lombardy. Elsewhere, in the mountainous Alpine and Apennine regions, a new class of peasant smallholders emerged.[17]

The tensions between the new agrarian middle class and old nobility, while not insignificant, were also far less acute in Piedmont than in Sicily. A kind of 'fusion' took place within the ranks of the rural élites; they tended to marry and socialize with members of the minor nobility, producing a new kind of ruling class in the provinces (if not in the more rarefied noble circles of Turin).[18] This process was by no means unique to Piedmont, but in Piedmont it produced a new rural élite with a fairly coherent set of political values and economic aims. Members of this class, whose power and wealth lay predominantly in the countryside, established agrarian associations for the dissemination of information about agriculture and began to seek political power through the elective councils in the municipalities and provinces before 1848.[19] These local groups eventually provided the popular basis for moderate liberalism in Piedmont.

The combination of dynastic loyalty, administrative efficiency, and relative social stability produced a far greater degree of political cohesion in Piedmont than in most of the other Restoration states in Italy. Furthermore, the ideology of the moderate liberal opposition was itself

---

[16] Romeo, *Cavour*, ii. 77.   [17] Ibid. 78.

[18] On the process of 'fusion' and on its limitations, see M. Meriggi, 'La borghesia italiana', in J. Kocka (ed.), *Borghese europee dell'Ottocento* (Venice, 1989), A. Lyttleton, 'The Middle Classes in Italy', in J. A. Davis and P. Ginsborg (eds.), *Society and Politics in the Age of the Risorgimento* (Cambridge, 1991), and A. Cardoza, 'Tra casta e classe: clubs maschile dell'élite torinese, 1840–1914', *Quaderni Storici*, 77 (1991), 363–88.

[19] G. Prato, *Fatti e dottrine economiche alla vigilia del 1848: L'associazione agraria subalpina e Camillo Cavour* (Turin, 1921).

well-suited to a compromise with the existing order in Piedmont. Moderate liberals defined themselves in opposition to both revolution and reaction, identifying themselves politically with the July monarchy in France and Peel's Conservative Party in Britain: Cavour might have been describing the party he would lead when he wrote in 1835 that 'the Tory party converted to conservatism has been joined by a group of honest, enlightened men, whose intentions are liberal but who fear the violence of radicals'.[20] Two years earlier Cavour had described his own political beliefs in similar terms as 'of the straightforward *juste milieu*, desiring, hoping, working for social progress with all my might but determined not to buy this at the price of general upheaval, whether political or social'.[21] Even the nationalism of moderate liberals was moderate. It was based on a sense of cultural and historical *italianità*, finding its political expression in an anti-Austrianism which fitted in easily with the conservative foreign policy of the king. Mack Smith writes that Cavour sought a 'middle way between Mazzini's utopian nationalism and Solaro dell Margherita's [the leading Piedmontese conservative] anti-Italian, Piedmontese nationalism',[22] and it is clear that this blend of conservative and revolutionary nationalism, when allied with the power of the Piedmontese army, was both a potent and practical force.

The success of moderate liberalism in Piedmont was also based in no small way on the skill and dynamism of its leaders. Cavour may not have been quite the canny realist sometimes portrayed by historians, but he did understand the need to appeal across a broad political spectrum (through newspapers and journals) as well as the importance of estab-lishing an effective bureaucracy. He also understood the importance of controlling parliament, and established a political alliance between the centre-Right and centre-Left—the so-called *connubio* ('unlawful marriage').[23] Without the *connubio*, Cavour could never have used parliament as he did to overcome the resistance of monarch and Church to his reforms. Moderate liberals in Piedmont also drew great strength from their leadership of the nationalist movement in Italy, and from the increasing numbers of liberals in Lombardy, Tuscany, Emilia-Romagna, and Southern Italy who supported their programme. The establishment

---

[20] 25 May 1835, in C. Cavour, *Diario Inedito* (Rome, 1888), 177.
[21] C. Cavour, *Epistolario* (14 vols.; Bologna, 1962–8, and Florence, 1973–94), i. 132.
[22] D. Mack Smith, *Cavour* (London, 1985), 71.
[23] On the crisis leading up to the *connubio* and the circumstances surrounding it, see Romeo, *Cavour*, ii. 527–644.

of the National Society in 1857 to promote Piedmontese leadership of a united Italy marked the emergence of moderate liberalism as a national movement. Finally, Cavour's extraordinary success in foreign policy enhanced the status of Piedmont, not just *vis-à-vis* the Italian states but, more importantly, among the Great Powers of Europe.[24] Piedmont's success in foreign policy became, in turn, one means by which the monarchy and army was reconciled to Cavour's more liberal regime.

However, the success of moderate liberalism in the 'decade of preparation' before 1860 also masked a number of contradictions and limitations. Cavour managed to balance the centre, but he never managed to reconcile the extremes of Left and Right to the new regime. An obvious problem was that the compromise between absolutism and liberalism did not include the Church, and ended by actively excluding it. Bad Church–state relations were a source of permanent tension between Cavour and the king and between Cavour and some of his colleagues. In 1854, during the passage through parliament of proposals to abolish non-charitable religious orders (the *crisi callabiana*), members of his party—including his own brother Gustave—spoke bitterly against the bill.[25] Moreover, republicanism remained a potent and destabilizing force throughout Italy. Some republicans remained staunchly opposed to the moderates and, as Garibaldi's expedition to Sicily showed, even those who supported the Piedmontese 'solution' proved difficult to control.

At the same time, while Cavour was prepared to manipulate nationalist pressure to gain support for his reforms he despised the notions of popular sovereignty and unity which Mazzini and others espoused. Thus, Piedmontese anti-Austrianism, however successful a force in Piedmont, could not find a stable basis for compromise with republican unitarianism. Nationalism in this respect proved a divisive, not a unifying force. According to Cavour's close friend, Salmour, the expulsion of Austria from Italy was 'the desire of his youth and his aim from the moment he came to power'. The unification of Italy was, on the other hand, something that Cavour had never even considered as a possibility

[24] On Cavour's foreign policy, see M. Walker, *Plombières: Secret Diplomacy and the Rebirth of Italy* (Oxford, 1968), F. Coppa, *The Origins of the Italian Wars of Independence* (London, 1992), 74–111.

[25] For a discussion of Church–state relations in Piedmont, see Scirocco, *L'Italia del Risorgimento*, 362–66, and A. C. Jemolo, *Church and State in Italy, 1850–1960* (Oxford, 1960), 10–26.

before the mid-1850s.[26] Few Northern moderates knew anything about the world south of Rome; Massimo d'Azeglio had travelled extensively in the South, but he was an exception. Cavour never made it further south than Florence. He and most of his contemporaries were more interested in the world north of the Alps, and spoke better French than Italian.

Even some of Cavour's greatest successes masked a more unstable reality. The parliamentary *connubio*, which enabled him to dominate parliament and bring in liberal reforms, also 'decapitated' the political opposition to the moderate liberals in the parliament, thus eroding parliament's function as a representative institution.[27] The *connubio* was, moreover, much more fragile than it looked, sustained largely by Cavour's tireless capacity for hard work and political intrigue. By 1860, political relations between Cavour and Urbano Rattazzi, the leader of the Piedmontese centre-Left, had become very strained. Cavour came to suspect Rattazzi of using his friendship with the king to undermine him, particularly as Cavour's own relations with the monarch were often openly hostile.[28] Cavour's colleagues were divided in their opinions of Rattazzi—Salmour wrote that Rattazzi had a 'haughty, vindictive personality' with 'a great lust for power and no desire to share it'—and this caused friction and rivalry within governing circles.[29]

Some historians argue that the instability of the *connubio*, and the demands of coalition politics, also accounts for the relative lack of institutional reform between 1852 and 1859.[30] In truth, the moderates' most lasting achievements during the 1850s were economic. Under a moderate liberal government, Piedmontese administrative and judicial institutions continued to be among the most centralized and authoritarian in Italy. One of the Left 'dissenters' in the Piedmontese parliament, Angelo Brofferio, complained to Cavour that:

---

[26] C. Cavour, *Carteggio Cavour-Salmour* (Bologna, 1961), 99.

[27] For a critical analysis of the *connubio*, see Maranini, *Storia del potere in Italia*, ch. 4, and P. G. Camaiani, *La rivoluzione moderata: rivoluzione e conservazione nell'unità d'Italia* (Turin, 1978).

[28] For examples see Mack Smith, *Cavour*, 109, 160–1, 171, and 180–1.

[29] *Cavour-Salmour*, 95.

[30] Mack Smith broadly follows this analysis in arguing that the *connubio* achieved little because of the needs of coalition government: see his *Cavour*, 122–3, 192–3. Romeo, however, is sharply critical of this kind of analysis, arguing that the *connubio* modernized moderate liberalism and revitalized the left, and that Mack Smith makes unrealistic comparisons with a bi-partisan British model which was not possible in Piedmont: Romeo, *Cavour*, ii. 570–80, esp. 573 n.

You ministers have never wished to harmonise the nation's legal codes with the Statute: you have promised much, it is true, but you have done nothing . . . Until these reforms are completed our institutions will remain an illusion and nothing else.[31]

Thus, Piedmont was not merely the only Restoration state in Italy which managed to reach a *modus vivendi* with liberalism; it did so without sacrificing many of the essentials of absolutist power.

Although recent historiography has made much of the moderates' admiration for English 'self-government', some aspects of the absolutist state—perhaps most notably its coercive aspects—were attractive to moderate liberals, and offered them obvious advantages. Liberal governments in Piedmont had no less hesitation than their predecessors in using the army (an unreformed institution from the absolutist system) to quell popular unrest or political disorder. For example, in 1849 Genoa was bombarded and martial law declared when the city revolted against the peace treaty with Austria. Food riots in Turin and elsewhere during 1853, where the population blamed Cavour's economic policies for the high price of bread, were dealt with harshly. Cavour announced his intention to 'adopt severe measures, extreme measures if needed', and his interior minister, San Martino, sent in troops to halt the riots in some areas.[32]

In common with the old Piedmontese nobility, moderates like Cavour were socially quite conservative. Justifying the narrow suffrage in Piedmont, they argued that the poor and uneducated needed to be educated and to own property before they could take on the responsibility of public life. Piedmontese peasants, according to one liberal observer, lived in a state of 'savage barbarism, which does not always permit them to tell the difference between good and evil'.[33] Baron Bettino Ricasoli, the leading Tuscan moderate, defined the business of government as 'doing good to the people who are entrusted to us'. This sense of paternalism, rather than any notion of popular political rights, guided moderate policies towards the so-called *paese reale* ('the real nation', meaning the mass of society). Popular unrest and mass disturbances horrified moderate liberals, confirmed their dislike of revolutionaries, and shook their paternalistic impulses toward the poor. In a letter which perfectly illustrates both the priorities of mod-

---

[31] Quoted in S. J. Woolf, *A History of Italy, 1700–1860: The Social Constraints of Political Change* (London, 1979), 442.   [32] Romeo, *Cavour*, ii. 715–23.
[33] Ibid. 74.

erate liberals and the nature of their compromise with absolutism, Cavour confessed that 'I can have Mazzini shot if he falls into my hands [or] have Genoa bombarded if it causes trouble' but that 'if I radically change the press laws I will lose all my prestige'.[34] For all their faith in progress and freedom, moderate liberals seemed to care much less about preserving the constitutional rights of those outside the *paese legale* (the 'legal nation'), or those, like the republicans, who rejected moderate values. In this respect, the liberal compromise with absolutism preserved much that was authoritarian from the old Piedmontese regime.

II

The unification of Italy was the result of a long and bitter power struggle in the Italian peninsula between conservatives and liberals and between moderate liberals and democrats. The plebiscites held in Southern Italy in October 1860, which voted overwhelmingly in favour of unification, also established the moderate liberals and Piedmont as the leaders of united Italy. Thus, with unification, the power struggles of the Risorgimento were finally resolved in the moderate liberals' favour. Historians have not, however, been slow to point out the ironies of this victory. First, in order to defeat the democrats, moderate liberals were forced to finish what the democrats had set out to accomplish. As Denis Mack Smith writes:

Few people were more surprised by the speed and success of this achievement [Italian unification] than Cavour, its chief architect; and few more disappointed than Mazzini and Garibaldi, the two men who had looked forward to this moment more keenly and who had sacrificed most for its attainment.[35]

The Piedmontese moderate liberals were not prepared for national unification and, on the whole, saw it as the means to a different end.

In the months that followed the October plebiscites, the subordination of the Left and the hegemony of Piedmont was confirmed. In January 1861 the first national elections were held, resulting in a clear victory for government candidates.[36] Two months later, in March,

[34] To the Conte di Salmour, 8 Aug. 1857, in *Cavour-Salmour*, 135. This letter was written in the aftermath of the crisis caused by Pisacane's expedition to Sapri in 1857, when Cavour was under pressure to curtail press freedoms.

[35] D. Mack Smith, *Cavour and Garibaldi: A Study in Political Conflict* (Cambridge, 1954; 2nd edn., 1985).

[36] For an analysis of this election see P. L. Ballini, *Le elezioni nella storia d'Italia dall'unità al fascismo* (Bologna, 1988), 43–58.

Vittorio Emanuele II of Piedmont was officially declared King of Italy by the Italian parliament. In October 1861 the separate administrations in Tuscany and Southern Italy were abolished, and the Piedmontese system of provincial administration was extended to the new Italian provinces (the separate administration in Sicily was abolished in January 1862). The construction of Italy's political and administrative institutions as a kind of 'greater' Piedmont then continued with fiscal and monetary union in 1862. Finally, in 1865, Piedmont's administrative and judicial institutions (including its police regulations, public works regulations, and its civil and civil procedure codes) were extended, in their entirety and without modification, to the rest of Italy.[37]

What took place, strictly speaking, after 1860 was the 'piedmontization' of Italy rather than political 'unification'. This process also shifted the power of initiative and decision away from parliament into the hands of the executive. Much of the legislative process of unification was introduced by decree, in a process which undermined the role of parliament and enhanced the role of the executive. In 1859 parliament had delegated full powers to the government to pursue the war against Austria; these powers were subsequently used to extend the whole body of Piedmontese legislation to the newly annexed province of Lombardy.[38] In 1865, Prime Minister La Marmora gave parliament the choice of either approving or refusing government proposals for administrative unification. No debate on the content of the legislation was allowed.

National unification also undermined the constitutional independence of the judiciary. The Rattazzi law of 1859 gave enormous powers of organization, recruitment, and surveillance to a newly created Min-

---

[37] There is a huge literature on the process of political, administrative, and judicial unification. See in particular the series of studies by C. Pavone, *Amministrazione centrale e amministrazione periferica da Rattazzi a Ricasoli* (Milan, 1964), A. Aquarone, *L'unificazione legislativa e i codici del 1865* (Milan, 1960), and d'Addio, *Politica e magistratura*. Other important studies include S. Cassese (ed.), *Storia della società italiana dall'unità ad oggi: l'amministrazione centrale* (Turin, 1984); R. Ruffilli, *Istituzioni, società, stato*, i: *il ruolo delle istituzione amministrative nella formazione dello Stato in Italia* (Bologna, 1989); E. Ragionieri, 'Politica e amministrazione dello stato unitario', in *Politica e amministrazione dello stato unitario* (Turin, 1967); and, most recently, F. Cammarano, 'La costruzione dello stato e la classe dirigente', in G. Sabatucci and V. Vidotto (eds.), *Storia d'Italia*, ii: *il nuovo stato e la società civile* (Rome and Bari, 1995). There are also useful, shorter analyses in R. Romanelli, *L'Italia liberale (1861–1900)* (Bologna, 1979), 36–63, and C. Ghisalberti, *Storia costituzionale d'Italia, 1848–1948* (Rome and Bari, 1989), 87–122.

[38] Ibid. 90–2.

ister of Justice. It circumvented the independence of the judiciary by stating that, in the newly annexed provinces, where magistrates' loyalty to the new system could not be taken for granted, the usual constitutional guarantees did not apply. The ministry was given the right to transfer magistrates and to decide whether or not a magistrate should continue in service after the age of 65. After 1860 the ministry also acquired the exclusive right to appoint judges; as d'Addio puts it, 'the new Italian judiciary was to be appointed and renewed solely on political grounds.'[39] The Rattazzi law also confirmed special public-order powers which could be used by the state to by-pass normal judicial procedures, and which were to be employed with increasing frequency in the decade which followed.[40]

Thus, the process of political and administrative unification was carried through rapidly by the government, often without consulting parliament and using powers which accentuated the most absolutist elements of the Piedmontese political system. Parliament itself was based on a narrow suffrage: those who were entitled to vote comprised slightly less than 2 per cent of the total population. In some areas the percentage was significantly smaller; for example, in Palermo only 1.06 per cent of the population had the vote.[41] So the second irony of the moderates' victory in 1860 was that it led them to create a state which was as centralized, interventionist, and, often, as authoritarian as anything produced by their Restoration predecessors. Hardly surprisingly, this process is also one of the most debated aspects of the Right's work.[42] Claudio Pavone states the controversy quite explicitly: 'how could these men . . . once in power have traced step by step the very road against which they had

[39] D'Addio, *Politica e magistratura*, 43.

[40] On the process of unifying the police and criminal justice system after unification see A. Berselli, 'Amministrazione e ordine pubblico dopo l'unità', in *Amministrazione della giustizia e poteri di polizia dagli stati preunitari alla caduta della Destra: atti del lii congresso di storia del Risorgimento italiano* (Rome, 1986). The application of this aspect of government policy to Sicily will be discussed in much more detail in the chapters which follow. Useful general analyses of this legislation are d'Addio, *Politica e magistratura*, 133, J. A. Davis, *Conflict and Control: Law and Order in Nineteenth-Century Italy* (London, 1988), 176–82, and R. Martucci, *Emergenza e tutela dell'ordine pubblico nell'Italia liberale, 1861–1865* (Bologna, 1980), esp. 9–67, 111–83.

[41] E. Iachello and A. Signorelli, 'Borghesie urbane dell'Ottocento', in M. Aymard and G. Giarrizzo (eds.), *La Sicilia* (Turin, 1987), 120.

[42] There are useful summaries of the historiographical debate about the nature of the Italian state in N. Tranfaglia (ed.), *L'Italia unita nella storiografia della seconda dopoguerra* (Milan, 1980), and F. Mazzonis, 'La riflessione degli storici', in *Divertimento italiano: problemi di storia e questioni storiografiche dell'unificazione* (Milan, 1993).

written, were writing and would continue to write so many learned pages?'[43] The answer seems to lie in the causes and circumstances of unification itself.

With national unification, the political advantages which Piedmont had possessed, and which had allowed a successful compromise between absolutism and liberalism to emerge, effectively ceased to exist. Unification revealed the costs of the moderate compromise between absolutism and liberalism, which had hitherto been well hidden. It revealed, for instance, the financial profligacy which had lain behind Piedmont's 'economic miracle' in the 1850s. The huge cost of investment in welfare, public works, and the military had increased the national debt from 120 million lire in 1847 to 725 million lire in 1859. By 1859 Piedmont was heavily in debt to foreign investors.[44] After the war against Austria (and with the amalgamation of the Lombard national debt) the debt rose to 1,170 million lire.[45] National unification also destroyed the myth of Piedmont's foreign policy. Cavour's diplomatic intrigues—notably, his cession of Nice and Savoy to France in 1860—ultimately undermined his reputation abroad. This was particularly the case among the British diplomats and statesmen who had been most favourably disposed to Italian nationalism, about whom Emanuele d'Azeglio wrote to Cavour on 14 April 1860 that 'although the English consider you a very clever minister, for a long time you will remain for them a person on whose word very little trust can be placed'.[46] Thereafter there remained considerable distrust of the Italian government in diplomatic circles; even Italy's leaders considered themselves to be 'more lucky than strong'.[47]

National unification also meant that any hope of a compromise with the Church, with whom relations had been deteriorating since the Siccardi laws of the early 1850s, receded indefinitely. The invasion of the Papal States by the Piedmontese army in 1860 led to a rapid worsening of relations. Despite Cavour's strenuous efforts before his death to reach a compromise with Pope Pius IX over Church–state relations, the Pope refused to recognize the new state and condemned

[43] Pavone, *Amministrazione centrale e amministrazione periferica*, 5.

[44] Scirocco, *L'Italia del Risorgimento*, 359.

[45] Candeloro, *Storia dell'Italia moderna*, iv. 204.

[46] D. Mack Smith (ed.), *The Making of Italy, 1796–1866* (London, 1968; 2nd edn., 1988), 306.

[47] F. Chabod, *Storia della politica estera italiana dal 1876 al 1896*, i: *le premesse* (Bari, 1954), 30.

all attempts at compromise with liberalism.[48] Furthermore, the breach between Church and state after 1860 harmed the state much more than the Church. Since the Church, unlike the new Italian state, was a truly 'national' institution, with representatives whose authority was respected in every community, its hostility undermined the legitimacy of the new political system. Christopher Seton-Watson writes that, after unification:

the Church fought back with every weapon at its disposal. Victor Emmanuel, his ministers and all who shared responsibility for secularist legislation were excommunicated. Pius IX refused to recognise the new state, even to the extent of never referring to the Italian kingdom, but always to the 'Subalpine usurper'.[49]

Furthermore, with the assistance of French troops, the Pope was able to hold on to Rome until 1870: this failure to make Rome the capital of the Italian kingdom was a lasting humiliation for the government. Venetia remained part of the Austrian Empire until 1866, which also made a mockery of united Italy's claim to national independence.

The 1860s saw a resurgence of social unrest and political extremism, making a stable 'middle way' much more difficult to find. In the early 1860s Bourbon 'reactionaries' were able to establish a strong movement based on discontented peasants and bandits on the Southern mainland. By the mid- to late 1860s the Right's republican opponents had built up new support among the urban poor. Links with anarchist movements in the First International were also being established.[50]

With unification, the Right also took on the administrative, social, and economic problems which had destabilized the old regimes. It took on the resentments of the provinces against the centre which had undermined both the Bourbon regime in the South and the Papal regime in Central Italy. It took from them all the old municipal and regional rivalries, the problems of policing, and of government administration; and it also inherited their financial difficulties. Moreover,

---

[48] On the complex negotiations between Church and state at the time of unification, see E. Passerin d'Entrèves, *L'ultima battaglia politica di Cavour: i problemi dell'unificazione italiana* (Turin, 1956), 265–75.

[49] C. Seton-Watson, *Italy from Liberalism to Fascism, 1870–1925* (London, 1968), 11.

[50] On the political threats to national unity, D. Mack Smith, *Italy: A Modern History* (Ann Arbor, 1959), 61–99 is a useful and important summary, but he probably overstates the difficulties. Mack Smith's book caused considerable controversy in Italy. For an analysis sympathetic to Mack Smith which also examines the significance of the internal threats to Italian unity, see Ragionieri, 'Politica e amministrazione', esp. 97–8. See also A. Caracciolo, *Stato e società civile: problemi dell'unificazione italiana* (Turin, 1959), 68–9.

unlike the Piedmontese kingdom, there was little loyalty to the Savoy dynasty in the new Italy. Administrative inefficiency and corruption was an everyday reality and, in many areas, a fundamental social instability threatened the existing order. Cavour's untimely death in June 1861 also left a huge vacuum at the centre of power.

Thus, the practical problems which faced Cavour's successors were immense. Recent historiography has tended to see the Right's decision to prioritize administrative unification as an unavoidable response to the instability which threatened the new kingdom's viability. Indeed, evidence suggests that many Italian liberals saw centralization as merely a temporary expedient to be followed, when the situation calmed, by a measure of 'self-government'. Romanelli argues that, for the Right, centralization was a means of bringing the benefits of liberalism to a part of Italy which had hitherto experienced only political 'corruption'.[51] Administrative centralization was thus 'judged to be the indispensable tool for holding on to power and for affirming their position as the national ruling class'.[52]

Yet, while neither the scale of the task nor the Right's faith in liberalism can be denied, it none the less seems clear that centralization was an inappropriate response to the crisis which the new government faced. The Right had set themselves what was, in Romanelli's words, an 'impossible task' (*un comando impossibile*). Instead of establishing the strong, legitimate, and effective government sought after by Cavour and his successors, administrative centralization actually led to the creation of a political system which was unstable, generally unpopular, and frequently inefficient. Thus, the third irony of the moderates' victory over the democrats was that it produced largely counterproductive results. In Sicily, as we shall see, the policies pursued by the new government meant that it was often not able to govern at all.

With unification, the government began to lose control of parliament. Shortly before his death, Cavour clashed violently with Garibaldi in the national parliament over the unification of the army: Garibaldi accused Cavour of provoking a 'fratricidal war'. This debate marked the end of the temporary truce between Left and Right in parliament.[53] Even within the Historic Right, there was considerable dissent over the government's handling of national unification. Not all Italian moderate

---

[51] R. Romanelli, 'Il comando impossibile: la natura del progetto liberale del governo', in *Il comando impossibile: stato e società nell'Italia liberale* (Bologna, 1988), 7.

[52] Romanelli, *L'Italia liberale*, 40.

[53] Extracts from the debate are reprinted in Mack Smith, *The Making of Italy*, 348–52.

liberals shared the secularizing zeal of Cavour and his Piedmontese followers; for Bettino Ricasoli and many others, bad Church–state relations were a source of considerable personal unease.[54] Even greater problems were caused by the centralization (or 'piedmontiza-tion') of political institutions. Centralization was resented by many non-Piedmontese government deputies; alternative proposals for decentralization were presented by Farini (who was from Modena) and Minghetti (who was from Bologna), but these were both shelved by the government.[55]

The core of the Right was a group of like-minded individuals rather than a political party with shared traditions and an agreed programme for government.[56] Reconciling the aims and attitudes of moderate liberals from all over the peninsula was never going to be an easy task. Regional loyalties resurfaced quickly in the national parliament, and they frequently determined the voting behaviour of deputies who were nominally within the Right.[57] Increasingly after 1860, the Right found itself divided along regional lines, between the Piedmontese *permanente* and the Lombard–Tuscan *consorteria*. The Historic Right was, in other words, a shifting, sometimes precarious coalition, not a monolithic ruling party; and this is reflected in the number of ministries (twelve in all) in the first decade after unification.

III

Of the issues facing the Historic Right in October 1860, by far the most urgent was that of protecting its political position and maintaining its control over the concluding events of the Risorgimento. Since the South had been annexed primarily to pre-empt the advance of the *garibaldini* on Rome, Piedmontese policy towards the Southern provinces tended initially to be dominated by strategic and political considerations. 'Our aim is clear,' Cavour wrote to the king in December 1860, 'to impose unity on the most corrupt and weakest part of Italy. . .

[54] Romanelli, *L'Italia liberale*, 95–101; Jemolo, *Church and State in Italy*, 34–9.

[55] For an analysis of the *progetto Minghetti*, see Pavone, *Amministrazione centrale e amministrazione periferica*, 120–51, and Candeloro, *Storia dell'Italia moderna*, v. 152–9.

[56] Romanelli, *L'Italia liberale*, 20. Romanelli describes the main personalities and ideology of the Right, ibid. 17–27.

[57] M. Serena Piretti and G. Guidi, *Emilia Romagna in parlamento (1861–1919)* (2 vols.; Bologna, 1992). The authors use a statistical analysis to show that regional loyalties played a determining role in the voting behaviour of the deputies, even while they continued to support the government.

MAP 4. The Kingdom of Italy in 1861 (adapted from J. A. Davis, *Conflict and Control: Law and Order in Nineteenth-Century Italy*, London, 1988)

[by] moral force and, if this is not enough, by physical force.'[58] The plan, according to Luigi Farini (the *luogotenente generale* in Naples), was to go 'and establish monarchic authority, morality and good sense in Naples and Sicily'.[59] If 'we resolutely bring in our government and our ideas', a colleague of Cavour's wrote to him enthusiastically, 'we will

---

[58] 14 December 1860, *Il carteggio Cavour-Nigra dal 1858 al 1861* (4 vols.; Bologna, 1926–9), iv. 290–3.   [59] Quoted in Mack Smith, *Cavour and Garibaldi*, 258.

come out of Palermo blessed and victorious'.[60] The government's main objective in Sicily went no further than to set up an effective administration to re-establish law and order in the cities and countryside. This task was considered all the more urgent because they feared the effects of Southern 'corruption' on the administration or, as Cavour put it, losing power to 'the tyranny of village know-it-alls [*dottoruzzi dei villaggi*]'.[61] An extremist (Bourbon and/or republican) resurgence based on the prevailing chaos was also considered to be a major risk.

It is striking that, on the whole, Italian leaders seemed to have had little interest in Sicilian problems *per se*. There was a mistaken belief that the island was one of the richest and most fertile regions in Italy. Early impressions confirmed this view. One correspondent—no doubt struck by the contrast between Palermo and Turin during the winter months—spoke glowingly of Sicily as 'the paradise of Italy' and 'an eternal Spring', where 'sulphur mines, wines, grains, olives, oranges, marbles' were found in glorious abundance.[62] The obvious appeal of this view was that it suggested that such problems as existed required no special treatment. It also reinforced the tendency to attribute the prevailing political and social chaos to the corrupting legacy of the Bourbons and to the administrative mess apparently created by the *garibaldini*.[63] 'Sicily,' Depretis told parliament in October 1860, 'is a true paradise . . . [which] has been governed by Satan.'[64] Popular unrest was often seen simply as the result of an organized conspiracy. Crispi noted in a letter of March 1861 that in Sicily 'the government sees the work of *mazzinians*, *republicans*, etc. to be the only cause of disorder'.[65] Little effort was made to inquire more deeply into the

---

[60] Cassinis to Cavour, 9 Dec. 1860, in C. Cavour, *La liberazione del Mezzogiorno e la formazione del regno d'Italia: carteggi di Camillo Cavour con Villamarina, Scialoja, Cordova, Fasini ecc* (5 vols.; Bologna, 1949–54) iv. 39.

[61] *Lettere edite e inedite di Camillo di Cavour* (Turin, 1885), iv. 238. For a fuller discussion, see M. Salvadori, *Il mito del buongoverno: a questione meridionale da Cavour a Gramsci* (Turin, 1960), 32.

[62] 9 Dec. 1860, in *La liberazione del Mezzogiorno*, iv. 35–40. Mack Smith suggests that what knowledge Northern Italians had of Sicily came from ancient history and poetry; D. Mack Smith, *A History of Sicily* ii: *Modern Sicily After 1713* (London, 1968), 454.

[63] Salvadori, *Il mito del buongoverno*, 31.

[64] Quoted in F. Renda, 'Garibaldi e la questione contadina in Sicilia nel 1860', in G. Cingari (ed.), *Garibaldi e il socialismo* (Rome and Bari, 1987).

[65] 25 March 1861, in ISR, b.657, n.14 (3). See also F. de Stefano and F. L. Oddo, *Storia della Sicilia dal 1860 al 1910* (Bari, 1963), 241–2, and Mack Smith, *Modern Sicily After 1713*, 454.

causes of disorder in Sicily, or to consult with those experienced in Sicilian affairs.

Policy-makers in Turin remained largely ignorant of Sicilian culture and political traditions. This is hardly surprising, since the political and economic centre of the new nation's affairs was so clearly in the North. Such difficulties as the government encountered in Sicily were often considered of irritating and peripheral concern compared to the main issues of the day—Rome and relations with the Papacy, the question of Venetia, and the mounting financial crisis. Little time was given over in parliament to debating Sicilian problems and, on those few occasions, government ministers made a clear effort to downplay any difficulties. Perhaps the most remarkable statement of government indifference to the situation in Sicily was made by Cavour's successor as Italian Prime Minister, Bettino Ricasoli, in December 1861. Despite having received a long and gloomy report from the special envoy, Diomede Pantaleoni, which clearly revealed the extent of discontent, lawlessness, hostility to the government, and support for opposition groups in the island, Ricasoli felt able to assure the deputies that in Sicily 'everything is proceeding as it should, laws are respected, there is no evidence of any party hostile to the government and, as far as we can tell, nobody is unhappy with the present situation'.[66]

According to Diomede Pantaleoni, the government was in fact extremely isolated in Sicily. The government party (which he called 'the party of the national society', La Farina *et al.*) lacked energy and purpose, was less than entirely committed to liberal values, and had links with some of the 'shady' elements of Palermo society. Pantaleoni concluded that the government party had made itself very unpopular, and that this was the real reason 'for the government's lack of support in the country.'[67]

When Sicily was annexed by Piedmont after the plebiscite of October 1860, a separate administration or *governo luogoteneziale* was established in Palermo. It consisted of a council of ministers in charge of the day-to-day running of the administration, as well as for introducing Italian (effectively Piedmontese) legislation into Sicily, reorganizing local government, and setting up new security forces. Its members were nominated by a *luogotenente generale* who was in turn appointed by Turin.

---

[66] *Atti Parlamentari, Camera dei deputati, discussioni*, 7 Dec. 1861, 131. Pantaleoni's report of 10 Oct. 1861 is in G. Scichilone, *Documenti sulle condizione della Sicilia dal 1860 al 1870* (Rome, 1952), 92–103.   [67] Ibid. 97–8.

There were three *luogotenente generale* in all: the Marchese di Montezemolo, General della Rovere, and General Pettinengo. None of these
appointments appear to have been particularly successful; the appointment of della Rovere and Pettinengo reflect the government's decision
to unify its military and political control of the island.

A former governor of Nice, Montezemolo was by all accounts
appalled by the administrative chaos he found in Sicily, and disturbed
by the confrontational nature of its politics. The Mazzinian agitator,
Giorgio Asproni (not the most impartial of observers), described with
glee Montezemolo's terror at the popular unrest in Palermo, and
observed that he was 'a mass of meat made inert by gambling and
gluttony, having no heart for anything except to show how capable of
harassment and how incapable of government the Piedmontese are'.[68]
Montezemolo's own unhappiness and sense of isolation are strongly
expressed in a series of letters to Turin, which end with a request to be
relieved of his post.[69] His successor General della Rovere was also
clearly unhappy and isolated, complaining that he was 'overcome' by
the amount of work which he alone could do.[70]

Supporters of the government were in a minority in the council of
the *luogotenenza*. Tensions between the government party and autonomists within the *luogotenenza* provided the focus of the first political
crisis after unification. Prior to the plebiscite of October 1860, Cavour
had reassured autonomists that Sicily would retain a measure of regional autonomy within the future kingdom,[71] and autonomists—who
dominated the council of the *luogotenenza*—hoped that it would provide the basis for a separate and permanent Sicilian administration. The
government in Turin, however, seemed increasingly to see the *luogotenenza* as merely a transitional government. In January 1861 growing
friction over the presence of the Cavourian agents La Farina and
Cordova in the council led to popular agitation in the streets of Palermo
and to the resignation of the council.[72] The effect of this was to divide
the autonomist movement into those, led by Torrearsa, who accepted
'piedmontization' and agreed to form a new government, and those who

[68] 20 Feb. 1861, in G. Asproni, *Diario politico, 1855–1876* (7 vols.; Milan, 1974–91), iii.
34.
[69] To the Minister of the Interior, Marco Minghetti, 20 Jan. 1861, in ASP, Prefettura di
Palermo, serie gabinetto, 1860–1905 (henceforth pref. gab.) b. 1, prat. 1, f. 1, n. 8.
[70] 4 May 1861, in *La liberazione del Mezzogiorno*, iv. 468.
[71] Mack Smith, *Cavour and Garibaldi*, 67–8, 72–6.
[72] Montezemolo to Cavour, 2 Jan. 1861, in *La liberazione del Mezzogiorno*, iv. 162–4.

continued to oppose it. Montezemolo hoped, as he put it to Cavour, to 'decapitate' the autonomist movement, by including prominent members in his government; and he was at least partially successful.[73] Alarmed by the growing disorder in Palermo, and fearing the consequences of an extended period without government, Torrearsa decided to throw in his lot unreservedly with Cavour and moderate liberalism.[74]

The government followed its victory over the autonomists with an acceleration of the process of administrative unification. In October 1861 it issued decrees which extended Piedmont's legal codes to the rest of Italy; in January 1862 the *governo luogotenenziale* in Palermo was abolished and replaced with the Piedmontese system of provincial and communal administration.[75] However, the Bourbon administrative boundaries (twenty-four districts and seven provinces) were retained. Intendants and sub-intendants (governors under Garibaldi) were simply replaced by prefects or sub-prefects. Moreover, this new system and these new terms were not immediately or uniformly adopted. In 1861 government reports make for confusing reading: some prefects went on calling themselves governors, sub-prefects called themselves intendants, and so on.[76]

Among the government's supporters, Pantaleoni had listed the *garibaldini*; they were, he wrote, the most popular, talented, and loyal supporters of the government in Sicily. By contrast, a Bourbon party, according to Pantaleoni, 'does not exist'. He also warned against alienating the Church in Sicily, arguing that the Sicilian clergy was 'above all . . . Sicilian in spirit and in origin', had supported the movement for autonomy, and had opposed Bourbon rule.[77] Others disagreed, and advised excluding the *garibaldini*. Cavour's agent, La Farina, wrote to him from Sicily at the end of December 1860 that 'all the administrative authorities have been appointed by Crispi and Mordini, and are therefore hostile to us'.[78]

In terms of the policy towards government employees, it was La Farina's advice which was followed. One of the government's first priorities, indeed, was to eradicate the traces left by Garibaldi's admin-

[73] Montezemolo to Cavour, 9 Jan. 1861, in *La liberazione del Mezzogiorno*, iv. 193–6.

[74] Ibid. 31 Jan. 1861, Torrearsa to Cavour, 263.

[75] For a more detailed description of the erosion of the *governo luogotenenziale*'s autonomous functions before October 1861, see F. Brancato, *La Sicilia nel primo ventennio del regno d'Italia* (Bologna, 1956), 148–56.

[76] Here the titles have been used according to those actually used by the correspondents.

[77] Scichilone, *Documenti*, 93.

[78] 22 Dec. 1860, *La liberazione de Mezzogiorno*, iv. 61.

istration. In November 1860 the minister of the interior, Marco Minghetti, instructed the Naples administration to remove the 'obstacles
and appendages' put in place by Garibaldi's 'so-called government
[*sgoverno*]' before replacing the Bourbon system. This policy was followed in Sicily as well.[79] Reflecting a general standpoint of moderate
liberalism to dismiss democrats as incapable of effective government,
the *garibaldini* who had held power during 1860 were viewed as dan-
gerously incompetent.[80] Where this was manifestly not the case, it was
feared that they would use their position of power to help the republicans. In March 1861, Minghetti told the Sicilian *luogotenente generale*,
Montezemolo, to compile a list of Sicilian governors and others who
should be transferred.[81]

In January 1861 the government decided to disband and reorganize
Garibaldi's national guard throughout Southern Italy and to replace it
with the more élitist Piedmontese system. In April further modifica-
tions were introduced which excluded men under 21 and those who
paid no taxes from service in the local militias.[82] In May 1861 the
Minister of War announced the conscription into the army of 4,500
Sicilians. Its determination to exclude the 'irregular' *garibaldini* was
even more evident in its policy towards his volunteer army. At the end
of the Southern campaign Garibaldi's volunteers totalled some 52,839
men, of whom 45,050 were from the mainland and 7,799 from Sicily.[83]
A government decree of November 1860 offered the volunteers a
choice between signing up in the regular army for two years or a
paid pension.[84] In practice, however, the number of volunteers
allowed to transfer into the army was strictly limited by a special
commission. Molfese argues that the procedures followed by the
commission involved excessive bureaucracy, humiliation, and discri-
mination so that, between November and December, nearly all the
non-commissioned officers resigned, while three-quarters of the officers did the same.[85]

Fear of the *garibaldini*, and perhaps even more of their links with
republicanism, was a factor in the government's otherwise surprising
decision to adopt a relatively tolerant attitude towards former employees

[79] *La liberazione del Mezzogiorno*, 12 Nov. 1860, iii. 349.
[80] On this subject, see Giacinto Carini's letter to Cavour, ibid. 96–8.
[81] 29 March 1861, ASP, pref. gab. b. 1, prat. 1, f. 1, n. 4.
[82] P. Pieri, *Le forze armate nella età della Destra* (Milan, 1962), 66–7.
[83] F. Molfese, *Storia del brigantaggio dopo l'unità* (Milan, 1964), 25.
[84] Pieri, *Le forze armate*, 58.   [85] Molfese, *Storia del brigantaggio*, 25.

of the Bourbon administration. Government correspondence of the period is full of alarmist reports about Bourbon activity. These fears were compounded by the war on the Southern mainland, where the government faced a large-scale and costly battle against brigandage which was supported by the Bourbons. In November 1861 the Minister of War wrote to the Sicilian *luogotenente generale* that the number of troops stationed in Girgenti might have to be doubled due to the threat of an invasion from Bourbons in Malta.[86] In February 1862 a spy sent details to Ricasoli's secretary, Bianchi, about attempts by Bourbons in Rome and Malta to foment unrest in Sicily.[87]

Nevertheless, when it came to the bureaucracy the desire for continuity and the fear of the *garibaldini* took precedence over the threat of Bourbon reaction. The governor of Girgenti wrote, in April 1861:

it clearly was not possible to wipe out with one blow all that was old and replace it with what was new. The machinery of government had to function, and the government not only found it useful but was actually obliged to leave some powers and some duties with those who had held them under the Bourbon government.[88]

In May 1861 the new Sicilian *luogotenente generale*, della Rovere, indicated to Minghetti that the vast majority of Bourbon employees placed more value on their jobs than on political loyalties. Given the unstable political situation, he suggested that a pragmatic approach should be adopted where only the completely inept should be dismissed, and then without political distinction.[89] In reply Minghetti agreed, adding that because of the problems of finding reliable replacements for those dismissed or transferred, caution should be used when condemning the past performances of employees.[90]

As Minister of the Interior, and responsible for the government's policy on employees of both former administrations, Minghetti seemed to favour administrative continuity and the retention of the Bourbon administration's long-term employees. By contrast, he was encouraged to regard those who had been employed under Garibaldi with much greater suspicion. The government's policy towards the judiciary in the Two Sicilies, using the Rattazzi law of 1859 which gave the Justice Minister significant powers to appoint and transfer magistrates, seems

---

[86] ASP, Luog. Polizia, b. 1683.   [87] Scichilone, *Documenti*, 122–8.
[88] 19 April 1861, in ASP, Luog. Polizia, b. 1683.
[89] 7 May 1861, *La liberazione del Mezzogiorno*, iv. 471–3.
[90] Ibid. 14 May 1861, 487–9.

to have been guided by similar considerations. Initially, under the Justice Minister, Giovanni Cassinis, and his successor, Vincenzo Miglietti, the government moved very cautiously, respecting the constitutional position of magistrates, and sometimes leaving blatantly pro-Bourbon or even entirely incompetent magistrates in their posts.[91] However, under Rattazzi himself, who was Justice Minister between March and April 1862 (as well as being Prime Minister and Minister of the Interior), the government moved swiftly, carrying out a full-scale 'purge' of Bourbon magistrates in Sicily during this period. Later in the same year the government caused a huge public outcry by transferring the popular president of the Court of Appeal in Palermo, the social-democrat leader Pasquale Calvi, to the court in Florence. Calvi had incurred the wrath of the government when he ordered the Procurator General of Palermo to pay damages to an ex-minister of Garibaldi, Giovanni Raffaele, whose illegal arrest had allegedly been ordered by Cavour's agent, Giuseppe La Farina, in January 1861.[92]

Although the main focus of government policy in Sicily was administrative unification, both Montezemolo and his successors also prepared a programme of social and economic reform. Here, too, the main aim of the government was to integrate Sicily more fully into the new Kingdom of Italy. In January 1861 Montezemolo complained to Turin about the lack of roads in Sicily, which in his view made it impossible to organize the upcoming parliamentary elections properly.[93] The governor of Caltanissetta wrote to Palermo in February that the province's inadequate infrastructure was responsible for 'the impossibility of developing huge areas of land between communities, the sluggish population growth . . . [and] the lack of incentive for labourers to improve their land's productive capacity'. Both he and the governor of Girgenti pointed out that the lack of railways and port facilities hampered the growth of sulphur-mining.[94]

The size of the budget deficit after unification acted as a severe constraint on public works of any kind. It is estimated that in the first decade after unification the government nevertheless spent three times

[91] See e.g. the complaint from the Governor of Girgenti, 19 June 1861, in ASP, Luog. Polizia, b. 1680.

[92] On this case see d'Addio, *Politica e magistratura*, documenti, nn. 134–6, 752–9.

[93] 21 Jan. 1861, ASP, pref. gab., b. 1, prat. 1, f. 1, n. 8.

[94] The long report from the Governor of Caltanissetta's office about the roads in the province, dated 16 Feb. 1861, is in ASP, Luog. Interno, b. 4176; that from the governor of Girgenti about the lack of port facilities, dated 19 April 1861, is in ASP, Luog. Polizia, b. 1682, f. aprile.

as much on roads in the South (taken as a whole) than it did in the North.[95] Even more emphasis was placed on the railways; in July 1861 the government modified and confirmed the agreement reached between the prodictatorship and the *Società Adami e Lemmi* for the construction of railway lines linking the provincial capitals of Sicily.[96] Similar efforts were made with regard to trade and commerce. In the early 1860s the number of credit institutions in Sicily increased rapidly; the Banco di Torino opened offices in Palermo, Messina, and Catania in 1861, and the Cassa di Risparmio opened a series of offices between 1861 and 1864. Internal and external barriers to trade were also dismantled.[97] Some of the greatest efforts made by the government were in the field of public education, where the Casati law providing for compulsory elementary education was put into effect. Renda estimates that the resources at the disposal of the educational authorities were nearly tripled after unification. In six years, between the 1861–2 school year and the 1868–9 school year, the number of communes with elementary public schools increased from 85 to 554 in the province of Palermo alone.[98]

Unfortunately, investment in education and infrastructure proved too slow a process to satisfy the government's urgent desire for economic and social unification. Road and railway building was difficult in Sicily, where new technologies and methods had to be introduced from scratch and where the mountainous and arid nature of the terrain, together with the absence of any other form of communication, meant that construction proceeded at a painfully slow pace. Despite substantial investment, road building also lagged behind relative to other parts of Italy. Although Sicily's network of national and provincial roads increased by some 27 per cent between 1861 and 1871, this represented only 10 per cent of the national total. The number of local roads, for which the communes were responsible, increased by a meagre 1 per cent of the national total.[99]

Railway construction, which demanded a vast initial investment of capital, was particularly hampered by financial constraints. The industrialist Quintino Sella, who was Minister of Finance for much of the

[95] A. del Monte and A. Giannola, *Il Mezzogiorno nell'economia italiana* (Bologna, 1978), 64.

[96] R. Giuffrida, *Politica ed economia nella Sicilia dell'Ottocento* (Palermo, 1980), 246–8.

[97] F. Renda, *Storia della Sicilia dal 1860 al 1970* (Palermo, 1984), i 116–17.

[98] Ibid. 251. For a more detailed discussion see G. Bonetta, *Istruzione e società nella Sicilia dell'Ottocento* (Palermo, 1981).   [99] Renda, *Storia della Sicilia*, 248.

1860s, looked to private investors to make up the difference, but their involvement became tied up in a series of personal and political considerations. The attempt to reach a loan agreement with the Rothschild bank in 1862 faltered due to a deterioration in Italo-French relations. Efforts by Bastogi, the Minister of Finance in 1862, to form a consortium of Italian investors came to nothing when a public scandal revealed his part in giving and receiving bribes.[100] Finally, the government assumed direct responsibility for the opening of the track between Palermo and Bagheria in 1863. A new company funded by French capital, the *Società Vittorio Emanuele*, completed the track between Bagheria and Termini Imerese in 1866. The Messina–Catania line was opened in 1867.[101] These were, however, all coastal tracks. They did nothing either to revitalize economic activity in the interior or to increase the government's control of the countryside. When Leopoldo Franchetti visited the Sicilian interior in the mid-1870s, he travelled on the railway line which was still incomplete and which, as he remarked, went on 'to lose itself in the centre of Sicily'.[102]

Investment in education also failed to bring about the desired results. By 1901, forty years after unification, rates for illiteracy in Sicily had fallen by only 16 per cent, from 89 per cent to 71 per cent. The figures for female illiteracy were even higher, falling only 14 per cent, from 91 per cent in 1871 (there are no separate figures for 1861) to 77 per cent in 1901. By comparison, the national average for illiteracy was much lower: 75 per cent in 1861 and 48 per cent in 1901. Piedmont had only 18 per cent illiteracy in 1901 (14 per cent for men). Hence, while Sicily's illiteracy rate was only 12 per cent higher than the national average in 1860, by 1901 this had risen to 23 per cent.[103]

The fiscal policies pursued by the government after unification did little to undermine regional differences or encourage an integrated national market. The traditional account of an economy devastated by unification has undergone substantial revisions in the light of recent research. It is clear, nevertheless, that the expected economic benefits to Sicily from unification were very unequally distributed. The new government's economic policies accentuated the uneven development of the Sicilian economy. Some Sicilian industries (sulphur-mining) and some branches of agriculture (market gardening and wine), already

---

[100] Candeloro, *Storia dell'Italia moderna*, iv. 262–73.
[101] Giuffrida, *Politica ed economia*, 246–8.
[102] L. Franchetti, *Condizione politiche e amministrative della Sicilia* (1876; Rome, 1993 edn.), 22.   [103] These figures are in Romanelli, *L'Italia liberale*, 436.

prospering before unification, benefited considerably from the introduction of free trade. However, many smaller industries (textiles) suffered a mortal blow as a result of the loss of protective tariffs. At the
same time, some social groups did better than others. For instance, the
new tax structure did little to benefit the small producer/consumer:
direct taxation accounted for 34 per cent of state revenue, while taxes
on consumption accounted for 54 per cent.[104] By far the most important direct tax was on land, but this was partly assessed on the basis of
the land's productivity. The tax thus favoured the large landowner who
used extensive farming methods with low productivity, and worked
against the smallholder, who used intensive methods. Moreover, since
local taxes were allocated by the commune, and the commune was
dominated by large landowners, the burden tended to fall most heavily
on its poorest members. Sonnino observed in 1876 that mules and
horses, which were owned by peasants, were heavily taxed in many
communes, while cattle, which were owned by rich landowners, were
rarely taxed at all.[105]

The government's efforts with regard to the land question also ran
into difficulties. Although Mordini's land reform of October 1860, and
the efforts of the Sicilian deputy, Simone Corleo, had put this issue
firmly on the political agenda, the Mordini land reform had remained
unenacted after October 1860. It was replaced by the plan which Corleo
himself presented to parliament in 1861 and which became law on 10
August 1862. The Corleo law concentrated exclusively on Church land
(removing common land from the sale) and made some 192,000 hectares available in perpetual leaseholds to be allocated by auction. There
was no provision for the extension of credit to the new peasant pro-
prietor. Corleo had become convinced that Mordini's system of allocat-
ing land by lottery would lead to inefficiencies. The new law thus
stipulated that instead of the allocation of leaseholds being entrusted
to the communes, the operation would be conducted by a special
commission which would hold auctions to divide up the property.
Barriers to the monopoly purchase of land were also removed.[106]

Although the intention of the Corleo law, like much of the legislation
on land in the years before unification, was to create a new class of small

[104] Del Monte and Giannola, *Il Mezzogiorno nell'economia italiana*, 61.
[105] Sonnino, 'I contadini in Sicilia' in L. Franchetti and S. Sonnino, *Inchiesta in Sicilia* (1876; Florence, 1974 edn.), 107–8.
[106] A. li Vecchi, 'Introduzione', in S. Corleo, *Storia dell'enfiteusi dei terreni ecclesiastici di Sicilia*, ed. A. li Vecchi (Caltanissetta and Roma, 1977), p. xxxviii.

landowners in the countryside, it was also governed by more urgent considerations. The government was in desperate need of money, and saw in the sale of Church land the possibility of raising revenue quickly and relatively uncontroversially; the law would also considerably weaken the economic power of the Church in Sicily.[107] As a result of the new provisions in the 1861 law, large landowners were able to take advantage of the reform to gain more land for themselves to the detriment of the peasants. Mack Smith writes that the use of auctions meant that 'peasants were excluded, the auctioneers were intimidated, and a few powerful buyers formed secret rings which eliminated competition and kept prices minimal'.[108] In the end, the government actually lost a valuable source of revenue. Only 7 per cent of the available land went to small proprietors: the remaining 93 per cent went into the hands of the powerful medium and large landowners.[109] The sale of Church property also damaged the credit assistance offered to the peasantry through the ecclesiastical institution, the *Monte di Pietà*.[110]

The combined effect of taxation, conscription, action against the Church, and land reform caused massive popular resentment against the new government. It is, therefore, not surprising that the peasant unrest which had been such a central feature of the 1860 revolution continued unabated in the years following national unification.

IV

To sum up, the relatively stable situation in Piedmont before 1859 had made possible a compromise between conservatives and liberals on the basis of loyalty to the monarchy, a sound administration, and economic growth. However, conditions prevailing during the same period in the other Italian states had made this kind of compromise impossible to sustain. Thus, after the wars of national unification in 1859–60, Piedmontese rulers encountered political conditions elsewhere in the peninsula which were in important ways very different from the ones which had helped them to success in Piedmont.

The new rulers of Italy saw strong and effective government as the solution to the political turmoil in the peninsula. Yet they, much like

[107] G. Luzzato, *L'economia italiana dal 1861 al 1914*, i: *1861–1894* (Milan, 1963), 36–40.
[108] Mack Smith, *Modern Sicily After 1713*, 457.
[109] Renda, *Storia della Sicilia*, 242.
[110] Ibid. 116–17. See, however, Sonnino's comments that, by unification, the credit made available by the Church was not a form of charity but simply another and more widespread form of usury: Sonnino, 'I contadini in Sicilia', 109–10.

their Restoration predecessors, failed to appreciate the necessity of obtaining support for the administrative changes which they proposed. As before, the task of electing government representatives, and of government itself, was confined to a fairly narrow ruling élite who were unable to represent society's diverse needs. This narrow élite was also internally divided: its members disagreed strongly about essential features of government policy. The gap between state and civil society, which had been such a destabilizing feature of Restoration Italy, continued to destabilize the business of government after national unification.

After 1860 many aspects of the Right's programme were deeply unpopular. Beyond the confines of the ruling élite, the government's programme of free trade and free speech did not always appeal. The opposition of the Church to the new state severely weakened the legitimacy of the new political system. The rhetoric of Italian nationalism failed to find much resonance beyond the small minority of Italy's population who could not only read and write, but who actually had the leisure to do so. Nationalism was, in any case, a double-edged sword which could be used by republicans to lament the failure to gain Rome and Venetia and so to criticize the limited achievements of the new government.

Finally, the construction of a strong central administration offered little to groups such as the Sicilian landed élites, whose political identity had been forged during the Restoration in opposition to the central power. Many of the difficulties in establishing a stable political system in Sicily can be attributed to this one fundamental problem. In Sicily, the new government inherited the bitter conflict between central and local power and the particular political practices which went with it. It also inherited the municipal and personal rivalries which had destabilized local government prior to unification. Worst of all, it inherited a peasant revolution. In Sicily, the new government had, in short, lost most of the advantages which had characterized the Piedmontese 'solution' in the first place.

Policy-makers in Turin were largely unaware of the intricacies of Sicilian politics, and often made short-sighted decisions based on ignorance. Their choice of political allies showed a lack of attention to Sicilian sensibilities and to political realities. The alienation of the *garibaldini* and the Church, while understandable in the national context, was a mistake in the Sicilian one. Government policy towards the personnel and the judiciary of the former regimes was similarly based on political considerations which, in Sicily, were largely inaccurate. As a result of these decisions, the liberal government found itself as isolated in Sicily as the Bourbons had ever been.

Many of the government's economic and social policies were well-intentioned. However, for the most part, they were also insufficiently funded and often inappropriate. In the case of railway building, the policy was too long-term to have any appreciable impact before the end of the century. The government's education policy, revolutionary in terms of its provision of compulsory elementary education, was simply not enough on its own. Agrarian reform, for which there was both an obvious need and an overwhelming desire among the peasantry, prob-ably worked to the advantage of the existing landed élite. Military conscription, conceived as a means of uniting the new nation, was to prove profoundly unpopular in Sicily.

All this reflects not so much pernicious intent as neglect and incom-petence. The reluctance to investigate the long-term causes of political instability in Sicily and (still less, for obvious reasons) to learn from the mistakes of their predecessors meant that the members of the new administration were destined to reinforce and repeat them. Good gov-ernment was supposed to bring its own rewards; economic prosperity, political legitimacy, and 'morality' were believed to follow the benefits of a liberal administration. In this environment it is hardly surprising that, as time went on, official ignorance was replaced by bewilderment and, ultimately, impatience at the sheer intractability of Sicilian problems.

5

Liberal Policy and the Control of Public Order, 1860–1862

I

As early as December 1860, one government correspondent in the South had pointed to the practical difficulties of implementing government policy. 'How', Giuseppe Finzi asked,

> would you introduce such a disorganized country to our liberal system, how would you bring those provinces with you which are not yet under your control, how would you hold elections for parliament, where you have neither the relevant provincial or municipal administrations nor any loyal personnel to implement your policies or to act as mediators?[1]

The following October, and referring specifically to Sicily, the envoy Diomede Pantaleoni was even more direct. The prevailing mood of opposition to the government was, he argued, reflected in the problems of government itself. The government:

> cannot find a chief of police, does not find mayors who are of use, the municipal elections do not take place, the provincial councils are frustrated in their work and even the national guard balks . . . . when it comes to paying its respects to a representative of the government.[2]

Without a degree of local support, in other words, good government could hardly exist at all.

The Piedmontese system of administration was more centralized than the Bourbon one, although both were based on the Napoleonic model. With unification, Palermo lost its remaining administrative functions as a capital city with a separate ministry for Sicilian affairs, although the prefect of Palermo seems to have retained a certain role as

---

[1] 9 Dec. 1860, C. Cavour, *La liberazione del Mezzogiorno e la formazione del regno d'Italia: carteggi di Camillo Cavour con Villamarina, Scialoja, Cordova, Farini ecc* (5 vols.; Bologna, 1949–54), iv. 45.

[2] G. Scichilone, *Documenti sulle condizione della Sicilia dal 1860 al 1870* (Rome, 1952), 98.

a source of information and policy-making for Sicily in general. In other respects, the principle of administrative uniformity was followed and Palermo became, with Messina, Catania, Siracusa, Caltanissetta, Girgenti, and Trapani, just another Sicilian provincial town. Every province was headed by a prefect who was appointed by the central government (nominally, by the king) and responsible to it. Each province was, in turn, divided into *circondari* (districts), headed by sub-prefects. The districts were divided into communes which were headed by a mayor. Unlike the Bourbon system, the sub-prefects and mayors were also appointed by the central government (under the Bourbons they had been appointed by the intendant).

The prefect was the instrument of the new 'liberal dictatorship', with substantial powers and responsibilities. He presided over various provincial bodies, and he controlled the administration of public order, health, education, and public works.[3] He held far-reaching powers over communal administrations: he could dissolve any association which he considered a threat to public order, and he could dissolve local councils and replace them with special commissions until public order was restored. He was responsible for organizing elections (in practice, this meant doing his best to ensure government candidates were elected) and was the main conduit of information from the centre to localities and vice-versa.[4]

Despite these powers, the position of the prefect was undermined in a multitude of ways. For instance, most of the other key positions at the provincial and communal level—including the provincial and municipal councils—were elective, and based on a wider suffrage than elections for the national parliament. Responsibility for taxation, policing, public works, and compiling electoral lists rested, as it had under the Bourbons, with local government and gave its members considerable power. Furthermore, the mayors and sub-prefects were almost invariably local men. Although answerable to the centre, they tended to be strongly influenced by local conditions and considerations. Generally, the only outsider in local government was the prefect. Thus, while the Piedmontese system deprived Palermo and Sicily of any political autonomy, in practice it gave a lot of informal autonomy to local administrations. Indeed, many prefects, when surveyed in 1869 over proposals to

---

[3] R. Romanelli, *L'Italia liberale* (Bologna, 1979), 43.
[4] R. Fried, *The Italian Prefects: A Study in Administrative Politics* (New Haven, 1963), esp. 94–119, 122–4.

increase local autonomy, argued that their capacity to direct local government was severely limited. What leverage a prefect possessed over local communities often derived more from his capacity to manipulate informal structures of power and intervene or mediate in the conflicts within local communities.[5]

Under the Bourbons, the amount of autonomy enjoyed by local administrations was increased by the huge distances which divided central from local power. These distances were compounded by poor communications which, particularly in the interior, made it almost impossible to move mail or troops at any speed from one town to another. With unification the demands of the central power may have increased, but little else did. In January 1861 Montezemolo complained that the isolation of so many communes created enormous obstacles when it came to organizing the general elections.[6] Turin was also considerably further away than Naples; it took at least three days of travel in good weather to reach even Palermo from Turin. The confirmation of Palermo as a provincial town rather than a regional capital in effect increased this 'distance', and thus probably also undermined control from the centre.

In the absence of a firm consensus in favour of the new government, the introduction of a new system of administration designed to reinforce rule from the centre could actually be used by local notables to strengthen their own power.[7] In Lercara Friddi the Nicolosi brothers continued to control all the key administrative positions in the commune. Described in one report as 'a bunch of evil men', they were said now to exercise their power 'through the development of free institutions'. Under the new liberal administration Luigi Nicolosi became director of public works, Vincenzo Nicolosi became the tax collector, Francesco Nicolosi became an alderman, and Giovanni Nicolosi became a commander of the national guard. Between them they had the town council sewn up. The town council had, according to the same report,

---

[5] Romanelli, 'Tra autonomia e ingerenza: un'indagine del 1869', in *Il comando impossibile: stato e società nell'Italia liberale* (Bologna, 1988). For further discussion of these issues, see L. Riall, 'Elite Resistance to State Formation: The Case of Italy', in M. Fulbrook (ed.), *National Histories and European History* (London, 1993), 59–63.

[6] 21 January 1861, ASP, pref. gab., b.1, prat. 1, f. 1 n.8.

[7] Paolo Pezzino suggests that the lack of a liberal/modernizing élite in the Sicilian provinces thwarted the liberal government after 1860, just as it had thwarted the liberals' predecessors. Pezzino, 'Monarchia amministrativa ed élites locali: Naro nella prima metà dell'Ottocento', in *Il paradiso abitato dai diavoli: società, élites, istituzioni nel Mezzogiorno contemporaneo* (Milan, 1992), 176.

'its origins in an irregular electoral list, in an assembly which violated all the best laws and in the *prepotenza* and intrigues of the reactionary family by which it is dominated'.[8]

Such was the hold of this 'reactionary family' over Lercara and its surroundings that complaints to the prefect of Palermo about their conduct achieved little. The Nicolosi brothers made much of their ability to maintain law and order and of their close relations with the sub-prefect of Termini Imerese. Indeed, advised by the sub-prefect of Termini, the Palermo administration even agreed to the transfer of a *carabinieri* brigadier named Balsamo, whose complaints about Giovanni Nicolosi had caused problems in the town.[9]

One of the problems facing the new government was the same one which had caused the *garibaldini* such problems: political control in the provinces and communes was often in the hands of those most hostile to the government. The governor of Caltanissetta, Baron Morillo di Trabonella, also continued to exercise power according to his own rules after October 1860, and to use his office to protect his friends and persecute his enemies. He was said to have harboured known criminals in his house.[10] Important orders to investigate reactionary activity or to carry out arrests of anti-government agitators were obstructed. On one occasion Trabonella ignored urgent government instructions, preferring to enjoy a break over ice-cream in his office.[11] Bourbon conspirators met openly in Caltanissetta with the apparent knowledge of the governor, who pursued instead a near-obsessive campaign against the republican enemies who threatened his vast landholdings.[12] 'He greets with indifference every outbreak of disorder, every outrage', the commander of the *carabinieri* wrote of Trabonella, 'and as far as I can tell

[8] 22 March 1862, ASP, prefettura de Palermo, ufficio provinciale di pubblica sicurezza, 1862–1879 (henceforth, pref. pubblica sicurezza), filza 3, f. 1, n. 31.

[9] In a report of 13 December 1861 the sub-prefect praised the work of the Nicolosi family and recommended the removal of Balsamo, ASP, pref. gab., b. 2, prat. 8, 3 div. For Balsamo's complaints and the remonstrances of his commanding officer see ASP, pref. pubblica sicurezza, filza 3, f. 1 n. 31.

[10] Information from the commander of *carabinieri*, 5 Apr. 1861, ASP, Luog. Polizia, b. 1683, f. 1.

[11] See the exchange of telegrams between the *luogotenente generale* and Trabonella over Trabonella's refusal to investigate reactionary activities, ASP, Luog. Interno, b. 4176, f. 4. An account of the ice-cream incident is in a letter dated 19 Aug. 1861, ASP, Luog. Polizia, b. 1679.

[12] 6 June 1861, in G. Scichilone, *Documenti* 76–7.

there is only one thing that concerns him—his fear of republicanism and communism.'[13]

Problems with government employees undermined the centralized administrative structure envisaged as the solution to Sicily's problems. The intendant of Termini warned in 1861 of the unsuitability of many government employees in his district:

> the current political employees, nearly all born and educated in the areas where they work, have been found to be unworthy of their important positions, and out of place and dangerous in all respects.[14]

Such employees, he added, were an obstacle to the establishment of law and order. One problem was an apparent lack of adeptness in, or enthusiasm for, public administration in any form. As early as January 1861, *luogotenente generale* Montezemolo wrote despairingly to Turin that:

> practical knowledge, administrative notions or traditions, men skilled and experienced in the handling of affairs, all of this is lacking with a few, a very few, exceptions.

Requests to provincial governors for information about local conditions had elicited responses whose 'stupidity' had 'terrified' him.[15] Honest citizens, according to the governor of Girgenti, were simply not interested in either the Bourbon government or its replacement.[16] The sub-prefect of Cefalù complained in February 1862 of the lack of 'upright and honest people who wish to assume responsibility for running municipal affairs'. Most liberals, he maintained, had neither the experience nor what he called the 'civic courage' necessary for such positions.[17]

Of course, the government's lack of familiarity with local affairs meant that it was actually impossible to assess accurately the loyalties or competence of employees and government representatives. Influential figures in disturbed areas would sometimes bombard the provincial administrations with allegations about their enemies. Bias was omnipresent, but the motives and underlying attitudes of the correspondents often remained obscure. Private loyalties often remained unclear to the outsider, and locals were notoriously reluctant to talk to government

---

[13] 23 Aug. 1861, ASP, Luog. Interno, b. 4176, f. 4.
[14] 10 Oct. 1861, ASP, Luog. Polizia, b. 1682, f. ottobre.
[15] 20 Jan. 1861, ASP, pref. gab., b. 1, f. 1, n. 8.
[16] 19 Apr. 1861, ASP, Luog. Polizia, b. 1682, f. aprile.
[17] 11 Feb. 1862, ASP, Luog. Polizia, b. 1683, f. 1.

representatives. It was often alleged that those who called themselves 'liberals' were in fact no such thing; they were republicans, 'revolutionaries', or simply criminals intent on seizing control of the commune. General Cadorna, who was sent to Sicily in 1861 and 1866, complained that 'the parties into which every community divides itself—claim political affiliations—but are based on local and personal schisms'.[18] His complaint was a familiar one, and would not have come as a surprise to a governor from either the Bourbon or the democratic era.

Factional struggle within local communities continued to disrupt administrative control from the centre after 1860. The violent outbreaks of feuding between factions which had been such a feature of the 1860 revolution continued more or less unabated throughout 1861 and 1862. More than ever, control of the commune became the vital element in achieving local supremacy. The governor of Girgenti wrote in January 1861 of the existence of two 'parties' in the town: 'one of which controls all the jobs and posts, the other which thinks it ought to, but does not'. The former were 'non-liberals'; the latter 'call themselves liberals'.[19] In April problems in the commune were again attributed to 'the spectacle of a fight between citizens and citizens'. The cause of this fight was said to be 'the perennial question of jobs and influence'. As a result of this rivalry, the 'revolutionaries' (the minority excluded from 'jobs and influence') were associating more and more with criminal elements.[20] In the same month it was reported that the commune of Contessa in Corleone district was in a state of continual agitation due to feuding between two rival families, one of which controlled all government appointments and was also involved in criminal activity.[21]

Local rivalries were also responsible for a number of more serious outbreaks of disorder. During March 1861, riots took place in Santa Margherita which, according to the governor, were caused by the feud between 'Bourbons' and 'revolutionaries'. Trouble broke out at the funeral of the liberal Giuseppe Montalbano, a champion of peasants' rights and commander of the National Guard, whose murder had allegedly been ordered by locally powerful landowners. After the funeral some National Guardsmen shot two landowners at the *casino* (notables' club), and when its members took refuge in the town hall,

---

[18] Information given by General Cadorna to the parliamentary commission, 11 May 1867, in M. da Passano (ed.), *I moti di Palermo del 1866: verbali della commissione parlamentare di inchiesta* (Rome, 1981), 102.

[19] 12 Jan. 1861, ASP, Luog. Interno, b. 4176, f. 6.

[20] 19 Apr. 1861, ASP, Luog. Polizia, b. 1682, f. aprile.   [21] Ibid. 30 April 1861.

they blew it up, killing three more.[22] A more famous revolt took place in Castellamare at the beginning of January 1862. It too had its origins in a feud between the faction which had ruled the commune before 1860 and the liberals who had subsequently managed to seize power.[23]

These feuds, centred on control of local government and accompanied by social disorder and crime, could paralyse the work of local administrations. Indeed, when it came to administrative affairs, local government was all too often an obstacle rather than a firm link in the chain of command. There were, as the example of Santa Margherita indicates, specific problems with all law-enforcement agencies. The susceptibility of magistrates to local pressure was often referred to in government reports. Frequently, according to the justice secretary in Palermo, the criminal courts would 'free, out of fear or out of leniency, the most noted scoundrels that have been arrested'.[24] The behaviour of the examining magistrate in Caltanissetta was the subject of a report by the governor in April 1861. He was, apparently, influenced by a corrupt procurator general and was given to questioning detainees in the comfort of his own home. Often he would release those arrested 'using lack of proof as the paltry pretext which, if this is the case, is the result of the feebleness of his own inquiries'.[25] In December 1861 the new (Piedmontese) prefect of Caltanissetta, Domenico Marco, also complained about the anti-government bias of the criminal court. As a result he feared that proceedings against those involved in riots during the previous November would come to nothing. The criminal court showed no inclination to issue warrants, make inquiries, or convict those responsible.[26]

The capacity of *prepotenti* to intimidate the courts, their victims, and even witnesses was apparently immense. De Stefano and Oddo, in their history of Sicily, comment that 'gentle and honest people, for the most part, had a great deal more fear of a criminal's revenge, than they had faith in the protection of the security forces'.[27] The reluctance of

---

[22] The report is sent by governor Scelsi of Girgenti, 10 March 1861, ASP, Luog. Polizia, b. 1680.

[23] The factionalism which lay behind the revolt at Castellamare has been studied extensively. See S. Costanza, 'La rivolta contro i "cutrara" a Castellamare del Golfo (1862)', *Nuovi Quaderni del Meridione*, 16 (1966), 21–30, and P. Pezzino, 'Leva ed ordine pubblico in Sicilia: 1860–1863', in *Il paradiso abitato dai diavoli*, 183–201. See also below, p. 150.   [24] 23 May 1861, ASP, pref. pubblica sicurezza, filza 4, f. 1, n. 2.

[25] 30 Apr. 1861, ASP, Luog. Polizia, b. 1682, f. aprile. Note, however, that the author of the report is Trabonella, which makes these allegations unreliable.

[26] 30 Dec. 1861, ASP, pref. gab., b. 2, prat. 8, 2 div.

[27] F. de Stefano and F. L. Oddo, *Storia della Sicilia dal 1860 al 1910* (Bari, 1963), 233.

witnesses to testify seems to have been widely accepted as normal; the code of silence even had its own name—*omertà*. Members of the judiciary were also easily intimidated. Complaints were made about the feeble conduct of examining magistrates in Sciacca and Castellamare following the riots there. The public's lack of trust in the judiciary, according to the intendant of Sciacca, meant that an increase in violence and vendettas was likely.[28] The mayor of Castellamare wrote that the investigating magistrate, Milone, had made little effort to question witnesses and had departed suddenly without completing his inquiry.[29] Some magistrates were also suspected of direct involvement with criminals. The Stajano brothers, wanted for their involvement in the riot at Santa Margherita, were seen in public shortly after fleeing the scene of the crime, passing the time of day with the local judge. The same judge later refused to issue a warrant for their arrest.[30]

Lack of education and lack of attention to duty were factors which undermined the service offered by the chiefs of police (*delegati di pubblica sicurezza*). In fact, the government faced a major practical and technical problem in finding individuals capable of fulfilling the demands of these posts. A series of reports indicated that many police chiefs were woefully incompetent. The governor of Caltanissetta asked that his police chief be dismissed, since his lack of familiarity with the relevant laws combined with a general 'negation of all intellectual culture' made him a liability.[31] 'Ignorant and debauched' was how the intendant of Corleone described his police chief in Chiusa: 'he is eager to do his duty but in large measure is incapable of doing any good'. In the same district, police officers tended to overestimate their power and position, and to interfere in areas outside their jurisdiction. Perhaps the worst case cited was in Prizzi, where the police chief considered himself 'superior to all the authorities in the commune, a notion which makes him quite ridiculous'.[32]

There were complaints of an even more serious nature about other branches of the police. The police, Antonio di Rudinì told a parliamentary commission of inquiry in 1867, 'as it is organized here, is a nonsense'.[33]

---

[28] 15 Oct. 1861, ASP, Luog. Polizia, b. 1682, f. ottobre.
[29] 28 Jan. 1861, ASP, Luog. Polizia, b. 1683.
[30] From the commander of the *carabinieri*, 14 July 1861, ASP, Luog. Interno, b. 4176, f. 6.   [31] 28 Oct. 1861, ASP, pref. gab., b. 2, prat. 8, 2 div.
[32] 22 Oct. 1861, ASP, Luog. Polizia, b. 1678.
[33] 17 May 1867, M. da Passano (ed.), *I moti di Palermo*, 434.

One report stated baldly that elements of the 'ordinary police' were a '*gamorra* [camorra?]', and that 'the most serious crimes committed are usually the work of individuals who carry arms in the name of the law, and in order to enforce it'.[34] Numerous reports also depicted the National Guard as disorganized, ill-disciplined, and completely unreliable.

Some of the problems with the National Guard can be directly linked to the government's decision in 1861 to reorganize it along the lines of the Piedmontese model. In most areas this reorganization created delays and ill-feeling. It also faced immense practical difficulties. In January 1861 Montezemolo wrote to Turin that the 'condition of the country-side, the demands of public services and the scarce number of troops' made the disbanding and reformation of the National Guard in all the towns and villages an all but impossible task.[35] In addition to existing delays in supplying guardsmen with uniforms and firearms, the new regulations caused delays in organizing disciplinary councils and enrolling officers.[36] Even in the district capital of Cefalù, it took a year and a half to set up the National Guard.[37] Moreover, according to Montezemolo, the new élitist regulations meant there were often not enough eligible men to form a militia. He told Turin in February that 'the small numbers of landowners and the absence of direct tax on anything but land, will make it impossible to have a National Guard unless . . . mercenaries and labourers are admitted into the ranks'.[38]

The introduction of new regulations also led to feelings of discontent and insecurity affecting the service. The methods used by the enlisting body (*consiglio di ricognizione*) were unpopular.[39] The inspector-general of the National Guard, Amato Poulet, confirmed his difficult reputation acquired during 1860 by continuing to tread on local sensibilities. An angry report from the town council of Parco on 18 March 1861 told how Poulet had reversed all their work. Poulet had included those formerly excluded by the council and excluded all the 'honest citizens', even promoting Giuseppe Murfia, recently dismissed as chief of police, and including his son, at the time languishing in prison in Palermo, on

[34] From the intendant of Termini, 10 Oct. 1861, ASP, Luog. Polizia, b. 1682, f. ottobre.
[35] 20 Jan. 1861, ASP, pref. gab., b. 1, prat. 1, f. 1, n. 8.
[36] According to a series of reports about the National Guards in the districts of the province of Palermo: Palermo (14 and 28 July), Termini (14 July), Cefalù (26 July), Corleone (28 July). ASP, prefettura di Palermo, archivio generale, 1860–7 (henceforth pref. archivio), b. 386.
[37] From the sub-prefect of Cefalù, February 1862, ASP, Luog. Polizia, b. 1683, f. 1.
[38] 5 Feb. 1861, ASP, pref. gab., b. 1, f. 1.
[39] Report on the district of Palermo, 14 July 1862, ASP, pref. archivio, b. 386.

the revised list of Guardsmen.[40] In Salemi, popular agitation over the reorganization of the National Guard was so great that a major suggested setting up a corps of scouts which could include former members.[41] In other towns the upper classes were reluctant to have anything to do with the National Guard. Feeling against the new government in Alcamo meant that prominent citizens refused to become involved with the National Guard. Similar problems were reported in Altavilla, where no officers would come forward.[42]

In such conditions it is not surprising that support for the government was not forthcoming in emergencies. The National Guard failed to support the government during riots over conscription in Sciacca during October 1861.[43] When, in January 1862, the town of Alcamo was threatened by disturbances in nearby Castellamare, the commander of the National Guard and all his men went into hiding. The commander openly admitted that his safety had been assured (he did not say by whom) on the condition that he did not show himself.[44]

The decision to reorganize the National Guard was intended to establish a more 'moderate' and therefore more reliable basis of support. This objective was never achieved. Problems of indiscipline and disloyalty remained. The National Guard in Monreale remained under the control of the notorious bandit 'Turi Miceli. It was described in a report of July 1862 as consisting of 'robbers, *cammoristi*, royalists and corrupt men'.[45] When the decision was taken in October 1861 to disarm the Sciacca National Guard, the intendant wrote that 'a good number of troops' might be necessary to enforce the order, since he feared that the militia would resist by using their service weapons.[46]

If the National Guard simply compounded the problems facing the government as it sought to control the situation in the interior, the service offered by the *militi a cavallo* (mounted militia) was even more susceptible to local influence. Revived from the defunct *compagni d'arme* by Garibaldi, the *militi a cavallo* were responsible for security in the countryside and along the roads, as well as providing an escort for the transport of mail, taxes, and so on. They also assisted in the arrest of

---

[40] ASP, Luog. Polizia, b. 1679.   [41] 10 Feb. 1861, ASP, Luog. Interno, b. 1762.
[42] 29 July 1862, ASP, pref. archivio, b. 386.
[43] From the intendant of Sciacca, 14 Oct. 1861, ASP, Luog. Polizia, b. 1682, f. ottobre.
[44] From the inspector of the *militi a cavallo*, 6 Jan. 1862, ASP, Luog. Polizia, b. 1655, ff. 50–1.   [45] 29 July 1862, ASP, pref. archivio, b. 386.
[46] 15 Oct. 1861, ASP, Luog. Polizia, b. 1682, f. ottobre.

wanted men. Although their intimate knowledge of the countryside made it possible to overcome problems caused by the absence of witnesses and the reluctance to testify, these very advantages also tended to make them unreliable. The *militi a cavallo* rapidly became notorious for their involvement with the activities of armed gangs.

The procurator general of Girgenti referred to the local *militi* as being made up of 'more or less criminal elements'. Many *militi a cavallo*, he wrote, who were supposed to maintain public order, to control crime, and to arrest criminals, 'not only do not arrest wrong-doers but join in protecting them, and sometimes are themselves prepared to commit crime'.[47] In some areas the *militi* themselves formed what amounted to a criminal organization. Their methods were described by the intendant of Termini as 'deceptions, threats, tortures carried out on real or supposed criminals who don't give the desired evidence'. The *militi* were, he wrote, 'nothing but a genuine school of depravity, a breeding ground of discontent and crime'.[48]

As a result, the *militi a cavallo* were of little assistance in the maintenance of law and order. Not only were their methods irregular, but they were also easily intimidated. One report described meeting some *militi*, 'gathered, frightened and uncertain, at some distance from the scene of the crime, although a number of shots had been heard and despite information from some of the robbers' victims'.[49] Franchetti gives the following description of methods and conduct of *militi a cavallo*:

in the evening they arrive in a community [*paese*] and go into an inn. Putting their firearms in a corner they will sit down at a table and drink with mule-drivers, with carters, with all kinds of different people. They speak with every-one, they know everyone. News arrives of a robbery or a blackmail. They get on their horses, they search the countryside, but more often than not they don't see, they don't know, they don't find anybody. The whole district has suddenly become unknown territory to them . . . in a majority of cases, the *militi a cavallo* either because they are frightened of vendettas or because they share in the fruits of the crime are the accomplices of criminals, at the least by their silence and inaction.[50]

[47] 22 March 1862, ACSR, Ministero di Grazia e Giustizia, direzione generali affari penali, miscellanea (henceforth, grazia egiustizìa), b. 1, f. 81.

[48] 10 Oct. 1861, ASP, Luog. Polizia, b. 1682, f. ottobre.

[49] From the commander of the National Guard in Misilmeri, 3 Jan. 1861, ASP, Luog. Interno, b. 1757, ff. 1–4.

[50] L. Franchetti, *Condizioni politiche e amministrative della Sicilia* (1876; Rome, 1993 edn.), 45.

All too often, the *militi* were prepared to share in the fruits of a crime. The inspector-general of the *militi a cavallo* noted on 10 August 1861 that they were using their licence, which allowed them free movement from one district to another, as a 'concession for crime'.[51] In December of the same year it was reported that the *militi a cavallo* of Valledaluno were leaving the district to search for stolen animals, only to use the opportunity to steal the animals themselves.[52]

II

The failure of law enforcement might have been less serious had it not been for the increase in many areas of riots and rural crime. As the riots which took place in 1861 and early 1862 reveal, unification had done little to settle peasant grievances. Along with the land question, taxation was an additional, and apparently increasing, cause of unrest amongst the poorer classes. After the announcement of new local taxes unrest was reported in Alcamo throughout the summer of 1861. Riots were reported in Mazara in December and in Caltanissetta, where a crowd of some 4,000 people attempted to march on the mayor's house, shouting, 'Down with taxes! Down with the mayor! Down with the council!'[53]

According to reports from Caltanissetta, 'some malcontents used the situation to shout "Down with conscription!" '.[54] Conscription, as Garibaldi's experiences had already shown, was deeply unpopular in Sicily. Moreover, its unpopularity transcended other divisions, uniting whole communities against the central government. Various cases of fraud and intimidation were reported, as commissioners attempted to enforce the decree. The commissioner in Cefalù was warned that 'if you don't want to die stabbed or shot, leave our families' sons alone'.[55] In S. Michele, a priest advised one mother:

they want your son for the military because Vittorio Emanuele is ambitious; who for the vanity of power wants even to usurp Rome from the Pope; and who in

---

[51] ASP, Luog. Polizia, b. 1655, f. 43–1.

[52] From the commander of the *militi a cavallo*, 3 Dec. 1861, ibid.

[53] On Alcamo, see the report of the intendant, 23 July 1861: ASP, Luog. Polizia, b. 1679, and on Caltanissetta, the report from the *carabinieri* commander, 24 Nov. 1861, ibid. b. 1682, f. novembre. There is also a longer, anonymous account which was sent to Crispi: 'Relazione anonima sugli incidenti avvenuti in Caltanissetta', in ACSR, Carte Crispi (ASP), f. 115, n. vi.

[54] 17 Nov. 1861, from the commander of *carabinieri*: ASP, pref. gab., b. 3.

[55] From the sub-prefect of Cefalù, 1 Apr. 1862, ASP, pref. pubblica sicurezza, filza 3, f. 1, n. 31.

order to do this needs soldiers. But, anyway, don't you worry—your son will not have to leave. Francesco II, so eagerly awaited, is already in Naples and will soon be here to liberate us from foreign slavery.[56]

During the call-up in December 1861 a series of disturbances took place in the province of Caltanissetta. Government officials expressed particular concern about the activities of Bourbon agents in some communes.[57] Elsewhere there were popular demonstrations against conscription reported in the province of Trapani (particularly in Alcamo, Marsala and, above all, Castellamare) and in Girgenti (Palma di Montechiaro, Racalmuto, Belmonte, and Sciacca). In Marsala conscription notices were ripped up to cries of 'Viva Garibaldi!'[58] In Sciacca, 'turmoil amongst the common people who are arming themselves with gunpowder and bullets' was reported by the governor of Girgenti.[59]

In the revolt which took place in Castellamare in January 1862, resentment over conscription combined with agitation over land and taxation to show how fragile the government's authority was. Factional rivalries between the élites of Castellamare confused the situation still further: this was a peasant uprising, led by a Bourbon landowner, which proclaimed republican ideals. A prominent landowner named de Blasi had controlled the community under the Bourbons and, upon finding himself on the losing side in 1860, had started to stir up resentment over the land 'usurpations' of liberals. With local republican organizations, he also made much of the popular fury over the introduction of conscription. During the revolt there were shouts of 'Long live the Republic! Out with conscription! Death to the liberals!'. It was reported that the republican flag was then publicly blessed to the reciting of the *Te Deum.*[60]

By the early part of 1862 there began to be reports of young men fleeing into the countryside to avoid conscription. It was feared that, once there, they would join the large numbers already evading arrest

[56] 3 Dec. 1861: this information is in a report from the colonel of the *carabinieri* in Palermo, ASP, Luog. Polizia, b. 1682, f. dicembre.

[57] From the commander of *carabinieri*, 22 Dec. 1861, ASP, Luog. Polizia, b. 1682, f. dicembre.   [58] 14 Aug. 1861, ASP, Luog. Polizia, b. 1679.

[59] 13 Oct. 1861, ASP, pref. gab., b. 3.

[60] See the report from the inspector of *militi a cavallo* about Bourbon involvement, 6 Jan. 1862, ASP, Luog. Polizia, b. 1655, ff. 50–1. Eyewitness accounts spoke of republican slogans and activity: see the report by the police chief, Fundaro, and other accounts in ACSR, grazia e giustizia), b. 1, f. 1, nn. 67, 121, 127.

and who were suspected of seeking to undermine the government's authority by criminal means. Concern about the numbers of bandits and other criminals at large in the Sicilian countryside was fuelled by two factors: the breakup of Garibaldi's Southern army, and the opening of the prisons in 1860. The return of large numbers of ex-*garibaldini* to Sicily from the mainland during 1861 caused considerable security problems. Many were disillusioned and displaced by their experiences, and often they became a source of agitation.[61] By the middle of 1861 the government had given serious consideration to rounding up and removing many of them; General della Rovere wrote to Cavour on 4 May asking for a 'steamship to transport the agitators of Garibaldi's army'.[62]

Even more serious problems were caused by the opening of the prisons in 1860 and by Mordini's subsequent decree of amnesty, passed on 17 October. Mordini's decree, which amnestied certain categories of escaped prisoners convicted before 27 May 1860, recognized that his government lacked the means to recapture these prisoners (15,000, according to one estimate).[63] The amnesty was essentially an attempt to reconcile convicts to normal life. By the end of 1860 it was already quite clear that the amnesty had completely failed. Luogotenente Montezemolo wrote to Cavour on 19 January that 'over and above the opening of the prisons, we have a Decree of Amnesty for violent crimes which is so designed that every murderer can get away'.[64] Very few criminals bothered to fulfil the conditions of the amnesty, and the government, lacking reliable magistrates or an adequate police force, was unable to enforce it.[65]

It was in response to this amnesty that the government began to adopt alternative measures. The secretary responsible for public order noted in October 1861 that, despite a revised set of instructions, magistrates were continuing to release transgressors of the amnesty. He thus suggested that the role of the courts be obviated by applying police measures—notably by treating escaped prisoners as 'idlers' or 'vagrants' and subjecting them to the system of *ammonizione* ('admonishment' or cautioning), which imposed restrictions on their movements and allowed police

---

[61] See the correspondence between Montezemolo and central government on this issue, ASP, pref. gab., b. 1, f. 1, 'corrispondenza dal luogotenente col governo piemontese'.

[62] *La liberazione del Mezzogiorno*, iv. 468.

[63] Given by the governor of Caltanissetta, 27 Apr. 1861, ASP, Luog. Polizia, b. 1682, f. maggio. [64] *La liberazione del Mezzogiorno*, iv. 235–6.

[65] See the circular from the councillor for public security, 22 Jan. 1861, ASP, pref. pubblica sicurezza, filza 4, f. 1, n. 20.

surveillance.[66] Since *ammonizione* could be imposed by applying direct to the magistrate without full recourse to the courts, it was a convenient means of circumventing the problems of finding witnesses prepared to testify and the delays caused by judicial procedures.[67] This suggestion of the secretary for public order seems to have been part of a more general shift in government policy with regard to law and order. In April 1862 no less an authority than Urbano Rattazzi, the new Minister of the Interior, drew the prefect of Palermo's attention to this system of cautioning, and noted that the law against idlers and vagrants could be applied widely and vigorously.[68]

As early as January 1861 there was a change in attitudes towards the situation in Sicily and how it could best be resolved. In a report to Cavour, Montezemolo had confessed that he would need special powers to deal with lawlessness in Sicily.[69] In February he had repeated his view in stronger terms, asking for a standing force of between 15,000 and 18,000 men, for crime and riot control to be under military jurisdiction, and for a law permitting local administrations under certain circumstances to declare a state of siege.[70] Montezemolo was backed up by the judicial and military authorities. The procurator general of Caltanissetta wrote in May that the only way to stop crime in Sicily was with troops,[71] and General Cadorna wrote in October that 'I have come to the sorry conclusion that this island's present generation will only be curtailed through force'.[72] The procurator general of Girgenti described Sicilians as being for the most part 'of a fiery disposition . . . quick to react to even the smallest disagreement . . . with criminal tendencies, particularly towards violent crime and theft'.[73] The attitude of the government was, finally, made explicit in January 1862, when a long internal report stated that since government policy on conscription and taxation could not be changed 'and thus there is no way of avoiding this genuine cause of discontent, it is

---

[66] 8 Oct. 1861, ASP, pref. gab., b. 1, prat. 2, 2 div. There is a useful account of *ammonizione* in R. Bach Jensen, *Liberty and Order: The Theory and Practice of Italian Public Security Policy, 1848 to the Crisis of the 1890s* (New York, 1991), 32–3.

[67] J. A. Davis, *Conflict and Control: Law and Order in Nineteenth-Century Italy* (London, 1988), 217–20.

[68] 6 Apr. 1862, ASP, pref. pubblica sicurezza, filza 4, f. 1, n. 19.

[69] 2 Jan. 1861, *La liberazione del Mezzogiorno*, iv. 162–4.

[70] Ibid. 27 Feb. 339–41.   [71] 27 May 1861, ASP, pref. gab., b.2, prat. 8, 2 div.

[72] 16 Oct. 1861, in R. Cadorna, *Il generale Raffaele Cadorna nel Risorgimento italiano*, ed. L. Cadorna (Rome, 1922), 429.

[73] 22 Mar. 1862, in ACSR, grazia e giustizia, b. 1, f. 81.

necessary to prevent or reduce the outbreak of insurrection by deploying forces in sufficient numbers so that fear will immediately and successfully repress any attempts'.[74]

By the beginning of 1862 the government began to respond with increasing force to the problems of policing the countryside. In his April letter to the prefect of Palermo referred to above, Rattazzi ordered an increase in the numbers of patrols by security forces which, he added, should stop and question every suspicious individual—even those who simply fled at the sight of a patrol. On 15 May, he wrote to Palermo that the use of 'mobile columns' of troops and *carabinieri* should be increased in the provinces 'most infested' with bandits.[75] Increasingly, mobile columns began to patrol the Sicilian countryside with instructions to pursue and arrest criminals, to capture recalcitrants, and to bring military deserters to justice. A letter from the sub-prefect of Termini in March 1862 reported on an operation by troops undertaken, as he put it, 'to finish with the fugitives once and for all'.[76]

The repression of the Castellamare revolt in January 1862 represented a watershed in this respect. In the immediate aftermath of the revolt, five of its leaders were executed without trial. A petition from Castellamare's inhabitants spoke of security forces 'terrorizing' the area, searching homes without warrants, and making arbitrary arrests.[77] A large number of people unconnected with the revolt were detained, charged with being idlers and vagrants, and made subject to an *ammonizione*. Even more interesting was how the government reacted to criticisms of its conduct. Prime Minister Ricasoli wrote to Miglietti (the Minister of Justice) on 17 February that the arrests of so many idlers and vagrants was a response to 'the necessity of an immediate guarantee of law and order in the island'.[78] One government deputy replied to legal objections over the summary executions with the argument that 'today public order is the principal legality' (that is, the need for public order took precedence over all other legal considerations).[79]

---

[74] Jan. 1862, in Scichilone, *Documenti*, 120–2.

[75] Both letters are in ASP, pref. pubblica sicurezza, filza 4, f. 1, n. 19.

[76] Ibid. 20 Mar. 1862, filza 2, f. 1, n. 55.

[77] 31 Jan. 1862, ACSR, grazia e giustizia, b. 1, f. 55, n. 345.   [78] Ibid. f. 81.

[79] The deputy was Francesco Paternostro (later prefect of Girgenti). In *Atti Parlamentari, Camera dei deputati, discussioni 1860–1867*, 15 Jan. 1862, 677, replying to a speech by the Sicilian opposition deputy, Vito d'Ondes Reggio, 674–5.

III

In February 1862 the sub-prefect of Cefalù wrote to the prefect in Palermo that control and improvement of the Sicilian countryside would need a miracle. Such miracles, he went on to argue:

are obtained neither by the rigours of justice nor by political surveillance, but are obtained by proper roads which allow effective communication between two communities, they are obtained by primary education . . . and, above all, they are obtained by time.[80]

However, as we saw in Chapter 4, most of the internal reforms which the government pursued in Sicily during the period 1860–1 were driven by the overriding aim to protect Italian unity against its perceived enemies and give the liberal state solid institutional foundations. Land reform, the improvement of communications, and the expansion of the educational system were all made subservient to the immediate needs of institutional unity.

Ironically, the effect of these policy choices was to increase the difficulties of organizing and controlling government in the interior. Here, as elsewhere, government policy was driven by the assumption that once 'good' (efficient and moral) government was established with control over the countryside, economic and social improvement would inevitably follow. It was soon, however, quite obvious that this assumption was both mistaken and inappropriate. Far from improving law and order, some government policies increased peasant unrest and violence. Moreover, without the support of local élites for good government, good government was essentially impossible.

Poor communications, mass ignorance, and corrupt, self-serving officials were themselves significant obstacles to institutional unity. All branches of law enforcement were unreliable and ill-equipped. Given the huge distances which separated central government from the periphery, local government officials could do more or less what they liked, hampered only by local opposition and local rivalry. In these conditions, the institutional reforms introduced by the Piedmontese were likely to create another layer of corruption and lead to greater inefficiency than before. Attempts at administrative centralization thus further undermined the centre's control over local government.

When news arrived of riots and other problems of law enforcement in the Sicilian interior, members of the government tended to blame the

---

[80] 11 Feb. 1862, ASP, Luog. Polizia, b. 1683, f. 1.

republicans (who they associated with the *garibaldini*) and/or the Bourbons. What is most striking, however, is how far ministers made the
same mistakes as their predecessors in Sicily. They ignored the causes
of unrest and concentrated instead on repressing it. In the course of
1862 the liberal government began to give itself substantial police
powers to deal with the growing problems of popular unrest and crime.
Thereafter, as we shall see in the following chapters, these powers were
used extensively and frequently to restore order both on the Southern
mainland and in Sicily. By bringing in these powers, the government
completed Italian unification and gave the Kingdom of Italy an institutional structure which was highly centralized, distinctly authoritarian,
and an enduring source of political controversy. Yet in Sicily at least,
this new authoritarian structure reflected nothing so much as the failure
of liberal policy and the government's basic inability to govern by any
other means.

6

The Breakdown of Authority, 1862–1863

I

Between 1862 and 1866 the government conducted a series of public order operations in Sicily. The methods used in these operations paralleled the so-called 'brigands' war' on the Southern mainland, where between 1861 and 1865 a substantial part of the Italian army was bogged down in guerrilla warfare with supporters of the deposed Bourbon monarchy. In 1862, following Garibaldi's ill-fated attempt to march on Rome, operations took place to arrest the *garibaldini* and, more vaguely, to 'restore order' in Sicily. In 1863, large-scale military measures were mounted to enforce the conscription laws (both these operations are discussed in this chapter). In 1865, another operation was organized, this time to bring to justice members of the '*maffia*', a name the government had adopted to describe the growing anti-government conspiracy in Palermo (discussed in Chapter 7). In 1866 a series of operations were carried out to arrest those involved in the Palermo revolt of September 1866 (discussed in Chapter 8). Yet, whoever these operations were nominally aimed at, the underlying motive for all these campaigns was more or less the same: they aimed to capture and to contain all those responsible for 'disorder' whose arrest and conviction had proved impossible by normal means.

In common with the brigands' war on the mainland, the public-order operations in Sicily had one striking feature—the use of a new system of legal repression, relying on the state of siege, military courts, *ammonizione* ('admonishment') and *domicilio coatto* ('enforced domicile') to re-establish public order.[1] The declaration of a state of siege meant that the military was given full jurisdiction over all the civilian authorities in a town or province. The military authorities could restore order by force and, if necessary, set up military courts to deal with the disturbances.[2] Used to quell an uprising in Genoa in 1849 and disturbances in

---

[1] R. Bach Jensen, *Liberty and Order: The Theory and Practice of Italian Public Security Policy, 1848 to the Crisis of the 1890s* (New York, 1991), 12.

[2] F. Contuzzi, 'Stato d'assedio', *Digesto Italiano*, 22/2 (Turin, 1895).

Sardinia in 1852, the state of siege was also declared in Sicily following Garibaldi's ill-fated expedition in 1862 and after the Palermo revolt of 1866 (when military courts were also used to try those arrested for involvement).

Ammonizione was, as we saw in Chapter 5, widely used by the police from 1861 onwards. Its provisions—which allowed for surveillance and restrictions to be imposed on certain categories of 'dangerous' or 'suspicious' individuals—were confirmed in the 1865 public-security regulations; it provided the legal justification for huge numbers of arrests in the Sicilian campaign of 1865. *Domicilio coatto*, administrative detention in a town or island remote from an offender's original home, was introduced by the Pica law of 1863.[3] This law was approved by parliament as an emergency measure for dealing with the threat posed by brigandage on the Southern mainland. Thus, Article 1 stated that in provinces which were declared 'in a state of brigandage', groups of three or more found in the countryside with the apparent intention of committing crimes would be judged by a military court, while those who resisted arrest could be shot. For those not immediately identifiable as bandits, but who were suspected of involvement with their activities, new categories of offence and a new penalty were introduced. This new penalty, *domicilio coatto*, could be applied not only to those defined as vagrants or idlers (and thus already subject to 'admonishment' under the 1859 law), but also to those defined by the new law as *camorristi* ('criminal types') and *manutengoli* ('aiders and abetters'). Responsibility for assigning *domicilio coatto* was given to a special provincial commission, usually composed of the prefect, the president of the court, the royal procurator, and two provincial councillors. After 1863, *domicilio coatto* was used extensively in Sicily as a means of dealing with all types of offenders; its provisions were confirmed in the 1865 public-security legislation, while other emergency powers contained in the Pica law were made permanent in the Crispi law of 1866.[4]

Thus, the public-order campaigns mark a moment when the government considerably expanded its police powers over the Sicilian population. It did this, arguably, by infringing the individual liberties and judicial prerogatives guaranteed by the 1848 constitution. Most

[3] P. Bach Jensen, *Liberty and Order*, 33.
[4] On the Pica law see J. A. Davis, *Conflict and Control: Law and Order in Nineteenth-Century Italy* (London, 1988), 223–6.

historians of the period detect a shift in government attitudes and policy towards the South and Sicily around the middle of 1862, when the outcome of a parliamentary debate favoured a far more restricted interpretation of Article 71 of the constitution (which guaranteed to every citizen the right to be judged by his peers). At around the same time steps were taken to curtail the right of association, also guaranteed by the constitution, by making a distinction between legitimate and illegitimate associations.[5]

John Davis notes that although special powers already existed in the Piedmontese criminal code for dealing with the threat of brigandage, the introduction of the Pica law in 1863 enabled the government to bypass normal judicial procedures and put in the hands of civilian authorities the summary methods of military justice.[6] *Ammonizione* and *domicilio coatto* also gave huge powers to police officers and to government officials that were not subject to strict procedural regulations. No law at all governed the conduct and operation of the state of siege by the military. *Ammonizione* involved the surveillance of 'suspicious' individuals: the burden fell on the accused to prove that s/he was not a vagrant and, subsequently, that s/he had not broken the conditions of 'admonishment'.[7]

Not surprisingly, the introduction of these new public-security regulations caused considerable controversy. In parliament, opposition deputies blamed the growing numbers of irregularities and abuses by members of the security forces on the new regulations. Criticisms of the operations were reported in the press, in official correspondence, and in private letters. One observer of the 1862 campaign in Sicily complained to Francesco Crispi (now a leading member of the parliamentary opposition) that 'the abuses committed by the *carabinieri* surpass those of the gendarmes and Bourbon police'.[8] In the parliamentary debate following the 1863 campaign, an opposition deputy told the government that 'in order to carry out one law, that for conscription, you have destroyed the prestige of . . . all the others by making their authority dependent on *brute force*'.[9] The unconstitutionality of the new regulations was also

[5] R. Martucci, *Emergenza e tutela dell'ordine pubblico nell'Italia liberale, 1861–1865* (Bologna, 1980), 20–31; Davis, *Conflict and Control*, 254–5.

[6] Ibid. 178–9, 223–4.

[7] F. S. Merlino, *Politica e magistratura dal 1860 ad oggi* (1925; Milan, 1974 edn.), 257–8; Bach Jensen, *Liberty and Order*, 33.

[8] 21 Sept. 1862, Giorgio (?) to Crispi, in ACSR, Crispi (ASP), f. 125 XXI.

[9] Speech by La Porta, in *Atti Parlamentari, Camera dei deputati, discussioni, 1860–1867*, 7 Dec. 1863, 2135.

widely criticized. Two Sicilian opposition deputies—Crispi and Vito d'Ondes Reggio—insisted that the application of the Pica law to Sicily was unlawful. According to d'Ondes Reggio, the law 'was never planned to be a law for the whole of Italy but only a law against brigandage in Naples'; it was the outcome of an inquiry concerned with the mainland and with a phenomenon (brigandage) which did not exist in Sicily in anything like the same form.[10]

This judgement of government action in the South is shared by many historians. Massimo d'Addio argues that government policy reflected a general conviction that nothing should be allowed to get in the way of internal order: 'the freedoms confirmed by statute should only be respected in normal times, since the moment that public order was endangered by the subversive forces in society, they became an obstacle to firm action by the government'.[11] Violante suggests that the use of military courts reflected a long-term policy which ignored the constitutional independence of the judiciary and aimed to make the courts a simple tool of the executive.[12] Other historians maintain that the use of special public-security powers in the early 1860s established an enduring pattern of dealing with unrest which persisted through the anarchist struggles of the 1870s to the socialist repressions of the late 1890s and, arguably, even to the Fascist period. Alatri writes that a

single thread from the cruelties committed in Sicily in 1863 to the Turin massacres in September 1864, from the excesses against the peasants united in the *fasci siciliani* during 1893 to the repression of the Milanese disturbances in 1898 [tied the] internal politics of the government towards every part of Italy in the first forty years of unification.[13]

In a different slant on this interpretation, Jonathan Dunnage argues that the institutions and methods created in the 1850s and 1860s were 'incompatible with liberal policies'; later these same institutions were to constrain Giolitti's more liberal policing strategy after 1901.[14]

Recent attempts to explain the harshness of public-order measures

---

[10] D'Ondes Reggio's speech was given on 5 Dec. 1863, ibid. 2099, and Crispi's on 10 Dec. 1863, ibid. 2217.

[11] M. D'Addio, *Politica e magistratura, 1848–1870* (Milan, 1966), 133.

[12] L. Violante, 'La repressione del dissenso politico nell'Italia: stati d'assedio e giustizia militare', *Rivista di Storia Contemporanea*, 5 (1976), 491–2.

[13] P. Alatri, *Lotte politiche in Sicilia sotto il governo della Destra, 1866–1874* (Turin, 1954), 83.

[14] J. Dunnage, 'Law and Order in Giolittian Italy: A Case Study of the Province of Bologna', *European History Quarterly*, 25 (1995), 384.

have focused on official representations of Southerners and/or Sicilians. Nelson Moe argues that a sense of 'otherness' expressed itself in the conviction that force was the only means of governing the South,[15] while John Dickie suggests that although 'the actual suppression of brigandage' was not the government's highest priority, brigandage 'was a central ideological concern which played a crucial part in reconciling the liberal principles and authoritarian practices of the new state'.[16] In this way, the use of special powers against specific categories of criminals can be linked to the battle for political hegemony in the South—especially to the need to crush the threat of reaction, or to contain the mounting popularity of republicanism.

There is, in short, a general assumption amongst historians that a single government policy relating to public order existed in the South and, moreover, that a study of the government's public-order policy can show us the reactionary 'face' which lay behind its liberal 'mask'. In fact, the conduct of the military operations in Sicily suggests otherwise. As we shall see in the chapters which follow, many of the leaders of the Right—most notably Ricasoli—wavered between a policy of repression and one of prevention.[17] A grim determination to crush unrest there may have been, but this was usually tempered by a concern for liberal principles. There were also clear disagreements over policy among government ministers, perhaps most obviously between Rattazzi and Ricasoli, and between government ministers and the generals in charge of operations. Rattazzi and Ricasoli disagreed about the suppression of the Mazzinian *società emancipatrice* in 1862. Rattazzi sought to make a distinction between legitimate and illegitimate associations, whereas Ricasoli maintained that all such organizations had a role to play—even when they caused trouble to the government.[18]

Thus, one problem with many explanations of government action in the South is that they attribute a level of clarity and decisiveness to government policy which, in reality, is hard to find. The danger of political upheaval, and of republicans or reactionaries in Sicily making 'common cause' with criminals, was clearly a factor in the government's harsh response to the situation. Equally, the decision to criminalize the

[15] N. Moe, '"Altro che Italia!": il Sud dei piemontesi (1860–61)', *Meridiana*, 15 (1992), 84–8.

[16] J. Dickie, 'A Word at War: The Italian Army and Brigandage, 1860–1870', *History Workshop Journal*, 33 (1992), 1–24.

[17] On this distinction, and its significance, see Bach Jensen, *Liberty and Order*, 21–9.

[18] Davis, *Conflict and Control*, 254.

republican opposition followed logically from this interpretation. But it is also difficult to make a clear distinction between the political bias and cultural perceptions of officials and the immediate policing tasks with which they were faced. On a day-to-day basis the government never made a clear choice between a liberal policy or a repressive one. Repression was often carried out in response to local pressure rather than orders from central government. Lack of up-to-date information often meant that central government had little control over events. Both local officials and government ministers justified the use of repression on the basis that the capture of 'trouble-makers' (*i cattivi*) was necessary to ensure the success of liberal policy—to encourage, as they often put it, the honest people (*i buoni*) of Sicily.

It is also worth remembering that after October 1860 the government never developed a detailed policy for its Sicilian provinces, aiming simply to integrate the Sicilian administration and economy into a united Italian kingdom. Its policy towards policing and public order was no exception to this. Indeed, what is most striking about the public-order operations of the early 1860s in Sicily is the lack of a single aim or focus. The operations were born out of a sense of political isolation, and what drove them forward was the lack of any obvious alternative. There were not always clear instructions from the centre, and the aims of the campaign were ill-thought-out and, often, short-term. In many respects the decision to use military force was an admission of weakness. From a purely practical point of view, troops were used to capture offenders and summary measures were used to try them for the very simple reason that the normal police were not reliable and the criminal courts proved ineffective.

Arguably, the trouble with government policy was not so much the policy as the means of enforcing it. The problem with government attempts to repress disorder lay with the repressive structure itself. An inefficient and often self-serving bureaucracy, the weak links between central and local power, and the consequent difficulty of policing by normal means lay behind the decision to proceed with military operations in Sicily. These same problems, moreover, ensured that the military operations themselves would not be a success.

II

It is arguable that a more severe political crisis in Sicily—similar in scale to the brigands' war being fought on the mainland—was only avoided because in the first eighteen months after unification the government's opponents were in disarray. Despite periodic panics, the Bourbons enjoyed little popular support in Sicily and were never the threat in Sicily which they were on the mainland. The blow to autonomist hopes also threw the autonomist movement in Sicily into confusion. Some autonomists simply withdrew from politics in disappointment, while many of the more energetic leaders left Sicily to become deputies in the new national parliament in Turin. After 1860, the democratic movement in Sicily was more internally divided than ever. It too was deprived of some of its most effective leaders—notably Crispi—whose centre of attention was now fixed well to the north of Palermo. Until the summer of 1862 this lack of effective opposition masked the extent of the government's isolation in Sicily.

However, in June 1862 Garibaldi returned to Sicily. Initially, no mention was made of any ulterior motive to his visit but, impressed by the enthusiasm of the crowd which followed him everywhere, he soon began to consider mounting an expedition in Sicily to take Rome from the Pope. By the middle of July, the cry of 'Rome or Death' (*O Roma O Morte*) was raised at every public meeting he addressed. Garibaldi, with his two colonels Trasselli and Bentivegna, then began a wide south-eastwards sweep through the towns and villages of Sicily, encouraging volunteers to join up in the new campaign. It was estimated that by mid-August he had collected some 4,000 volunteers, many of whom were deserters from the army. In some places, notably in San Stefano near Sciacca, the movements of Garibaldi's army were accompanied by skirmishes with regular troops.[19]

Popular disturbances were reported in many areas. The prefect of Girgenti wrote on 8 August that the sub-prefect of Sciacca was unable to control popular unrest in many areas. The next day he requested troops for Racalmuto, where revolt was imminent.[20] Also on 8 August, the sub-prefect of Cefalù reported to Palermo that criminals in the town had intensified their activities, hoping for impunity resulting from a revolution.[21] The prefect of Messina warned of popular demonstrations in favour of Garibaldi on 9 August.[22] The prefect of Caltanissetta wrote on 13 August that Garibaldi's stay had led to considerable disturbances (he was subsequently dismissed on 17 August for having dined with

---

[19] On the incident in San Stefano, see the letter from the procurator general in Palermo to the justice minister, ACSR, grazia e guistizia, b. 1, f. 357.

[20] ASP, pref. gab., b. 4, nn. 71 and 104.   [21] ASP, pubblica sicurezza, filza 1.

[22] ASP, pref. gab., b. 4 n. 106.

Garibaldi).[23] There were demonstrations in Catania on 13 August, and the prefect warned that any attempt to arrest Garibaldi would be seen in the city as 'a signal to revolt'.[24] Finally, concern was expressed about security in the prisons; requests arrived from Sciacca,[25] Palermo,[26] and Cefalù[27] for transport to move prisoners elsewhere.

The Italian government was slow to react to Garibaldi's actions. The Prime Minister, Rattazzi, may well have hoped to collude with Garibaldi, at least by his inaction. In fact, the government was eventually forced to resign in December, largely as a result of controversy over its whole handling of this affair.[28] Local officials in Sicily simply felt bewildered and isolated. The sub-prefect of Cefalù complained on 8 August that it was impossible to stop Garibaldi while people believed he had the support of the government.[29] On 10 August the sub-prefect of Caltagirone requested from Palermo 'clear, precise instructions as to how to handle the forthcoming arrival of Garibaldi with his volunteers; . . . not having . . . received any instructions from either Palermo or Turin, subordinates cannot deal with such excessive disorder'.[30] General Cugia, appointed as prefect of Palermo in July 1862 to replace the former democrat, Giorgio Pallavicino-Trivulzio, later confessed to parliament that he did little to stop Garibaldi, since, had he done so, his position in Palermo would have become untenable.[31]

In the absence of clear instructions or decisive action, Garibaldi was able to cross unimpeded over to the mainland with his volunteers on 25 August. The next day, however, central government finally decided to act. The arrest of all those 'who were part of the band of Garibaldi or took part in any way in the rebellion' was ordered.[32] On 29 August the volunteers were halted by Italian troops in a skirmish at Aspromonte in Calabria, where Garibaldi was shot and badly wounded in the foot. Military action against the remnants of his army in Sicily took place shortly after the events of Aspromonte. On 2 September the column of *garibaldini* led by Trasselli was arrested near Acireale. Four deserters

---

[23] ASP, pref. gab. b. 4 n. 207. G. Scichilone, *Documenti sulle condizione della Sicilia dal 1860 al 1870* (Rome, 1952), 137. On the prefect's dinner with Garibaldi, see E. Amari, 'Cronaca della venuta in Sicilia di Giuseppe Garibaldi nell'anno 1862', Biblioteca Comunale di Palermo, 5Qq B 39.

[24] ASP, pref. gab., b. 4, n. 199, Scichilone, *Documenti*, 138.   [25] Ibid. n. 71.
[26] Ibid. n. 96.   [27] Ibid. n. 208.
[28] D. Mack Smith, *Italy: A Modern History* (Ann Arbor, 1959), 63–4.
[29] ASP, pref. pubblica sicurezza, filza 1.   [30] ASP, pref. gab., b. 4, n. 134.
[31] See the debate on the repression in Sicily, *Camera dei deputati, discussioni*, 25 Nov. 1862.   [32] ASP, pref. gab., b. 4, n. 571.

from the Italian army were shot after summary procedures, while three civilians met the same fate.[33]

Soon after the disastrous end to Garibaldi's expedition the government introduced additional public-order measures and decrees. It declared a state of siege throughout the Southern mainland and in Sicily, and gave the military commanders in Palermo, Messina, and Siracusa full military and civil powers to deal with the emergency. Any armed gang or 'disorderly gathering' could now be broken up by force. The freedom of the press was also suspended. On the same day the freedom of association was radically curtailed when the Mazzinian *società emancipatrice* and its 500 affiliated organizations were dissolved by government decree.[34] Enrico Cialdini, the general in charge of preventing Garibaldi's expedition, issued a further decree on 30 August which stated that 'all those who are caught armed and vagrant in the countryside and villages without being able to justify their presence there will be considered and treated as brigands' (this meant being subject to military jurisdiction and, in case of conflict with the security forces, shot). It also stated that *garibaldini* would only be treated as prisoners of war if they gave themselves up within five days.[35] In particularly disturbed areas, such as Catania, even more stringent measures were introduced.[36]

The declaration of a state of siege led to widespread unrest. The noted autonomist Emerico Amari noted that Palermo was '*agitatissima*' after the decree was published.[37] Over a thousand people demonstrated for over two days in the streets of Messina, and all the notices proclaiming the siege were destroyed.[38] News from Girgenti indicated that the decree was unenforceable due to the opposition of the local police forces.[39] Only in Caltanissetta and in Modica was the reception of the decree actually reported as favourable.[40]

Popular agitation combined with existing anxiety about the activities of bandits and *facinorosi* ('lawless people') to provide the impetus for a general security crackdown throughout Sicily which lasted into Novem-

---

[33] Four of these were presumed deserters. An account of these events based on contemporary newspaper accounts is in A. Maurici, *Il regime dispotico del governo d'Italia dopo Aspromonte* (Palermo, 1915), 50–2.

[34] This move was particularly controversial. Martucci, *Emergenza e tutela dell'ordine pubblico*, 30–6, Davis, *Conflict and Control*, 254.   [35] ISR, b.668, n.34(6).

[36] Ibid. n.34(5).

[37] Amari, 'Cronaca della venuta in Sicilia di Giuseppe Garibaldi'.

[38] ASP, pref. gab., b.4, nn.411, 427, and 440.   [39] Ibid. n.413.

[40] Ibid. nn.430 and 432.

ber. The Piedmontese general appointed by Cialdini to restore order in Sicily, Filippo Brignone, announced the beginning of this campaign on 12 September. He instructed the mobile columns and standing troops to respect persons and property, but gave greater priority to enforcing respect for government authority: 'in every case I will be more inclined to condone excessive repression, than weakness and indecisiveness'. Any riotous assembly should be immediately broken up, with force if necessary. If armed bands were found in the vicinity, a detachment of troops should:

under instructions from the prefects and sub-prefects or local commander, and in an emergency even spontaneously, not hesitate to search them out and attack them using every effort. If fighting should take place with these gangs, those captured while armed should be treated as brigands.[41]

The commitment to using exceptional powers is also indicated by the appointment, on 14 September, of Alessandro di Monale as temporary commissioner for the Sicilian provinces, with additional responsibility as prefect of Palermo.

Operations by the military were initially concentrated on the province of Girgenti, where the prefect Enrico Falconcini, recently arrived from Tuscany, was pursuing a keen campaign of his own against lawlessness. In a letter to all the police chiefs on 19 September, Falconcini instructed that:

with the presence of troops and the exceptional powers granted by the state of siege, there is an opportunity to restore law and order once and for all, by depriving ruffians and criminals of the liberty which they currently enjoy.[42]

Operations were reported in Sambuca, Grotte, Aragona, Casteltermini, and Castrofilippo.[43] Troops were also used to repress serious outbreaks of violence and rioting in the towns of Canicattì and Racalmuto. A series of unlawful arrests were reported in Canicattì; some sixty people in all were arrested in Racalmuto.[44]

---

[41] The orders are published in *Il Giornale di Sicilia*, 15 Sept. 1862.

[42] E. Falconcini, *Cinque mesi di prefettura in Sicilia* (Florence, 1863), doc. xliii, 112–13. The experiences of Falconcini as prefect of Girgenti have recently been studied by Paolo Pezzino as a case study of the difficult relationship between central and local power in Sicily. P. Pezzino, 'Un prefetto "esemplare": Enrico Falconcini ad Agrigento (1862–1863)', in *Il paradiso abitato dai diavoli: società, élites, istituzioni nel Mezzogiorno contemporaneo* (Milan, 1992).

[43] According to a report sent to Francesco Crispi in Oct.; ACSR, Crispi (ASP), f. 126 II.

[44] For an account of the events in Canicattì and Racalmuto, see Falconcini, *Cinque mesi di prefettura*, 50–5, 57–8. For a very different account of what happened in Canicattì, see the reports to Crispi in ACSR, Crispi (ASP), f. 126 II.

On 1 October the military commander of Girgenti, Colonel Eber-hardt, announced that within five days all firearms should be consigned to the military authorities. Although the National Guards were allowed to retain their arms, they would henceforth take their orders from the military. Anyone caught after that time in possession of firearms would be shot.[45] The next day the military ordered the disarming of all the Sicilian provinces. Provincial police commissioners were given special powers of search in private homes, and a semi-curfew was imposed where shops, hotels, and other public places had to be closed by 10 p.m.[46]

The immediate cause of this additional crackdown was the apparently motiveless stabbing (*pugnalazione*) of thirteen citizens in separate inci-dents in Palermo on the night of 1 October. This bizarre episode was initially attributed to the work of a Bourbon committee aiming to challenge government authority.[47] It marked the start of a new round of military operations to enforce the disarmament, lasting until the beginning of November, which involved house-to-house searches as well as reported cases of brutality and torture. Vincenzo Cacioppo wrote to Crispi that his home in Santa Caterina had been invaded by sixty soldiers at 2 a.m.; the town itself was continually occupied by troops, and women who refused to sleep with members of the *carabinieri* saw their families arrested.[48] Cases of serious abuse were reported in Alcamo: one individual was tricked into consigning a weapon and then shot for possessing it, a bandit was shot in bed as he prepared to leave with the soldiers, and others were subject to beatings and tortures to obtain confessions.[49]

The state of siege was lifted in Sicily on 16 November. However, on the same day the temporary commissioner announced, 'I remain invested with ample political powers over the whole of the island.'[50] Although in some quarters the emergency powers had provoked pro-tests and accusations, in others there was strong pressure to make the ban on firearms permanent and to give the emergency provisions the

[45] ISR, b. 668 n. 34(10).   [46] *Il Giornale di Sicilia*, 2 Oct. 1862.
[47] There is a long report on the *pugnalazione di ottobre* in ACSR, grazia e giustizia, b. 3, f. 79. The incident gave rise to a number of conspiracy theories and a long, convoluted trial; see F. Orestano, *Processo e condanne degli imputati della pugnalazione del 1 ottobre 1862* (Palermo, 1865), L. Sciascia, *I pugnalatori* (Turin, 1976), and P. Pezzino, *La casa dei pugnalatori: un caso politico-giudiziario alle origini della mafia* (Venice, 1992).
[48] 3 Nov. 1862, ACSR, Crispi (ASP), f. 126 XXXV.
[49] M. S. Caracciolo to Saverio Friscia; ibid. f. 125 XLIII and f. 126 II.
[50] Quoted in Maurici, *Il regime dispotico*, 102–3.

status of law. By the beginning of 1863 it was also clear that there had been little or no long-term improvement in law and order. The government came under severe attack in parliament during April 1863 for its indifferent and 'illegitimate' handling of security problems in Sicily.[51] Moreover, existing concerns about high levels of crime were further increased by rumours of a mounting political conspiracy against the government.

III

During the winter of 1862 and the following spring and summer, political agitation against the government took a new and increasingly shady turn. In January 1863 reports reached the Minister of the Interior of a republican sect in Palermo which, led by a priest named Brother Pantaleo, had established links with the Bourbons to undermine the government. In June, the commander of *carabinieri* in Misilmeri wrote that the secretary of the commune, an associate of Pantaleo, was conspiring with the *garibaldino* colonel, Carlo Trasselli, and the socialist, Saverio Friscia, against the government.[52] The events of Aspromonte seem to have been largely responsible for this new development. For one group of Sicilian democrats, led by Francesco Perroni Paladini, Aspromonte confirmed the need for a commitment to strictly parliamentary means of agitation.[53] However, another group, led by Giovanni Corrao and Giuseppe Badia, became more convinced that violence and popular insurrection played a central role in political action. Corrao had fought with Rosolino Pilo in the April 1860 insurrection in Palermo, and had subsequently been accepted as a colonel in the reorganized National Guard. Despite this, in 1862 he resigned his commission and joined Garibaldi in the attempt to march on Rome.

Corrao and Badia were largely responsible for the increase in conspiratorial activity after 1862. They were involved in a republican demonstration in support of the recent revolt in Poland at the church of San Domenico in Palermo on 1 March 1863. Government fears were apparently roused by speeches calling for a march on Rome and, in consequence, the arrest of prominent republicans was ordered on 13 March. However, both Corrao and Badia managed to go into hiding;[54]

---

[51] *Camera dei deputati, discussioni,* 17 Dec. 1863, 6341–61.

[52] 25 Jan. and 30 June 1863, Museo Storico dell'Arma dei Carabinieri, Archivio Storico, Rome (henceforth, MSAC), cartella 49.

[53] F. Brancato, *Francesco Perroni Paladini* (Palermo, 1962), 60–5.

[54] Maurici, *Il regime dispotico,* 183–8.

thereafter rumours circulated about conspiracies in Palermo and the nearby area. One government informer, Andrea di Salvatore, said that Corrao's cousin had attempted to form armed gangs in Monreale which would invade Palermo with the help of the English.[55] The head of police in Monreale reported on 10 March that the inhabitants were buying bullets, gunpowder, and cartridges in large numbers and, between 14 and 17 March, a general 'ferment' amongst the population was noted in many areas.[56] During April, Corrao was reported to be organizing gangs of draft-evaders in Bagheria and Misilmeri with the aim of invading Palermo on 4 April.[57] Similar activity was reported in Monreale, Borgetto, Toretta, Cinisi, and Carini—towns which were strategically placed to the west of Palermo. Together with a committee of Bourbons, and with the hope of obtaining English assistance, Corrao also made efforts to provoke unrest in Partinico.[58]

It was the nature of Corrao's conspiratorial alliances which caused particular concern and confusion. Along with his republican sympathizers, he was said to be enlisting the help of the Bourbons and of the English, to be organizing gangs of draft-evaders against the government, and encouraging bandits. According to the informer di Salvatore, Corrao cast his net widely: 'depending on whom he was with, Corrao would at one moment speak of the Republic, then of the English, and then of Francesco II'.[59] The procurator general of Palermo wrote on 30 April that Corrao 'spoke Bourbon words to the Bourbons, Mazzinian words to the Mazzinians, criminal words to the brigands and, to encourage and give hope to all, spoke of disorder, of Garibaldi's arrival, of warships, the English etc. etc.'.[60] When Corrao was arrested, in Palermo's *giardino inglese* on 29 April, he was charged in connection with the bizzare Palermo stabbings (*pugnalazione*) of the previous October, which the government suspected to be the work of Bourbon reactionaries. However, he was later released without charge. His nefarious activities finally caught up with him on 3 August, when he was murdered in an ambush about two miles outside Palermo.[61]

The effect of Corrao's various conspiracies was to heighten govern-

[55] 7 Apr. 1863, in ACSR, grazia e giustizia, b. 2, f. 213.

[56] 10 and 30 March 1863, ibid. f. 184.   [57] 30 Apr. 1863, ibid. f. 213.

[58] Ibid. These activities are also described in a letter from the Palermo chief of police: Scichilone, *Documenti*, 148–9.

[59] 7 Apr. 1863, ACSR, grazia e giustizia, b.2. f. 213.   [60] 30 Apr. 1863, ibid.

[61] On his murder see the letter of 4 Aug. from the prefect of Palermo (from Jan. 1863, Augusto Nomis, conte di Cossilla) to the Minister of the Interior, Ubaldino Peruzzi, ASP, pref. gab., b. 5, cat. 11, f. 3.

ment anxiety about the numbers of vagrants, 'lawless people', and draft-evaders (*renitenti*) at large in the Sicilian countryside. Problems had, for instance, persisted in Girgenti despite the previous year's operations. Gangs 'composed of escaped convicts, draft-evaders and criminals of every kind' were said to be creating havoc in the countryside.[62] By 1863, the government estimated that some 19,298 Sicilians had ignored or refused the call-up. This meant that, along with some 5,608 deserters from the army, there was a total of over 26,000 men unaccounted for and, it was feared, ready to be recruited by Corrao and his followers.[63]

The new campaign planned by the Minister of the Interior in May 1863 aimed not just to capture draft-evaders but also to proceed with the arrest of many other criminals—even those for whom an official arrest warrant did not exist.[64] Under the command of a new general, Giuseppe Govone, troops were initially sent to search the countryside around Palermo in mobile columns, where they planned to hold all young men and suspicious characters until their innocence could be proved. However, since these methods were generally unsuccessful, they were soon supplemented by even tougher ones aimed at forcing the population to co-operate with the military. The second, 'more energetic' (to use della Rovere's phrase) stage of the campaign,[65] involved throwing a military cordon around a community, searching the homes of suspected draft-evaders, and, if he or they failed to come forward, placing these homes under permanent surveillance. As a last resort, the families of draft-evaders would be arrested. In practice, supplies of water were also cut off as the troops put up their cordon. In this way, although the campaign was aimed against crime and fugitives in the open countryside, rural communities came to be the locus of action by the military.

From the start these new methods caused controversy. In Misilmeri, where the methods used during 'phase two' were first tried, there were protests about the behaviour of troops, notably from the mayor against the military commander Besozzi, who had jostled him in public and called him a '*vile borbonico*'.[66] In July, at the height of the Sicilian

---

[62] 13 Apr. 1863, from the procurator general of Girgenti, ACSR, grazia e giustizia, b. 2, f. 184.

[63] These figures are given by General della Rovere and differ slightly from those given later in the same debate. *Camera dei deputati, discussioni*, 5 Dec. 1863, 2104. See below, p. 173.

[64] According to evidence presented to parliament; ibid. 8 Dec. 1863, 2155.

[65] Ibid. 5 Dec. 1863, 2105.   [66] Letter in *L'Arlecchino*, 10 June 1863.

summer, military operations began in earnest. Troops were concentrated in Caltanissetta and Girgenti, the provinces considered to be 'most infested' with bandits and draft-evaders. At one point the entire town of Caltanissetta was cordoned off and around 2,000 troops were involved in the search for draft-evaders. Smaller towns were also put under siege.[67] In mid-August the centre of operations was moved to Trapani and Palermo, although four mobile columns continued to patrol the Girgenti countryside.[68] Trapani, Menfi, Salemi, and Castelvetrano were surrounded by military cordons. In a bid to rid Alcamo and Castellamare of the armed bands which continued to trouble this district, troops put up a forty-kilometre-long cordon which cut off the mountainous peninsula of San Vito and 'flushed out' criminals in a house-to-house search.[69]

By late August the use of military cordons and of penalties applied indiscriminately to whole towns and villages had become the accepted norm for the campaign. Public opposition to the military was also growing. A report in the opposition newspaper *Il Precursore* on 9 September described an operation in Partanna where 'the usual stories of arbitrary acts are told, indiscriminate mass arrests and known violations of the law and the constitution'. Since most of those wanted had fled into the countryside, 'the arrest of their relatives was ordered, with far worse to take place at night . . . front doors were simply knocked down and domestic privacy violated, and in the confusion whole families were carried off to prison'.

The powers available to the military had, in fact, been considerably increased by the application of the Pica law to the Sicilian provinces in August 1863. The Pica law was subsequently widely used to assist operations in the province of Palermo, and was also used retrospectively to try detainees in Girgenti against whom normal judicial proceedings had proved ineffective.[70] Military tribunals were set up at the beginning of September, and the provincial commission to assign *domicilio coatto* at the beginning of October. As troops moved into the Madonie mountains, allegations of abuses became more vociferous and more numer-

---

[67] According to reports in *Il Precursore*, 3 July 1863.

[68] 16 Aug. 1863: information from the major commanding the national guard, in Archivio di Stato di Agrigento (henceforth, ASAg), Carte di pubblica sicurezza, 1862–1932 (henceforth, pubblica sicurezza), f. 249.

[69] *Camera dei deputati, discussione*, 5 Dec. 1863, 2111–19.

[70] Letter from Govone to the prefect of Girgenti, 11 Oct. 1863, ASAg, pubblica sicurezza, f. 249.

ous: in Petralia Soprana troops trying to burn one 'rebel' out of his house succeeded in killing almost his entire family; in Gangi they seized the pregnant wife of a wanted man, causing her to miscarry the child.[71]

The most damaging allegations concerned the torturing of a severely handicapped man named Antonio Capello, on suspicion of simulating muteness in order to avoid enlisting. This case came to public notice through the efforts of a journalist, Antonio Morvillo, who visited Capello in the military hospital and found him covered with 157 festering burns and lesions. Although the doctors claimed that the burns were part of a treatment, and a judicial inquiry even confirmed this, when Capello was questioned through an interpreter he 'indicated that when he entered hospital he was not ill, and that there they tortured him with a red-hot iron to make him talk'.[72] A public outcry ensued. Morvillo published his account in *Il Precursore* on 4 November, and Capello's case was brought up in parliament in December. When Capello was finally released by the authorities in January 1864, photographs were taken of the wounds on his body and distributed around Palermo with an accompanying poem.[73]

IV

A pattern emerged during the operations of 1862 and 1863 which persisted for the remaining campaigns. Lack of support for government policy meant that the government was, in a sense, compelled to keep increasing its powers, both over local government and over the judicial authorities. These powers, and the use of them, grew with every campaign. And it is easy to see why, at the time, there seemed to be little alternative to the operations. In the event, however, it is difficult to see what benefit the government derived from them. The operations produced a clamour of public opinion against the government. They produced remarkably little else, for all the disruption they caused, in terms of arrests or a return to order. The powers acquired by the government were used to a chorus of criticism in Sicily, once again

[71] On the incident in Petralia, see the report of 19 Oct. 1863 in ASP, pref. gab., b. 5, cat. 11, f. 3. See also the petition from Pietro Gennaro, 22 Oct. 1863, ibid. On the incident in Gangi, see the petition from the wanted man, Gilibasi, 19 Oct. 1863; the letter from the military commander, Major Volpi, to Govone, 31 Oct. 1863; and Govone's letter to the prefect of Palermo, 6 Nov. 1863, ibid.

[72] According to reports of 7 and 17 November 1863, ACSR, grazia e guistizia, b. 3, f. 24.

[73] See the account in A. Maurici, *Genesi storica della rivolta del 1866* (Palermo, 1916), 36–7.

to very little effect. The government, according to one observer, had 'the misfortune of satisfying nobody', and its representatives in Sicily increasingly bemoaned the effects of their political isolation.[74]

The operations aggravated existing problems. Instead of calming political unrest they seem to have accentuated it. Giuseppe Badia took over the republican leadership after the death of Corrao and adopted all of Corrao's tactics and connections, which further polarized the Sicilian democratic movement. The disarmament ordered in 1862 and the additional security measures introduced at this time did not particularly improve public order. In a parliamentary debate in April 1863 Ubaldino Peruzzi, the Minister of the Interior, candidly admitted that only 'honest people' consigned their firearms, which left them defenceless against criminals who did not.[75] Inevitably, the disruption caused by the operations caused security problems of their own. The presence of troops halted commerce and economic activity, and encouraged anyone on the wrong side of the law to flee from their homes. The prefect of Palermo, Nomis di Cossilla, warned in May 1863 that military measures could be counter-productive; public order was deteriorating partly because of 'the continuous search for draft-evaders who take off into the countryside where . . . they commit robberies and hold-ups'.[76] The opposition newspaper *Il Precursore* also pointed out on 16 September that military measures could actually encourage criminal activities, since many draft-evaders and others 'escaped through the military cordon and, being wanted men, would form new groups of brigands or would swell the ranks of those existing'.

One problem seems to have been that both the 1862 and the 1863 operations were hurriedly put together, with little attention to specific preparations and local conditions. The 1862 campaign in particular was little more than a footnote to other concerns—to the need to contain the political fallout from Garibaldi's expedition and to deal with a more serious set of disturbances on the mainland. In 1862 the judicial system was clearly not adapted to the needs of the campaign. The numbers of those convicted was surprisingly small compared to the numbers arrested; even deserters from the army who joined Garibaldi received light sentences. Lists from the military courts in Palermo reveal that, by December 1862, some seventy deserters had been convicted of treason

[74] Letter from Giorgio (?) to Crispi, end of September 1862, ACSR, Crispi (ASP), f. 125, XXI.   [75] *Camera dei deputati, discussioni*, 17 Apr. 1863, 6351.
[76] 28 May 1863, Biblioteca Nazionale di Firenze (henceforth, BNF), Carte Peruzzi, Carteggi (henceforth, Peruzzi), XX, 17.

and/or rebellion, but only three had been condemned to death and they all later had their sentences commuted.[77] Moreover, the judicial and penal system seemed unable to cope with the numbers arrested. At the beginning of 1863 a large number of those detained during the state of siege still languished in gaol awaiting trial.[78] Nomis di Cossilla then complained in May about the 'release from prison of the majority of those arrested during the state of siege'.[79]

The increased powers made available to government forces in 1863 seem, however, to have brought about little improvement. The scope and nature of this campaign was, if anything, more vague than in 1862. In 1863 General Govone made up his methods as he went along. In June he wrote that the Minister of War had given him no detailed instructions 'and perhaps cannot, since these instructions would either be too violent and cause a scandal, or else they would be meek and obtain little. I have done as I see fit so as to bring about results.'[80] Assessing the results of Govone's operations, a few figures speak volumes. In parliament it was reported that of a total of 22,000 draft-evaders and deserters, approximately 4,000 had been apprehended. 1,200 criminals had also been arrested, and half a million lire in unpaid taxes collected. An astonishing 8,000 draft-evaders, however, were found to be female 'or to be dead or to have changed address or else to have never existed'. Some 10,000 draft-evaders were still unaccounted for at the end of operations.[81] Thus the 1863 campaign seemed neither justified nor particularly worthwhile. The arrests that were made appeared random and ineffective, rather than the expression of a strong government intent on enforcing its 'moral' authority.

The failure to establish local assistance was probably the greatest weakness of both these campaigns. Comparatively little attention was paid to the practicalities of operating in the vast open spaces of the *latifondo* in the fierce heat of a Sicilian summer, using troops unfamiliar with their surroundings, and relying on communications which were practically non-existent. The task of identifying wanted men in a village

---

[77] ACSR, Tribunali militari di guerra di Palermo, Messina, Catania e Catanzaro, 1862, b.4.
[78] According to correspondence from the Minister of the Interior, Ubaldino Peruzzi, 20 Jan. 1863, in ASP, pref. pubblica sicurezza, filza 23, f. 2, cat. H. His letter also instructed that a special commission be set up to deal with detainees against whom it was difficult to obtain proof. [79] 28 May 1863, BNF, Peruzzi, XX, 17.
[80] Letter to General la Marmora, 25 June 1863, in G. Govone, *Il generale Giuseppe Govone: frammenti di memorie*, ed. U. Govone (Turin, 1902), 156–7.
[81] These figures are given in *Camera dei deputati, discussioni*, 5 Dec. 1863, 2114.

full of their friends and families was also not really considered before-hand. Govone himself came to recognize this, lamenting that bandits in Sicily did not behave like their mainland counterparts. Far from being permanently wedded to the life of an outlaw, a Sicilian bandit would often maintain normal working habits. They lived, Govone wrote:

at home or with friends or with landowners or with the municipal authorities who look after them from fear or for interests of their own; and they go out from time to time into the fields; and they even send letters of extortion while they are at home.

No-one, he added, ever dared to report their activities to the author-ities.[82]

In the mean time, military action, however prompt, often came to nothing because troops became bogged down making arrests *en masse* in the towns. Even the Minister of the Interior admitted to parliament that many innocent people were arrested during the state of siege in 1862.[83] Wanted men were tipped off and escaped into the countryside, where they knew hiding-places which the military could not reach. During the disturbances in Racalmuto in September 1862 troops rushed in to restore order, but to little avail:

a band of about 150 strong . . . established an armed encampment in the nearby mountains, practically throwing out a challenge to the troops, who could do nothing about it since they were fully occupied with disarming the town, placing those under arrest in custody and maintaining order.[84]

In this context, the problems of establishing adequate co-operation with the civilian police and authorities had particularly grave consequences. As early as January 1861 a report referred to an incident of jealousy and rivalry between the *carabinieri* and local police.[85] Although the Sicilian National Guards were placed under military control in 1862 they did not always respond positively to requests for assistance, and sometimes they had to be disarmed by the troops themselves.[86] General Brignone

[82] 1–4 July 1863, *Il generale Giuseppe Govone*, 159.
[83] *Camera dei deputati, discussioni*, 17 Apr. 1863, 6351.
[84] Falconcini, *Cinque mesi di prefettura*, doc. xxxiv, 88.
[85] 25 Jan. 1861, from the councillor for public order, ASP, Luog. Polizia, b. 1674.
[86] As in, for example, the Canicatti disturbances when the National Guard was actively involved: Falconcini, *Cinque mesi di prefettura*, doc. xxxviii, 97–8. See also the circulars sent by di Monale in October, which instruct the civilian authorities to co-operate with the military so that the two bodies 'do not contradict each other'. ASP, pref. pubblica sicurezza, filza 23, f. 4, cat. H.

later recalled of his experiences in Palermo that 'he had to say that he had not been supported by any of the municipal or civil authorities'. The National Guard, whose support he had particularly sought, had 'made common cause with the rebels'.[87]

Far worse was to come in 1863. The enforcement of the conscription laws was almost universally unpopular, and even the local authorities were often openly hostile to the military. Govone described these difficulties in vivid terms:

> Troops arrive with a list of 100 draft-evaders. The authorities are asked to identify the houses and they tell you they don't know them. You contact the municipal guards and caretakers who turn you down. The whole town is questioned and no-one knows anything. Suspicious individuals are arrested and no-one is prepared to identify them. What can a commander do then, with a list of which two-thirds of the names are dead, emigrants or have never existed?[88]

In Misilmeri Govone called on the town council to identify draft-evaders, but 'they prevaricated and were unwilling to give information'. He then enlisted the help of 'eight trusted men'; but, he complained, 'they were no more prepared to help us than the council'. Efforts to identify draft-evaders using parish registers were largely unsuccessful, because the registers were disorganized, and the council refused to put names to faces.[89] The assistance given by the government informer, Antonio Sticchi, was so negligible that he himself was eventually arrested.[90]

Despite Govone's claims, the methods subsequently adopted, which aimed as he put it 'to frighten people a bit', were hardly more success-ful.[91] Feelings ran very high as a result of the use of military cordons and holding families hostage, but they did not run in favour of the government. According to the Minister of War, the court clerk in Burgio (province of Girgenti) was arrested at the beginning of August for encouraging draft-evaders not to enlist as the Bourbons would return soon. Burgio's mayor was also placed 'under surveillance' for helping a wanted man to escape through the military cordon.[92] In Castrofilippo (again in Girgenti), the mayor refused to find lodgings

---

[87] 14 May 1867, in M. da Passano (ed.), *I moti di Palermo: verbali della commissione parlamentare di inchiesta* (Rome, 1981), 110–11.

[88] 1–4 July 1863, *Il generale Giuseppe Govone*, 159.   [89] Ibid. 151–5.

[90] 10 June 1863, ASP, pref. pubblica sicurezza, filza 22, f. 79.

[91] 1–4 July 1863, *Il generale Giuseppe Govone*, 160.

[92] *Camera dei deputati, discussioni*, 2107–8.

for the troops; a murder attempt was reported on one of their number who had, it was alleged, simply asked the townspeople where they were hiding their draft-evaders and bandits.[93]

The application of the special powers contained in the Pica law to assist operations in the province of Palermo also seems to have made little difference. Indeed, some of the worst moments of the whole campaign were encountered by Govone in the city of Palermo itself. As Govone later told parliament:

I found myself with a list of 4,000 draft-evaders without knowing which were true draft-evaders nor where to find these names nor which ones were dead and I had, therefore, to verify every one of those 4,000 names.

This is where the real problems began. Officers made house-to-house searches for particular individuals. Those questioned:

came out and replied 'I don't know'. In a street, a passer-by would be asked: 'Is this the via Toledo? Is that the casa Riso?' He would answer 'I don't know' and the house would be right there beside him.[94]

Everyone, it seemed, opposed conscription, and nobody was prepared to help Govone's troops put the law into effect.

In this context it is hardly surprising that a distinct hardening of government attitudes towards the situation in Sicily can be detected in the course of 1863. In April 1863 Govone wrote a long memorandum to Giuseppe Massari, who was in charge of the government inquiry into brigandage on the Southern mainland. There were, he told Massari, real problems with using the state of siege for any length of time, and he recommended that the scope of the military authorities be limited: 'confusion is increased by the lack of any fixed rules or any regulations which determine military assignments'. Arrests, he continued, did not always have the desired effect: 'out of ten people brought in, five are honest, and more bad is done than good'.[95] By June, however, his views had changed drastically, at least regarding Sicily. To both the Minister of the Interior and the Minister of War he wrote that only military force would restore order to Sicily.[96] In December, at the end of the campaign, Govone made his instantly notorious statement that Sicilians were not yet ready for liberal government, as they had not yet devel-

[93] 10 Aug. 1863, ASAg, pubblica sicurezza, f. 249.
[94] *Camera dei deputati, discussioni*, 5 Dec. 1863, 2119–20.
[95] 4 Apr. 1863, in ISR, Carte Massari, n. 36(4).
[96] *Il generale Giuseppe Govone*, 151–7.

oped beyond barbarism.[97] For Govone at least, Sicily was an exception even in the context of Southern 'exceptionalism'.

The prefect of Palermo in 1863, Augusto Nomis di Cossilla, wrote an extraordinary series of letters to the Minister of the Interior in Turin which detail his personal, and growing, despair of the situation in Sicily. In his first letter, written a month or so after his appointment, he noted merely the strength of autonomist feeling in Sicily and described the island as an 'unfortunate' (*disgraziata*) place. In April, he recommended the use of force to 'return' Sicily to the peaceful conditions enjoyed by the other (presumably Northern) provinces of the kingdom, adding in a second letter that existing problems had been exaggerated by Sicilian deputies.[98] In May, however, he demanded the deportation of prisoners as the only means of avoiding a prolonged crisis (a 'plague') of public disorder. In the same month he began a long litany of complaints about the *militi a cavallo* ('who do more bad than good'), the Palermo National Guard, and the local bureaucracy (the only 'cultivated people' are 'autonomists'), complaints which continued until his transfer to Genoa in March 1865.

On 12 August, at the height of the military campaigns, Nomis di Cossilla wrote a bitter letter to the Minister of the Interior. Di Cossilla, it seems, experienced the government's isolation in Sicily on a personal as well as a political level. After spending 6 months and 10 days in Palermo, he told Peruzzi, nobody ever came formally to call or to invite him and his wife to dine: 'they are frightened to compromise themselves by being seen with a government representative in their house'. Indeed, Sicilians were like 'unknown persons' to him. He had never seen the inside of a Sicilian home. No-one, he complained, would work with him; they only knew how to work against him or to make up intrigues of their own. Nomis di Cossilla's thoughts on Sicily conclude with the comment that the proposed visit by the crown prince Umberto would raise public spirits: 'the islanders are like old women', he wrote, they were used to being neglected, but would fall in love with the first person who showed any interest in them.[99]

Thus, the perceptions of 'otherness', which were tied up in the Italian government's handling of public order in Sicily, was clearly derived from the sense of vexed frustration and bewilderment felt by

---

[97] D. Mack Smith (ed.), *The Making of Italy 1796–1866* (London, 1968; 2nd edn., 1988), 373.   [98] These letters are in BNF, Peruzzi, XX, 17.
[99] Ibid. 17 bis.

those personally involved. Moreover, this frustration was not just aimed at a particular source of disorder (whether 'brigandage', 'mafia', or draft-evaders) but at the very people who were expected to be the government's closest allies. The evidence from the 1862 and 1863 campaigns suggests that it was the civilian government's basic ineffectiveness, as much as an attempt to criminalize or otherwise categorize the political opposition, which led to the systematic use of special powers. As we have seen, however, both the presence of the military and the special powers at its disposal simply added an extra layer of confusion to the existing political and bureaucratic chaos. In the event, the use of special powers failed to resolve in any way the problems which had led to the adoption of these powers in the first place.

7

Criminals, Republicans, and Reactionaries, 1864–1865

I

Garibaldi's attempt to march on Rome in 1862 marked the beginning of a period of crisis for the Historic Right. When Rattazzi's government was forced to resign in December 1862, largely as a result of its handling of the Aspromonte affair, it was replaced by an 'anti-Piedmontese' ministry whose Prime Ministers, Luigi Farini and Marco Minghetti, were both from Central Italy. They had also been the most prominent opponents of administrative centralization in 1860–1.[1] Unfortunately, by the time Farini became Prime Minister he was already suffering from a severe mental illness. In March 1863 he was replaced as Prime Minister by Minghetti.

During the Farini–Minghetti ministry, an agreement was reached with the French government over Rome (the so-called September convention), whereby the French agreed to withdraw their garrison from Rome and the Italian government agreed to transfer its capital from Turin to Florence. The effect of this agreement, which seemed initially to represent a step forward in negotiations over Rome, was disastrous for the internal unity of the Right. There were riots in Turin in 1864 over the transfer of the capital, which were harshly suppressed by the army. The government fell and, when the capital was moved by order of the new Prime Minister, General La Marmora in December 1864, a permanent breach was formed within the Historic Right between the Piedmontese *permanente* and the Tuscan *consorteria*.[2] La Marmora's decision to finalize administrative unification in the decrees of 1865 also did little to heal the rifts within the Right.

A series of political realignments were also taking place on the Left. Some prominent opposition deputies (the most well-known of whom

[1] See above, Ch. 4, p. 123.
[2] G. Candeloro, *Storia dell'Italia moderna*, v: *la costruzione dello stato unitario* (Milan, 1968), 212–18, and D. Mack Smith, *Italy: A Modern History* (Ann Arbor, 1959), 64–6.

was the Tuscan democrat and former Sicilian prodictator, Antonio Mordini) voted with the government over the transfer of the capital. Another group of deputies, led by Francesco Crispi, refused to accept the deal with France, and continued to claim Rome as the only legitimate capital of Italy. However, in a public break with Mazzini and with the republicans, Crispi did declare himself to be a firm supporter of the Italian monarchy. Thus the parliamentary Left began to identify itself, albeit in disparate ways, with the existing regime to form what was known as thc 'loyal opposition'. The non-parliamentary Left, by contrast, became progressively more alienated from the regime. Reflecting what was a general trend among European revolutionaries in the early 1860s to move to the Left and towards socialism, these 'drop-outs and deviants', as Clara Lovett calls them, increasingly became involved in workers' alliances (*società operaie*) and in anarchist activities.[3]

Amid all this political infighting and confusion, the difficulties facing the government also mounted. Far from easing relations between Church and state, the conclusion of the September convention led to a hardening of the Church's attitude towards the kingdom of Italy. In 1864, the papal encyclical *Quanto cura* was issued together with a 'Syllabus of Errors', which condemned liberal principles and sanctioned radical clerical opposition to the new state.[4] The growing budget deficit, and the need to reorganize the state's fiscal structures, was an additional constraint and pressure on government policy.[5] On the Southern mainland, the period between August 1863 and the end of 1865 saw perhaps the most bitter fighting of all. In these two years, the government threw all the resources and powers at its disposal to defeat what came to be called '*il grande brigantaggio*'.[6] There was, moreover, growing international condemnation of government policy in the South. This condemnation threatened both ministerial attempts to attract financial backers from overseas for public works projects and diplomatic efforts to win the support of a 'Great Power' over the issues of Rome and Venetia.

The central government's policy towards Sicily was affected by these problems in the following way. For Sicily, the years between the conclusion of Govone's campaign in 1863 and the Palermo revolt of

[3] C. M. Lovett, *The Democratic Movement in Italy* (Cambridge, Mass., 1982), 187–217; R. Romanelli, *L'Italia liberale* (Bologna, 1979), 102–5.　　　　　　　　[4] Ibid. 98–9.
[5] Ibid. 74–84.
[6] F. Molfese, *Storia del brigantaggio dopo l'unità* (Milan, 1964), 260–322; J. A. Davis, *Conflict and Control: Law and Order in Nineteenth-Century Italy* (London, 1988), 168–82.

September 1866 were characterized largely by political neglect, while government ministers sought to grapple with these other, apparently more pressing concerns. Many Sicilian deputies (whether pro-government or opposition) were also caught up in the parliamentary wranglings of 1864–5, and had little time to spare for Sicilian affairs. The stormy debate which took place in parliament over Govone's campaign in December 1863 ended without conclusion, but with bitterness on all sides. There followed a series of parliamentary sessions, which ended only with the Palermo revolt of September 1866, when the 'Sicilian Question' was hardly referred to at all.

In practice, during the years between 1863 and 1866, whoever was in charge of Palermo and the other Sicilian provinces enjoyed a significant amount of autonomy. After the end of Govone's campaign, there was a tendency to let policy drift in Palermo, and this seems to be true of the other provinces of Western Sicily as well. Nomis di Cossilla continued—rather unhappily, from the available accounts—as prefect of Palermo until March 1865, and no further public order operations were undertaken while he was prefect. Although the emphasis on maintaining public order remained, so did complaints about the reliability and effectiveness of the local security forces.[7] The Pica law was renewed twice in 1864 (until December 1865), now referring specifically to Sicily, and its powers continued to be used by the police and *carabinieri*.[8]

In 1865, a number of developments occurred which affected the drift of government policy in Sicily. While popular unrest over conscription, taxation, and land persisted in many parts of the country throughout 1864, it seems to have actually increased at the beginning of 1865. This was largely the result of proposed government legislation abolishing religious orders, which was to destroy the Church's vital charity work among the poor. Agitation in opposition circles also increased in early 1865. After Giuseppe Badia took over the leadership of the republicans in Sicily, following Giovanni Corrao's murder in 1863, the movement moved further away from parliamentary methods

---

[7] Nomis di Cossilla made complaints about the security forces to the Minister of the Interior on 7 Mar., 23 Mar., 29 July, 12 Sept., and 21 Nov. 1864: BNF, Peruzzi, XX 17 bis. In May 1864 the procurator general of Palermo wrote a number of reports which complain, in particular, about the public security guards. ACSR, grazia e giustizia, b. 3, f. 84.

[8] 7 Feb. 1864, announcement by the Ministry of the Interior, ASP, gab. pref., b. 5, cat. 11, f. 4.

and towards exclusively conspiratorial action. These conspiratorial activities in and around the Palermo area caused the split between the republicans and the increasingly loyal 'loyal opposition' in Palermo (under Francesco Perroni Paladini) to widen and to become more bitter than before. Moreover, during 1864, and partly through the efforts of the socialist Saverio Friscia, Badia developed new links with the workers' and socialist societies gaining in popularity in Sicily.[9] He maintained his movement's close relationship with the *squadre* who the republicans had worked with during the revolution in 1860. Badia also established an additional, and still mysterious, alliance with Bourbon supporters. According to the bandit Giuseppe Cangelosi, arrested in February 1865, bandits were certainly involved in anti-government activity. His leader, Gandolfo:

in order to bring down the present government and to return to that of Francesco Borbone, hired some young men from around here [Bagheria] about six months ago . . . the first aim of this revolutionary armed band was to commit highway robbery, blackmail and such like so as to discredit the government . . . and bring the revolution closer. Gandolfo . . . did not pay the men with his own money but with funds that he would go and collect in Palermo, I don't know from whom.[10]

In all of these activities, Badia followed the precedents set by Corrao during 1862 and 1863.

It was the evidence of an alliance between the disparate anti-government elements which provoked action by government representatives in Palermo. In January 1865 a public meeting held by prominent democrats to discuss the suppression of religious orders was broken up by demonstrators who shouted '*Viva Francesco!*' and '*Viva la religione!*' and threatened and jostled participants in the meeting.[11] On the night of 12 May there were attempted insurrections in Palermo, Bagheria, Monreale, Misilmeri, and Carini. In Carini the government uncovered evidence of a complicated plot involving republicans, Bourbons, and *mafiosi*.[12] The procurator general of Palermo, Giovanni Interdonato, wrote to the Minister of Justice (Giuseppe Vacca) that 'the public are of the opinion that a Bourbon reaction is being attempted in Palermo and

[9] F. Brancato, 'Origini e carattere della rivolta palermitana del 1866', *Archivio Storico Siciliano*, serie iii, 5 (1952–3), 162–4.
[10] 'Allegato' to 4 Mar. 1865, ACSR, grazia e giustizia, b. 4, f. 15 bis.
[11] See Interdonato's telegram of 22 Jan. 1865 and his report of 24 Jan. ibid.
[12] 10 Aug. 1865, in G. Scichilone, *Documenti sulle condizione della Sicilia dal 1860 al 1870* (Rome, 1952), 164–5.

the surrounding area' with, it was generally assumed, the assistance of Badia.[13] In a subsequent letter he informed the minister that he had uncovered clear evidence of a conspiracy involving Badia, with links to the disturbances in January. The aim of the conspiracy was:

a return to the past dynasty under the flag of a federation . . . using bandits, highwaymen, thieves, swindlers, murderers [and] escaped prisoners, recruited and paid for the dual objective of robbery, murder, creating disorder and insurrection.[14]

However, all this activity might have generated a more muted reaction had it not been for a further development which altered the direction of government policy—the arrival of a new prefect, Filippo Gualterio, in Palermo in March 1865. Gualterio's sympathies were unquestionably moderate liberal and pro-Piedmontese. He had been a prominent opponent of the papal regime in his native Umbria during the 1840s and 1850s and, while in exile in Turin in 1851, he had published a famous work, *Gli ultimi rivolgimenti italiani* (*The Recent Events in Italy*) which wholeheartedly endorsed the moderate compromise between reaction and revolution. It also earned him the hostility of many democrats.[15] Gualterio was clearly trusted by the government in Florence, and he was equally clearly not the man to alter the prevailing emphasis on maintaining public order in Sicily. He was, however, quite inclined towards making this policy a great deal more effective.

Like his predecessor, Nomis di Cossilla, Gualterio does not seem to have particularly taken to life in Palermo. Although initially Gualterio's appointment was welcomed by many, it was soon observed that he was suspicious and fearful of everyone. Gualterio's negative attitude seems to have made him generally unpopular.[16] The series of reports about the province which Gualterio sent to the Minister of the Interior, Giovanni Lanza, certainly made for alarming reading. Famous for the first mention of the word 'mafia' (in this case, spelt 'maffia') in an official document, Gualterio's report of 25 April describes what he saw as the conspiratorial web made up of republicans and Bourbons consorting with a 'criminal association' ('the so-called maffia'). Public opinion (*lo*

---

[13] ACSR, grazia e giustizia, b.4, f. 15 bis.
[14] 26 May 1865, ASP, pref. gab., b.7, cat. 35.
[15] H. Hearder, *Italy in the Age of the Risorgimento* (London, 1983), 2.
[16] Statement made by General Caderina to the parliamentary commission of inquiry, 28 June 1867, M. da Passano (ed.), *I moti di Palermo del 1866: verbali della commissione parlamentare di inchiesta* (Rome, 1981), 373–4.

spirito pubblico) was, in his view, 'gravely disturbed'. There was, he added, a complete 'misunderstanding' between government and governed.[17] Later, on 2 May, Gualterio was more explicit. Giuseppe Badia was, in his view, 'the link between the Bourbons and the bandits', and measures had to be taken to combat this threat.[18]

Gualterio was rapidly convinced that a new series of military operations was needed to break up both the conspiracy and the criminals on which it relied. To this end he received a great deal of encouragement from General Giacomo Medici, the commander of the military division in Palermo, and Giovanni Interdonato, the procurator general of Palermo. Medici, who was from Milan, had been a military strategist for Mazzini in the early 1850s, but had thereafter distanced himself from Mazzini and become a supporter of the Piedmontese 'solution'.[19] He had also played an important military role in Garibaldi's Sicilian expedition of 1860.[20] Incorporated into the Italian army after 1860, Medici seems to have then entirely transferred his loyalties to the Right. In 1865 he was convinced that the political and popular disorder in Sicily—and particularly the threat from the 'maffia'—could be cured with efficient military measures. He assumed personal responsibility for organizing and co-ordinating the military aspects of the new public-order campaign.

These three men, Gualterio, Medici, and Interdonato, together conceived of and planned a campaign in 1865 to rid the province of Palermo of the mafia conspiracy against the government, and to bring the criminals who 'infested' the countryside to justice. All the initiative seems to have come from them rather than from central government. Gualterio requested permission for the campaign from the Minister of the Interior on 25 April; Medici reported to Gualterio on 20 April that he had already been given 'full freedom of action' by the Minister of War.[21] Gualterio was also encouraged by the prefect of Catania, Alessandro Bossini, who wrote that operations against 'Bourbons' could proceed relatively unhindered: 'With all this riff-raff you can let yourself go a bit: once you have the agreement of the ministry it is quite simple to legalize your methods.'[22]

---

[17] 25 Apr. 1865, ACSR, interno, b. 7, f. 4, n. 4.   [18] Ibid. n. 5.

[19] G. Candeloro, *Storia dell'Italia moderna, iv: dalla rivoluzione nazionale all'unita* (Milan, 1964), iv. 100–1.

[20] R. Grew, *A Sterner Plan for Italian Unity: The Italian National Society in the Risorgimento* (Princeton, 1963), 291–2, 300–2.

[21] ASP, pref. gab., b. 7, cat. 2; also in ACSR, interno, b. 7, f. 4, n. 7, allegato a.

[22] Scichilone, *Documenti*, 158–9.

Although Giovanni Interdonato's role in the campaign is less well-known than the other two, in many respects his influence was crucial. He was, of course, the only local man among them—he was both Sicilian and a former revolutionary. During the 1848 revolutions, and for a time afterwards, he had been identified with the extreme Left of the democratic movement in Sicily (the socialist group of Francesco Milo Guggino and Saverio Friscia). Subsequently, his political loyalties became ambiguous amid the general confusion of Sicilian politics at the time of the 1860 revolution. In a *carabinieri* report written in 1861, Interdonato's politics seem complex to the point of impenetrability:

He is of a republican hue, protects wrong-doers, popular with the *accoltellatori* ['knifers'?], among which can also be found people of the upper class, and for this reason has little influence over the population who actually hold him in great loathing.[23]

By 1865, however, one aspect of Interdonato's politics had become very apparent. He was a virulent opponent of Badia and all his associates. Equally, he was convinced—and most likely it was he who convinced Gualterio—that Badia was involved with the forces of reaction. It was Interdonato who specifically linked Badia to a number of well-known reactionaries and bandits. It was also Interdonato who first linked Badia to the disturbances of January 1865 and the attempted insurrection of May 1865.

Interdonato was determined to improve the administration of public order in the province of Palermo. Indeed, his intentions were made clear long before Gualterio's arrival. In a circular sent to all government officials in January 1865 Interdonato described the criminal justice system in some detail, so that everyone would be familiar with its workings. He chose to emphasize the importance of *ammonizione*, which he referred to as 'one of the most powerful expedients, and at the same time one of the most legal ways, of distinguishing between the criminal and the honest man', and he went on to recommend its wide application.[24] A month later Interdonato's opinions had become, if anything, even more forthright. An improvement in public order in the Palermo area would, he told the Minister of Justice, require among other things an increase in the number of *carabinieri*, a change in judicial personnel, changes in the trial process, a wider use of *domicilio coatto*, and an

---

[23] The excerpt from this report, and other information on Interdonato, is in da Passano (ed.) *I moti di Palermo*, 51.   [24] 12 Jan. 1865, ACSR, grazia e giustizia, b. 4, f. 15 bis.

increase in public works (which would mean better communications and, above all, roads).[25]

Interdonato was obviously determined to use all the legal and police powers at his disposal to bring about as many arrests and convictions as possible. Hardly surprisingly, he responded enthusiastically to a letter from Gualterio requesting advice on the legal aspects of the upcoming campaign. Not only was he able to reassure Gualterio that such operations were perfectly within the bounds of the law, but he went on to offer various 'hints' on making legal arrests. Interdonato's instructions to Gualterio excluded the courts from a substantial area of criminal justice and confirmed the military's extensive and unsupervised powers of arrest. Thus, in cases where the absence of witnesses made it impossible to obtain a warrant from the court (a chronic problem in Sicily), Interdonato told Gualterio that legal arrests could still be made. They could be made where the offender had been caught either *in flagrante* or shortly after the crime was committed; all suspected members of armed bands could be immediately arrested, as special provisions applied; anyone defined as a 'vagrant' or 'idler' could be arrested for failing to fulfil the conditions of their 'admonishment'; and, finally, all those amnestied in 1860 could be arrested for not fulfilling the conditions of their amnesty.[26]

The correspondence between Interdonato and Gualterio, and between Gualterio and Medici, offers interesting insights into the nature of the 1865 campaign and, more generally, into policy-making at this time. According to Brancato and to Alatri the whole campaign marks the beginning of a long series of 'errors and illegalities' in government policy as it sought to deal with the growing political opposition in Sicily.[27] Duggan also emphasizes the growth of political opposition, and places great significance on Gualterio's decision to criminalize political activity. For Duggan, Gualterio was the first to realize what subsequent generations of government officials in Sicily were to realize in their turn: that 'the concept of "the mafia" was a powerful instrument for dealing with political unrest'. Gualterio, he concludes, sought to manipulate a particular concept of criminality in order to maintain the government's hold over Sicily.[28]

---

[25] 14 Feb. 1865, ibid.   [26] 23 Apr. 1865, ASP, pref. gab., b. 7, cat. 35.
[27] The phrase is Paolo Alatri's, *Lotte politiche in Sicilia sotto il governo della Destra, 1866–1874* (Turin, 1954), 151. In his study of the Palermo revolt of 1866 Brancato sees the campaign of 1865 as a kind of prelude to the main events, 'Origini e carattere della rivolta palermitana', 172–6.   [28] C. Duggan, *Fascism and the Mafia* (London, 1989), 27.

There is a danger, however, of using the benefit of hindsight to read too much into Gualterio's plans. In reality, government policy was not nearly so far-seeing or as calculating as Duggan suggests. The problem facing government officials was the difficulty of distinguishing between what was criminal and what was political; many officials were convinced that there were well-established links between these two 'spheres' which went back at least as far as the Restoration period. Nor does this assumption set Gualterio and his officials apart; like many of their contemporaries elsewhere in Europe, their fear of disorder derived from the belief that, as Robert Tombs puts it, 'those most likely to participate in revolution were also those most likely to indulge in crime, for crime and revolution were symptoms of the same disease'.[29] It is also probably a mistake to blame Gualterio alone for this decision; he was not the only 'player' in government circles and, as a newcomer to Palermo, he seems to have relied heavily on the advice of Interdonato. Interdonato had, from all appearances, a complicated political and legal agenda all of his own.

The concerns of both Gualterio and Medici in 1865 reflect the tendency to treat the situation in Sicily as a local problem, one apparently not, at least not in 1865, of any national significance. Everyone, including probably central government, was anxious that it remain so. Gualterio and Medici were anxious, above all, about the logistics of the campaign. On the whole, the operations of 1865 showed a remarkable concern with both legal and military detail. Gualterio wrote to the Minister of the Interior at the beginning of May:

I must tell you here and now that the zeal and activity of Medici in preparing and conducting this operation, his prudence and care to avoid the appearance of illegality . . . promises good and effective results.[30]

It is also worth noting that, beyond the arrests which needed to be made, both Gualterio and Medici had high expectations of the campaign. In separate letters they argued that force was not a long-term solution in Sicily, but was only a means to a better end. They were confident once they had managed to restore order, support for the government and obedience to its laws would resume.[31] As operations

---

[29] R. Tombs, 'Crime and the Security of the State: The "Dangerous Classes" and Insurrection in Nineteenth-Century Paris', in V. A. C. Gatrell, B. Lenman, and G. Parker (eds.), *Crime and the Law: The Social History of Crime in Western Europe since 1500* (London, 1980), 214. [30] 2 May 1865, ACSR, interno, b. 7, f. 4, n. 5.
[31] Ibid. Medici to Gualterio, no date, ASP, pref. gab., b. 7, cat. 35.

commenced in late April 1865, they must have felt every justification for expecting their campaign to be a success.

II

Medici's campaign had three official aims—to arrest wanted men and contravenors of the *ammonizione*; to enforce a general disarmament of the Sicilian population; and to arrest draft-evaders and deserters. Gualterio supplied him with various lists of wanted men and suspects,[32] and he planned the campaign with all the military skill for which he was renowned. Nothing was to be left to chance: detachments of troops were to be sent to occupy designated areas, and mobile columns organized to capture those who managed to slip through the cordon. In all, Medici had some 15,000 soldiers under his command, of whom 8,000 alone were in the province of Palermo.[33] Reflecting some understanding of the terrain to be crossed, Medici insisted on having two cavalry squadrons. All permits for firearms were to be withdrawn, and those wishing to travel outside their commune of residence would have to obtain an internal pass.[34] Operations were to be concentrated in the province of Palermo, and to include the city of Palermo itself—known, Gualterio told Lanza, as a 'citadel' by the mafia.[35] Medici also wrote to the prefects of Trapani and Girgenti asking for their permission to extend operations into these provinces.[36]

The commencement of military operations was first announced in the *Giornale di Sicilia* on 25 April. On 27 April the National Guard was mobilized in the province of Palermo, and on 30 April troops were mobilized throughout Palermo, Trapani, and Girgenti. At first operations were confined to the province of Palermo; clashes with bandits and/or arrests were reported in Monreale, Corleone, Altavilla, Misilmeri, Petralia Soprana, and Termini Imerese.[37]

Some celebrated bandits were arrested in the district of Termini, among whom were members of the infamous gang of Don Peppino 'il

---

[32] 26 Apr. 1865, ACSR, interno, b. 7, f. 4, n. 3.

[33] These figures are given by the prefect of Palermo on 7 Sept. 1866 in a letter to the Minister of the Interior. Scichilone, *Documenti*, 186.

[34] Medici to Gualterio, 20 Apr. 1865, ASP, pref. gab., b. 7, cat. 2, and ACSR, interno, b. 7, f. 4, n. 7, allegato a. See also his letter of 5 May, ASP, pref. gab., b. 7, cat. 35.

[35] 2 May 1865, ACSR, interno, b. 7, f. 4, n. 5.

[36] 26 Apr. 1865, ASP, pref. gab., b. 7, cat. 2. This was at Gualterio's suggestion, and permission was obtained (see Medici to Gualterio, 29 Apr., ibid. cat. 35).

[37] See the newspapers *Il Precursore* and *Il Corriere Siciliano* for May 1865.

Lombardo' and a related group led by Giuseppe del Santo.[38] In Monreale, in July, one bandit was shot and horribly mutilated, apparently for co-operating with the security forces.[39] Giuseppe Badia was arrested by a mobile column on 20 July; interestingly, the mobile column was commanded by Colonel Trasselli, a leader of Garibaldi's volunteers in 1862, who had now sided with the 'loyal opposition'. According to the newspapers, Badia was captured hiding in the tobacco plants on an estate near Palermo and, when spotted by the troops, called out 'Don't shoot! I am not a bandit!'.[40]

Operations seem to have proceeded more quietly in the other provinces. Operations in the province of Girgenti were relatively low-key, and concentrated on areas—Sciacca, Santa Margherita, Caltabellota, Grotte—already well-known for criminal activity.[41] There are no reports of significant operations taking place in the province of Trapani.

The main phase of the campaign came to an end at the beginning of September. It was, in general, a better-organized and more efficient campaign than the preceding two, with a greater concern for military discipline being probably responsible for fewer reported cases of abuse by troops and mobile columns. On 1 September Gualterio wrote to Natoli, the new Minister of the Interior, that the campaign had worked out well and that the political situation was now much calmer. In his opinion the threat of reaction and republicanism had been more or less quashed.[42] Medici confirmed this view a week later, writing to Gualterio that 'every day I become more and more convinced that, through the use of troop manoeuvres, we have achieved all the improvements in the condition of public order that we could have hoped for', although he qualified this claim by adding 'given the enormous difficulties we were faced with at the beginning of our mission'.[43] In purely military terms the 1865 campaign was a greater success than those of preceding years, resulting in many more arrests than before.

Despite all Medici's efforts, however, the campaign failed to bring about a long-term improvement in public order. In their letters commending the results of the campaign, both Gualterio and Medici tacitly admitted as much. In his letter to Natoli, Gualterio noted that the

[38] On these arrests, see the letter from the sub-prefect on 6 May, ASP, pref. gab., b. 7, cat. 35, and from the Duca di Castelmonte, 5 Nov., ibid. cat. 2.

[39] The incident in Monreale is reported in *Il Precursore*, 6 July 1865.

[40] Ibid. 21 July 1865.   [41] *Il Giornale di Sicilia*, 12 May and 23 June 1865.

[42] ACSR, interno, b. 7, f. 10, n. 12.

[43] 9 Sept. 1865 in Scichilone, *Documenti*, 168.

'disintegration' of government forces—the decline of authority and morale within the government—was now almost more worrying than the strength of the opposition.[44] Since crime levels were not brought under control by the new round of operations, Medici seems to have abandoned his hope for a short campaign followed by a period of liberal peace. He attached proposals to his letter to Gualterio suggesting that a permanent military presence be set up in the Palermo countryside for the purposes of policing, and that the military should have special jurisdiction extending over the other three provinces of Western Sicily.[45]

In reality, the 1865 campaign hardly dented the threat of reaction and/or republicanism at all. Despite the arrest of Badia, anti-government activities intensified during the following year. In April 1866 rumours of a revolt were rife in Palermo, red flags were flown, and there were reports of attacks on policemen.[46] Medici's campaign also led to increased friction between the two wings of the opposition movement in Palermo. A few days after the arrest of Badia, the leader of the 'loyal opposition' in Palermo, Francesco Perroni Paladini, was stabbed and seriously wounded while walking on the Corso in Palermo. All the evidence pointed to the involvement of Badia's associates in revenge for his arrest. A colleague of Perroni Paladini's, Enrico Albanese, told the investigative tribunal that he had heard the assassination being planned in his local bar. Rumours also circulated about plans to murder Trasselli and other prominent moderate democrats, and witnesses testified that famous bandits (Lorenzo Minneci, Giuseppe lo Bue) were involved in the plot.[47]

By 1865 the obstacles to effective liberal government in Western Sicily were mounting rather than diminishing. No amount of military and legal planning could alter this basic fact. Indeed, in one important respect at least the campaign of 1865 was killed by its own success. The large numbers detained by Medici's troops in the course of operations meant that the arrests made soon began to exceed the capacity of the authorities to deal with them. Gualterio had alluded to this potential problem at the start of the campaign when he instructed Medici to

---

[44] 1 Sept. 1865, ACSR, interno, b. 7, f. 10, n. 12.

[45] *Allegato* to letter of 9 Sept., Scichilone, *Documenti*, 168.

[46] See the series of letters between 17 Apr. and 31 Aug. 1866 from the new prefect, Torelli, to the Minister of the Interior: ibid. 170–84.

[47] Statement by Enrico Albanese to the investigative tribunal, 26 July 1865, ACSR, interno, b. 8, f. 1, n. 319, and by a painter named Perdichizzi, 21 Sept. 1865, ibid. n. 330.

proceed with the arrest of more serious criminals first, otherwise the numbers arrested might cause the government difficulties.[48] A letter dated 16 May from Interdonato to the Minister of Justice, which expressed concern about the large numbers arrested, indicates that this began to be a problem almost immediately.[49] Although it is difficult to state with accuracy how many people were arrested as a result of Medici's manœuvres, the number is put at 500 in the middle of July;[50] and, in all, some 3,684 arrests were made by *carabinieri* and public-security guards between January and the end of October.[51] As a result, the courts were thrown into chaos and the prisons became seriously overcrowded.

At least twice during the campaign bandits were able to escape from custody. The *capo-banda* Salvatore Marino escaped from custody in Monreale,[52] and Antonio Mistretta (part of the infamous band of Don Peppino il Lombardo) escaped from custody in Cefalù.[53] As we shall see in Chapter 8, Badia was able to continue his conspiratorial activities while awaiting trial in Palermo's main prison. The danger of mixing hardened criminals with those charged with more minor offences also began to cause official concern. In July, around 200 of those detained for minor offences were transported to the Tremiti islands (off the Gargano peninsula in Puglia).[54] Nearly a year later, in May 1866, the number of prisoners in Palermo's gaols alone was put at 1,937, of whom approximately 1,500 were still awaiting trial. By then the prisons had become a dangerous source of anti-government agitation; the prefect of Palermo wrote to the Minister of the Interior that detainees were 'expecting a repeat of 1860' (meaning a revolution accompanied by a mass breakout).[55]

By a horrible misfortune, troops brought into Sicily to assist in operations also brought cholera with them and spread it throughout

[48] 26 Apr. 1865, ibid. b. 7, f. 4, n. 3.   [49] ACSR, grazia e giustizia, b. 4, f. 15 bis.
[50] 15 July 1865, in a letter from the Minister of Justice to the procurator general, ibid. b. 5, f. 232.
[51] 'Stato numerico degli arresti operati nella provincia di Palermo dal 1 gennaio a tutto il 31 ottobre 1865 dai carabinieri e dalle guardie di p. s. divisi secondo la designazione del codice penale', ASP, pref. pubblica sicurezza, filza 54, f. 68. It should be noted that not all of these arrests were made during the course of Medici's operations.
[52] From the commander of the sub-zone of Monreale to Medici, 11 Aug. 1865, ASP, pref. gab., b. 7, cat. 35.
[53] The sub-prefect to Gualterio, ASP, pref. pubblica sicurezza, filza 54, f. 39.
[54] See the correspondence between Interdonato and the justice minister on 15 July, and the information sent by Interdonato on 11 Aug., in ACSR, grazia e giustizia, b. 5, f. 232.
[55] 6 May 1866, Scichilone, *Documenti*, 175–6.

Western Sicily. As in other parts of Europe affected by cholera, the effect of the 1865 epidemic in Sicily was devastating to government authority.[56] Mentions of cholera first appeared in government reports towards the end of July 1865. Between September and December 1865 the epidemic raged, leaving 5,688 dead in the province of Palermo, 734 in Trapani, and 98 in Girgenti.[57] The spread of the disease was all the more damaging to government authority because of the popular belief which held the cholera morbus to be part of a deliberate government plot to decimate an innocent population. In the past this belief had been encouraged by liberals in an effort to 'make the Bourbon government more hated';[58] in 1865 it harmed the liberal government's own image and reputation.[59] The district judge of Petralia Sottana wrote to Gualterio in July that 'the common people here associate the cholera with poison', that they believed he and the local priest had 'accepted the government's mission to spread the disease . . . that the casks containing the poison have already arrived and are in storage at the archpriest's home', and that twenty agents had been ordered to spread the poison around the town.[60] Amongst the educated public, the government's handling of the epidemic was generally viewed as no more effective than that of the Bourbons; the government, it was alleged, had mismanaged the epidemic and delayed introducing the necessary sanitary measures.[61]

III

The 1865 campaign showed that military action, however well-organized and executed, was simply not enough by itself. The support of local government was often far more important than the number of government troops. As we have seen, Medici and Interdonato had between them attempted to neutralize the role of local authorities

[56] For a discussion of the effects of cholera on public order, see R. J. Evans, 'Epidemics and Revolutions: Cholera in Nineteenth-Century Europe', in T. Ranger and P. Slack (eds.), *Epidemics and Ideas: Essays on the Historical Perception of Pestilence* (Cambridge, 1992).

[57] Alatri, *Lotte politiche in Sicilia*, 101. There were also 60 victims reported in Catania and 6 in Messina.

[58] According to the procurator general of Catania, 22 July 1865, ACSR, grazia e giustizia, b. 5, f. 239.

[59] For a comparison with the government's handling of cholera epidemics in Naples, particularly those of 1884 and 1910–11, see F. M. Snowden, *Naples in the Time of Cholera, 1884–1911* (Cambridge, 1995).   [60] 12 July 1865, ASP, pref. gab., b. 7, cat. 2.

[61] F. Maggiore Perni, *Palermo e le sue grandi epidemie dal secolo xvi al xix* (Palermo, 1894), 39.

through military strategy and through the consistent use of special police powers. Accordingly, little attempt was made to assess or to gain the support of local government for the campaign. Civilian police forces were simply placed under military jurisdiction. This procedure soon came to look like a mistake. Without a voluntary show of local support for the military's presence, and without the willing assistance of local officials in identifying wanted men, operations had much less chance of success.

Thus, the public-order operations of 1865, like those of 1862 and 1863, met their defeat at the hands of local communities. The mayor of Monreale—an area notorious for its high levels of crime—was known to be undermining the activity of the troops based there. Described by Medici as young, ignorant, and with no apparent attachment to the liberal government, he did little to uphold government authority. During the threatened disturbances in Palermo in May 1865, he:

shut himself in his house and locked the doors: inactive to the point of treachery, he simply waited on the favourable or unfavourable outcome of events, [he] gathered around himself twelve strong lawless men (*dodici bravi gente facinorosa*), members of the maffia . . . and they all enjoyed the wine which had been allocated to the municipal tax office.[62]

The mayor of Mezzojuso, in the same mountainous region above Palermo, was reported to be consorting with bandits rather than with the military. With other members of the Mezzojuso council (apparently known as 'the thieves' by the local population), he had also refused to comply with any of the hygiene measures introduced by the government against cholera.[63]

Where operations were successful, it was often the result of local co-operation. The arrests in July of the bandit Don Peppino and his various famous associates was brought about largely because their powerful and long-term 'protector', mayor Giovanni Nicolosi of Lercara, decided to turn them all in.[64] Presumably, Nicolosi's action was part of an attempt to win favour with the government. If so, he was

[62] 1 June 1865, ASP, pref. gab., b. 7, cat. 35.
[63] Medici to Gualterio, 9 June 1865: Scichilone, *Documenti*, 61–2; 21 July 1865, ASP, pref. gab., b. 7, cat. 35.
[64] Don Peppino actually fled to Tripoli in the middle of 1865, and was arrested there. See the procurator general's report of 5 May 1868 on Don Peppino's extraordinary confession about his activities and his links with the Nicolosi brothers in Scichilone, *Documenti*, 218–20, and, for an analysis, R. Mangiameli, 'Banditi e mafiosi dopo l'unità', *Meridiana*, 7–8 (1990), esp. 76–81.

successful; in October 1865, Medici even recommended him for a medal.[65] Elsewhere, friction between local authorities and the military became a serious problem. In June the municipal council of Termini Imerese received a rebuke from Gualterio for failing to assist troops in their inquiries.[66] A month later the military commander reported to Gualterio that, despite repeated requests, no help had been forthcoming in compiling lists of draft-evaders. The whole town, including the National Guard, resisted the military. Nobody dared to declare themselves pro-government.[67] The mayor of Campofelice, inland of Termini, refused to give the troops decent lodgings.[68] In Casteldaccia, the mayor became involved in a fight with the *carabinieri*.[69]

The behaviour of the local police forces often caused additional problems. A private letter written to the Minister of the Interior in May spoke of the chaos inside the mobile columns caused by local police.[70] Medici wrote angrily to Gualterio on 28 July, telling how a well-organized operation against a group of bandits hiding out near Monreale had come to nothing, simply because the public security guards involved in the operation had insisted on 'resting from their fatigue' overnight in Carini.[71]

These problems had a marked effect on the conduct of the campaign and the attitude of the government in Palermo towards the local population. Increasingly, if the prefect's dissolution of National Guards and town councils is anything to go by, the public-order operations involved the 'correction' of whole communities. Once dissolved, town councils would be replaced by a temporary delegate (*delegato straordinario*), whose job it was to organize new elections and, on this basis, set up a new council and/or militia with members loyal to the liberal government. Various reports indicate that this work was being undertaken at the time of military operations. For instance, in Montelepre and Borgetto the National Guards were dissolved, and in Mezzojuso the National Guard had also to be disarmed.[72] In Partinico, which had

---

[65] In a letter to Gualterio, 26 Oct. 1865, ASP, pref. gab., b. 7, cat. 35.
[66] Gualterio to the sub-prefect of Termini, 2 June 1865, ASP, pref. gab., b. 7, cat. 35. On 8 June, the mayor of Termini replied that he had done all he could to help the troops, ibid.   [67] 1 July 1865, Scichilone, *Documenti*, 162–3.
[68] 22 July 1865, Medici to Gualterio, ASP, pref. gab., b. 7, cat. 35.
[69] See the letters of 14 and 29 June 1865, ibid. cat. 2.
[70] From *Cavaliere* Paratore, 26 May 1865, ibid. cat. 35.   [71] Ibid.
[72] On Borgetto and Montelepre see the report of the police chief of Partinico, 8 May 1865, ASP, ibid. cat. 2. On Mezzojuso, see Medici to Gualterio, 9 June 1865, Scichilone, *Documenti*, 161–2.

apparently been ruled by a violent criminal organization presided over by two brothers, both the National Guard and the town council were dissolved.[73]

However, attempts to alter the composition of local councils in this way did not always meet with success. One problem was that both the use of special powers and the staging of elections were compromised by the factional struggles which they were supposed to replace. Gualterio came to recognize this after a fashion, writing to the Minister of the Interior in September 1865 that 'elections here are not a struggle over political principles but are over individual issues, and they all go back to the families who hold excessive power (*prepotenza*) or those who seek to hold it for themselves'.[74] Thus, local elections held at this time did not change matters greatly one way or the other. Gualterio noted that elections in Cefalù and in Termini 'were simply a confirmation of the old order'. In Corleone, they resulted in a 'preponderance' of the 'less liberal' party.[75]

Special powers, as the experience of the temporary delegate in Partinico suggested, did not always count for very much. The delegate wrote to Gualterio in early May, once he had dissolved the existing administration and was seeking to organize a new council. To enforce his decisions, however, he still needed local assistance and, in particular, he needed the support of the local police force. As it turned out, the chief of police in Partinico had suddenly (and quite irregularly) departed for a private visit to Palermo, ignoring all the delegate's orders and his pleas to remain. The unfortunate delegate, the supreme representative of the government's power in Partinico, thus found himself 'alone, without a council, without a commission, without a National Guard' and, by his own admission, incapable of enforcing his authority.[76]

IV

Central government did not involve itself particularly with the 1865 campaign against political unrest in the Palermo countryside. If anything, it was concerned simply to contain and underplay the situation. Gualterio, Medici, and Interdonato consulted with their respective

---

[73] One was the mayor, the other commanded the National Guard. From the police chief of Partinico, 8 May 1865, ASP, pref. gab., b. 7, cat. 2.

[74] 6 Sept. 1865, in Scichilone, *Documenti*, 168. It should be noted that Gualterio is referring here to the larger urban centres.   [75] Ibid.

[76] To Gualterio, 11 May 1865, ASP, pref. gag., b. 7, cat. 2.

ministers in April 1865, who then left them largely in control. The 1865 campaign was not the result of any new initiative on the part of central government, but was largely the result of local efforts to make the usual public-order policy more efficient than before, and to respond to an apparent threat from the government's (various) extremist enemies.

The experience of the 1865 campaign suggests that this policy was fundamentally misconceived. It was based on the assumption that the public-order problem in Western Sicily was due simply to excessive criminality or, in this case, criminality mixed with political conspiracy. It followed logically that the problem could be 'cured' by large numbers of arrests. Thus the only difficulty, in the eyes of Gualterio and Medici, was how to make these arrests and how, once having made them, to keep those arrested behind bars or otherwise out of harm's way. In the event, however, the most serious problem faced by them was the lack of local support for government policy.

Medici was a military man, and Gualterio was a tremendous enthusiast for Piedmontese rule. Hardly surprisingly, neither man had much appreciation of the problems of government in Sicily. Medici seemed, despite the obvious lesson of the 1862 and 1863 campaigns (and even of the democrats' experience in 1860) not to have realized the various ways in which the opposition of local communities to the use of military force could undermine the task of law enforcement. They seemed unaware of the extent to which local government officials and the police forces themselves were caught up in the prevailing factionalism of local communities. They ignored the mounting evidence of popular discontent over taxation and conscription and, in the rural areas, they did nothing to alter the still-unresolved conflict over land. Finally, they were powerless to prevent the rising tide of political and popular agitation over the government's proposed abolition of religious orders.

As an outsider, Gualterio allowed himself to be guided by Interdonato's political opinions and by his own fear of political extremism. He never gave much thought to the importance of establishing local support for the campaign. It seems that no-one looked much beyond the end of operations. Medici hoped for a short, efficient campaign which, by virtue of its superior planning and its observation of legal procedure, would succeed where the other ones had failed. Interdonato hoped successfully to conclude a by now bitter feud between rival groups within the Sicilian democratic movement. Gualterio hoped to undo the link between criminality and political opposition and, by putting the criminals behind bars, expected to dissolve the connections between these criminals and local communities. All three men were unaware of how far their decision to criminalize political opposition could undermine the business of government itself.

8

Revolt Against the Government, 1866

I

The decision to declare martial law in the city and province of Palermo on 23 September 1866 followed a week-long rebellion and the collapse of government authority. On the night of 15 September 1866, only six years after Garibaldi's victorious entry into Palermo, armed gangs organized in Monreale and the surrounding countryside invaded the city. The invasion sparked off a huge popular uprising. Barricades were thrown up, all telegraph links with the mainland were cut, and government buildings were attacked and seized. As one *carabinieri* report put it, 'almost all of the Palermo poor joined in . . . the mass of insurgents numbered several thousand and all were armed to the teeth'.[1] The most important assault took place on the main prison, led by the famous bandit 'Turi Miceli, in an attempt to liberate Giuseppe Badia and his associates. Although this attack was beaten back by troops and prison guards (and Miceli was killed in the fighting), elsewhere government forces were not so lucky. Numerous public buildings were attacked and looted, including the military hospital, the military college (the *istituto Garibaldi*), court buildings, municipal offices, and army barracks. Bandits also occupied a number of convents to serve as prisons for those they had captured.[2] The majority of officials and policemen fled for their lives.[3] The remaining troops and government representatives, including the prefect Luigi Torelli and the mayor Antonio di Rudinì, were forced to retreat after a violent skirmish with the rebels on the morning of 16 September. They were to remain besieged inside the old

---

[1] 7 Dec. 1866, Major Benassi to the Colonel in command, MSAC, cartella 49.

[2] See the cases of Paolo Giarmi, Girolamo Scaduto, Antonio Ferro, Francesco Orefice, Vincenzo Corona, Vincenzo Agata, Salvatore Cagliardi, and Andrea Nicosia in ACSR, Tribunali militari di guerra di Palermo, 1860–1866 (henceforth, tribunali militari), b. 4.

[3] See the letter from the *avvocato generale* to the Minister of Justice, 23 Sept. 1866, ACSR, grazia e giustizia, b. 8, f. 8, n. 11.

Royal Palace in Palermo until their rescue by government reinforcements on 21 September.

On 18 September a revolutionary committee was formed in Palermo by members of the old Bourbon élite. It was headed by the Prince di Linguaglossa, and included prominent aristocrats and clerics.[4] Although all its members later claimed they were forced to take part, the committee made clear efforts to control and direct the revolution. Its first act was to call on the National Guard and 'citizens of every class' to support the revolution. It later announced that any looting would be treated as an offence and urged the *capisquadra* to control their men.[5]

There were striking similarities between the events of 1860 and those of 1866. As in 1860, as soon as the rebels had struck a successful blow against government authority in Palermo the population turned against the government and many government officials abandoned their posts. In the surrounding countryside the scenes of violence were, if anything, worse than in the city. Bandits were reported on all sides of Palermo: along the coast in Bagheria, Villabate, Tommaso Natale, Cinisi, Terrasini, and Carini, as well as further inland in Partinico, Montelepre, Piana dei Greci, Ogliastro, Marineo, Misilmeri, Lercara Friddi, and Campofelice.[6] In Bagheria an armed crowd attacked the prison shouting 'Death to the *carabinieri*!' and 'Let the prisoners go free or you are all dead!'; and when the prison guards ran out of ammunition they opened the prison gates and fled for their lives.[7]

While towns in the district of Palermo were at the centre of the revolt, the districts of Termini and Corleone were also affected by disturbances. A detachment of *carabinieri* stationed in Corleone 'was absolutely the salvation of the city', in the words of its commander; despite widespread panic and the presence nearby of 'some brigand squads', the government remained in control.[8] In Termini an armed gang came down from the mountains 'and penetrating the town, firing their guns in the air, so terrified the inhabitants that many fled into their houses while other wrongdoers joined up with the squad'. The

---

[4] They were: Baron Pignatelli, Baron Riso, Prince di Ramacca, Prince di Galati, Baron Sutera, Prince di Niscemi, Prince di Vincenzo, Don Onofrio di Benedetto, Monsignor d'Acquisto, and Canon Bellavia. See the various reports about these men and their activities in ASP, Questura di Palermo, I divisione, gabinetto, 1860–1880, b. 1 and b. 4.

[5] G. Ciotti, *Cenni storici sugli avvenimenti di settembre 1866* (Palermo, 1866), 77–9.

[6] See the series of reports from Cadorna in ASP, pref. gab., b. 8, f. 38 cat. 2 and f. 4 cat. 2 bis.

[7] 6 Oct. 1866, from Major Benassi to the commander of the 12th legion, MSAC, cartella 49.   [8] 3 Oct. 1866, ibid.

carabinieri put up no resistance; the barracks was sacked and they were disarmed and robbed.[9] Outside the province of Palermo armed gangs were reported in Alcamo, Castellamare, Calatafimi, and Monte San Giuliano (Erice).[10] In Caltanissetta a conspiracy linked to the Palermo revolt involving priests and bandits was reported.[11] In Noto on 20 September telegraph communications were cut. Messina, however, was reported to be 'in complete calm'; in fact, it 'gave open signs of distinct disapproval' of the events in Palermo.[12]

Disturbances in Monreale, home of the bandits 'Turi Miceli and Lorenzo Minneci, preceded the invasion of Palermo by a few hours. A further battle took place during the morning of 16 September between the *carabinieri* and insurgents shouting '*Viva la Repubblica!*'; a number of *carabinieri* were subsequently shot.[13] The Monreale National Guard 'far from repressing the subversives, actually joined up with the *squadre*'.[14] In many of these towns, local government simply collapsed at the outbreak of disorder. Although reports reached the government that the town councils in Partinico and Carini remained loyal, more frequently, government officials went into hiding and in some cases joined in the disturbances.[15] Officials sometimes took advantage of the collapse of government authority to settle private scores. In Lercara, the captain of the National Guard and commander of the *militi a cavallo*, Giovanni Nicolosi, led his men in an attack on the *carabinieri*: 'pretending to be attacked by a band of brigands, they rushed into the town [and] fired two shots against the detachment of soldiers.'[16] One soldier, Luigi Alessandrelli, was killed in the fighting.[17]

---

[9]   7 Oct. 1866, from Major Benassi to the commander of the 12th legion, MSAC, cartella 49.   [10] 21–30 Sept. 1866, ibid.

[11] 1 and 29 Oct. 1866, ibid.   [12] 28 Sept. 1866, ibid.

[13] 7 Dec. 1866, ibid.

[14] General Cadorna to Bettino Ricasoli, 12 Oct. 1866, in G. Scichilone, *Documenti sulle condizione della Sicilia dal 1860 al 1870* (Rome, 1952), 202.

[15] Ricasoli wrote to Cadorna on 9 Oct. praising the mayor of Partinico, ASP, pref. gab., b. 8, f. 49, cat. 2; see also the letter of 25 Sept. from the mayor of Carini to the prefect of Palermo, ibid. f. 4, cat. 2 bis, and from the commander of *carabinieri* in Partinico praising the National Guard of Carini, 30 Sept. 1866, MSAC, cartella 49.

[16] 18 Sept 1866, from commander Malvezzi, MSAC, cartella 49.

[17] It emerged later that Nicolosi, whose brother Francesco was the mayor of Lercara, was still involved in a feud with the *carabiniere* Marshall Balsamo. Balsamo had long opposed the Nicolosi family's domination of Lercara and supported their political rival, Francesco Sartorio: the commander of the 12th legion of *carabinieri* to Cadorna, 2 Oct. 1866, ASP, pref. gab., b. 8, cat. 2, f. 38. For more details see the report to the Minister of the Interior on the Nicolosi brothers and their feud with the Sartorio family: 24 Nov. 1866, ACSR, interno, b. 8. f. 1, n. 300.

MAP 5. Province of Palermo: Towns Affected by the Revolt

A great deal of popular violence was directed against the *carabinieri*. They were not only the most visible symbols of government authority, but were also the only government organization to remain unreservedly loyal to it. Ironically, perhaps, it was only the *carabinieri* who remembered the revolt with a measure of official pride.[18] Some *carabinieri* being escorted into Palermo from Tommaso Natale managed to escape when their escort attempted to 'execute' them in the *giardino inglese*.[19] In the small town of Campofelice near Lercara more than one detachment of *carabinieri* were forced to flee the town, on one occasion chased by a bloodthirsty mob led by Campofelice's mayor, on another by a crowd of some 800 people crying 'Long

---

[18] See the text of a speech on the Palermo revolt by General Boella of the *carabinieri* in 1939, in MSAC b. 49. Clive Emsley has analysed how the experience of the Palermo revolt reinforced the *carabinieri*'s sense of 'Italian' identity in 'The Nineteenth-Century Gendarme: Attitudes and Mentalities,' unpublished paper.

[19] See the cases of Filippo and Gaspare Messina and Vito Riccobuono in ACSR, tribunali militari, b. 4, and of Antonio Graziano, in F. L. Oddo, 'Le sentenze del primo tribunale di guerra di Palermo per i fatti del 1866', *Archivio Storico Siciliano*, serie iii, 31–2 (1971–2), 326.

live the republic and religion!'.[20] Mobile columns of *carabinieri* spent
the week patrolling this remote area of the Palermo *latifondo*, attempting to uphold government authority and sometimes seeking a refuge
from the disturbances. Their reports convey an acute sense of the
government's predicament and of the suffering of its loyal representatives. They found, for instance, a *carabinieri* captain at Mezzojuso:

without his uniform and showing on his face the only too visible signs of the
anguish he had endured [hiding] for a good twelve hours in a tomb, for thirty-
six hours under the roof of the church . . . . for two days in a barrel in the
mayor's cellar and for three days in the vestry of the same church.[21]

The entire population of Mezzojuso, 'not just the men but also the
women and children', took part in the revolt; all the communal and
police papers were publicly burned together with the Italian flag.[22] In
Campofelice, the family of the communal assessor was 'massacred'.[23]

In the towns of Misilmeri, Ogliastro, Montelepre, and Torretta there
were even more violent attacks on the *carabinieri*. In Montelepre and
Torretta, most of them were able to go into hiding; in Montelepre a
local priest also stepped in to save the lives of all but two who were
discovered by the rebels.[24] However, in Ogliastro bandits reportedly
killed three *carabinieri* and dragged their naked and mutilated bodies
around the town before dumping them in the countryside. Another
four, led by the brigadier Taroni, chose suicide rather than be captured
by the rebels. In a celebrated gesture, Taroni seized the Italian flag and
shouted 'Long live the king! Long live Italy! You will never have the
honour of taking me alive!' before shooting himself.[25] The same group
of insurgents led by Francesco and Cosimo Lo Bue were also said to be
involved in a mass assault on the *carabinieri* barracks in Misilmeri,
where some thirty-one *carabinieri* were killed. Rumours abounded
that their bodies were cut up and displayed as meat for sale in the local

[20] 2 Oct. 1866, the commander of the 12th legion of *carabinieri* to Cadorna, ASP, pref.
gab., b. 8, cat. 2, f. 38; 1 Nov. 1866, from Major Benassi to the commander of the 12th
legion, MSAC, cartella 49.
[21] 2 Oct. 1866, the commander of the 12th legion of *carabinieri* to Cadorna, ASP, pref.
gab., b. 8, cat. 2, f. 38.   [22] 7 Dec. 1865, from Major Bonassi, MSAC, cartella 49.
[23] 1 Nov. 1866, from Major Benassi to the commander of the 12th legion, ibid.
[24] 1 Oct. 1866, ibid.
[25] Reports from Major Benassi, 14 and 18 Oct. 1866, ibid. On Taroni, Emsley, 'The
Nineteenth-Century Gendarme' is useful. On Ogliastro see Cadorna to Ricasoli, 14
Nov. 1866, ISR, b. 552, n. 4(8); and, on the trial of those involved, Oddo, 'Le sentenze',
315.

market.[26] The *carabinieri* themselves gave lurid accounts of the atrocities committed; telling that one rebel—Pietro Costa—had cut off the head of *carabiniere* Florio Rappieri and drank the blood which flowed out of it; while another, Domenica Bonanno, had cut off the nose of *carabiniere* Angelo Sartori 'and ate it in the company of her daughter Nicoletta'.[27]

The reconquest of Palermo by government forces began on 18 September. General Raffaele Cadorna, a veteran of the government's campaign against brigandage in the Abruzzi, was appointed as temporary commissioner of Palermo with full civil and military powers by the Prime Minister, Bettino Ricasoli.[28] Troops were also sent from the mainland to quell the revolt. They arrived by ship in the port of Palermo on 18 September, but the rebels resisted and prevented them from disembarking.[29] It took the troops three days of bitter street-fighting to win back Palermo for the government. During this time, the looting and violence continued with renewed vigour. Although efforts were made to throw a military cordon around the city, most of the rebels managed to escape through it into the hills.[30]

On 23 September General Cadorna declared a state of siege. The next day he instructed that all firearms should be surrendered and orders were given to arrest contravenors and, if necessary, shoot them. Nobody was to be allowed to leave the city between 6 p.m. and 6 a.m. without a special pass. Public meetings of more than three people were banned. The return of goods stolen during the revolt was ordered; those who failed to do so were to be treated as bandits. Finally, on 26 September, the Palermo National Guard was ordered to disband.[31] The local press was allowed to operate normally, largely because of its endorsement of government action.[32] On Cadorna's instructions a series of military operations got under way in the province of Palermo to arrest

---

[26] On Misilmeri, see the report of the temporary delegate in Misilmeri to the prefect of Palermo, 26 Sept. 1866, ASP, pref. gab., b. 8, f. 4, cat. 2 bis. On the trial, see Oddo, 'Le sentenze', 313–15, and ACSR, tribunali militari, b. 3. The report about the bodies of dead *carabinieri* being sold for meat was first published in V. Maggiorani, *Il sollevamento della plebe di Palermo e del circondario nel settembre 1866* (Palermo, 1867).

[27] 18 Oct. 1866, from Major Bonassi, MSAC, cartella 49.

[28] ACSR, interno, b. 8, f. 1, n. 2.

[29] M. Gabriele, 'La marina militare alla riconquista di Palermo (settembre 1866)', *Nuovi Quaderni del Meridione*, 16 (1966), 442–52.

[30] 23 Sept. 1866, from the *avvocato generale* to the Minister of Justice, ACSR, grazia e giustizia, b. 8, f. 8, n. 1.   [31] Ciotti, *Cenni storici*, 80–8.

[32] Cadorna to Ricasoli, 2 Oct 1866, ASP, pref. gab., b. 8, f. 4, cat. 2 bis.

the insurgents who had fled at the end of the revolt and to enforce the disarmament.[33] Finally, on 1, 19, and 28 October, Cadorna issued orders to set up three separate military courts to try the insurgents.

General Cadorna was convinced that the Palermo revolt was the result of a vicious criminal conspiracy also involving Bourbon supporters and the Church. 'Whatever the character of these anarchic disturbances,' he wrote to Ricasoli on 2 October, 'the motor force was provided by Bourbon and clerical elements.'[34] Cadorna particularly blamed the Church, publicly accusing the Archbishop of Palermo of collusion with the rebels, and writing, in another letter to Ricasoli, that the government's unpopularity had been 'spread amongst the masses by the shady activity of monks and priests'.[35] Six months later he told the parliamentary commission of inquiry that the September revolt 'was due to a clerical and Bourbon conspiracy' and that 'nearly all the convents were a hotbed of insurrection'.[36]

Others in Palermo insisted that the revolt was caused by a republican conspiracy. The leading proponent of this view was the procurator general, Interdonato, who wrote to Cadorna that Giuseppe Badia was behind the uprising:

We have every reason to believe that the above events are simply the development and completion of a single conspiracy, which having failed on the first attempt in May 1865, reorganized the plot to erupt as it later erupted in September 1866.[37]

Many of the moderate democrats agreed with this assessment. A colleague of Francesco Crispi's wrote to him from Palermo that the revolt was the continuation of a long conspiracy. He was, as he put it, 'convinced that the recent uprisings were linked to Badia . . . that Badia was linked to Corrao—Corrao was linked to Aspromonte—even to the *pugnalatori*'.[38] At the same time, everyone was equally determined to deny any kind of political legitimacy to the insurgents. 'There are no

[33] Cadorna to Ricasoli, 25 Sept. 1866, ibid. b. 9, cat. 2.

[34] Scichilone, *Documenti*, 196.

[35] This letter, dated 28 Sept. 1866, was published in the *Gazzetta Ufficiale del Regno* on 4 Oct. and in the *Giornale di Sicilia* on 17 Oct. Cadorna's later letter to Ricasoli, dated 30 Oct., is in Scichilone, *Documenti*, 204–5.

[36] 11 May 1867, M. da Passano (ed.), *I moti di Palermo del 1866: verbali della commissione parlamentare di inchiesta* (Rome, 1981), 101–2.

[37] 15 Oct. 1866, ASP, pref. gab., b. 8, cat. 2 bis, prat. v.

[38] 10 Oct. 1866, in R. Giuffrida, 'Aspetti e problemi della rivolta palermitana del settembre 1866', *Archivio Storico Siciliano*, serie iii, 7 (1955), 190.

political crimes in the Palermo events,' Prime Minister Ricasoli firmly told Cadorna in November.[39]

In some respects the tone of these reports say more about the prevailing fear of the Church and of reaction than they do about the character of the Palermo revolt. At the time, Cadorna's accusation against the Church was vigorously rebutted by Archbishop Naselli of Palermo.[40] Other observers suggested that Cadorna was generalizing on the basis of a few isolated incidents. The lawyer Pietro Crispi told the parliamentary commission that the clergy had little or nothing to do with the revolt.[41] Guiseppe Puglia wrote to Francesco Crispi that he knew of only one priest who had fought with the rebels, and he had been defrocked twenty years previously. For the rest, the idea of the clergy being behind the revolt was 'utter slander'.[42] Even Prime Minister Ricasoli was sufficiently doubtful as to instruct Cadorna to carefully re-verify all the sources for his allegations.[43] There was also some doubt as to the extent of the Bourbon threat. Although Bourbon agents were reported in the Palermo area, and although the Bourbon government in exile in Rome allegedly expressed disappointment that the revolt had failed, many of those questioned by the parliamentary commission insisted that there was no organized Bourbon party in Palermo.[44] The Left deputy, d'Ondes Reggio, told the commission that there 'had never been a Bourbon party' in Palermo, and that any nostalgia for the previous government came from opposition to the present one.[45] Francesco Lanza-Scalea, another deputy, confirmed this; no Bourbon party existed in Palermo, 'although discontent is great and it is said that under the Bourbon government life was better'.[46]

That said, there had been clear evidence from at least as early as 1865 of a Bourbon/republican conspiracy in Palermo which also included some members of the Church. The involvement of Giuseppe Badia and the noted 'Internationalist' Francesco Bonafede in the revolt, and the

---

[39] 28 Nov. 1866, ACSR, Ricasoli-Bianchi, B. 2A, f. 13(i) c.

[40] 23 Oct. 1866, in ISR, b. 552, n. 4(3). The letter was also published as a pamphlet, *Lettera dello arcivescovo di Palermo indirizzata al presidente del consiglio di ministri in difesa del clero palermitano intorno gli avvenimenti di settembre 1866* ('Letter from the Archbishop of Palermo to the Prime Minister defending the Palermo clergy in relation to the events of September 1866') (Palermo, 1866).   [41] 27 May 1867, *I moti di Palermo*, 296–7.

[42] 7 October 1866, in R. Giuffrida, 'La rivolta palermitana del settembre 1866 nella diagnosi del Crispino Giuseppe Maria Puglia', *Nuovi Quaderni del Meridione*, 16 (1966), 499.   [43] 1 Nov. 1866, ISR, b. 552, n. 4(5).

[44] 3 Oct. 1866, from a government informer in Rome: Scichilone, *Documenti*, 198–9.

[45] 4 May 1867, *I moti di Palermo*, 43.   [46] 8 May 1867, ibid. 57–8.

formation of a revolutionary committee by members of the old Bourbon nobility and clergy, certainly point to the establishment of some kind of an alliance by the government's enemies to bring down the government. Militarily, the conspiracy seems to have been well-organized. The rebels had established firm links with the *squadre* and the *squadre*, in turn, had organized themselves to take specific towns and attack particular targets. There seems to be little doubt, however, that this was a marriage of mutual convenience. Those involved had little in common with each other. At his trial in 1867, Badia justified his activities in nationalist terms—pointing to the need to win the war against Austria and complete the process of national unification.[47] According to Brancato, Francesco Bonafede always maintained his distance from Badia, 'believing that his [Badia's] republicanism was a mask that he could use to give Sicily back to the Bourbons'.[48] According to the socialist, Rosario Bagnasco, those who followed Badia and the republicans 'used the propaganda of the movement and thought to profit from it for their own ends'. He concluded that 'despite the republican flag, the movement can be characterized as entirely reactionary'.[49] The aims of the *squadre* were more confused still; the bandit leader Lorenzo Minneci reportedly told an autonomist, 'If you don't like the word "Republic", let's get rid of it—you are an autonomist, I support the Bourbons—the distance between us is not great.'[50] A bandit leader in Torretta had simpler ambitions, allegedly shouting to the crowd: *'Avanti picciotti!* Now we shall be mayors and commanders of the National Guard!'.[51]

A common opposition to the liberal government tied these disparate groups together. Although less is known about popular involvement in the revolt, anti-government sentiment seems to have motivated the crowd as well. Most commentators at the time dismissed popular participation in the revolt as the work of a disorganized mob, whose sole aim was to overthrow all established authority so as to engage in a mindless orgy of criminal violence. According to Palermo's mayor, Antonio di Rudinì, the mass of the population in Palermo was naturally

[47] 30 Jan. 1867, information sent by the procurator general to the Justice Minister, ACSR, grazia e giustizia, b. 8, f. 2.

[48] F. Brancato, 'Il Marchese di Rudinì, Francesco Bonafede e la rivolta del 1866', *Nuovi Quaderni del Meridione*, 16 (1966), 465.

[49] 30 Oct. 1866, in Giuffrida, 'Aspetti e problemi', 206–7.

[50] 3 Oct. 1866; the remark is quoted in a letter from the procurator general to the Justice Minister, ACSR, grazia e giustizia, b. 8, f. 8, n. 1.

[51] 30 Sept. 1866, MSAC, cartella 49.

corrupt and inherently predisposed to disobey the law.[52] Borsani, Palermo's procurator general, wrote to the Minister of Justice that 'in no other part of the peninsula are there so many anarchic elements as there are in Sicily'.[53] In the opinion of the Sicilian senator, Prince Torremazza, the poor of Palermo were quite beyond government control: 'the notorious rabble of this city', he told Ricasoli on 23 November, 'ready for any opportunity to loot, answers only to the call of criminals.'[54] Contemporary studies of the revolt also described in meticulous detail the criminal behaviour of the mob during the week-long revolt.[55]

In fact, popular involvement with the revolt was far from being without direction. If the cries of 'Long live the republic!' and 'Long live religion!' are anything to go by, the crowd understood only too well the various messages of the leadership. Although no-one tried by the military courts described himself as a revolutionary, there is evidence of popular support for the republicans in some of the cases. One group attempted to steal papers relating to Badia's trial.[56] Some insurgents wore red shirts and caps, indicating a conscious link with Garibaldi and the experience of 1860. The soldier and ex-*garibaldino* Pietro Leone was seen wearing a red cap during the revolt, as was a gang seen in the *convento santo agostino* and a gang seen near Porta Carini. Nunzio Barone, who took part in the attack on (and looting of) the *carabinieri* barracks at Olivella, was also seen wearing a red cap and shirt.[57] There was evidence of anti-government sentiment everywhere—in the trial records, in eye-witness statements, and in the *carabinieri* reports. Pietro Terravecchia, an ex-pupil of the military college, was heard during the revolt shouting obscene slogans against the government and the king: 'from now on the squads are in control and Vittorio Emanuele will take it up the arse'.[58] Michele lo Bue, arrested in Lercara in November, had shouted at the *carabinieri*: 'we should cut the heads off these cops (*'sbirri*) and send them as a present to the chief cop (*capo sbirazzo*), repulsive Vittorio Emanuele the polenta-eater and robber of Sicily

---

[52] 11 Oct. 1866, in G. Pagano, *Avvenimenti del 1866: sette giorni d'insurrezione a Palermo* (Palermo, 1867), 243–6.

[53] 18 Nov., ACSR, grazia e giustizia, b. 8, f. 8, n. 1.

[54] ACSR, grazia e giustizia, b. 7, f. 'lettere del senatore Torremazza sui moti di Palermo'.

[55] For example, Ciotti, *Cenni storici sugli avvenimenti di settembre 1866*, Pagano, *Avvenimenti del 1866*, and Maggiorani, *Il sollevamento delle plebe di Palermo*.

[56] ACSR, tribunali militari, b. 4; Oddo, 'Le sentenze', 312–13.

[57] ACSR, tribunali militari, b. 4.   [58] Ibid.

(*mangia polenta, schifoso e ladro della Sicilia*)'.[59] It is also significant that, in the main, only government buildings and government representatives were attacked, and that looting and destruction of property was confined to government property and government records. As Brancato points out, the only two private houses that were attacked in Palermo during the revolt were those of the mayor, Antonio di Rudinì, and of the democrat leader, Francesco Perroni Paladini, both of whom had taken a very public stance against the rebels.[60]

Moreover, very few of those who came before the military courts conformed to the criminal stereotypes put forward by di Rudinì and others.[61] First, the court records indicate that the vast majority of those tried were workers of fixed abode and occupation. Many were married with children; indeed, the average age of those convicted was 33. Of the 297 detainees brought before the courts only one, Ruggiero Oneto from Palermo, was listed as a vagrant (*vagabondo*), and he was later released. Although a number of women, arrested for looting along with their husbands, were listed as having no profession (*senza professione*), only one man, Giuseppe Cuccia from Piana dei Greci, was listed as *senza professione*, and he too was released.[62] Almost all of the 124 individuals convicted by the military courts were engaged in trade, the provision of services, or were artisans. Among the occupations listed were tavern-keepers, traders, carters, porters, waiters, greengrocers, bakers, butchers, and barbers. Cabinet-makers, carpenters, tailors, tanners, blacksmiths, ropemakers, and stonemasons also figured prominently among the list of those sentenced. None of these occupations identify the defendants as coming from the 'dangerous classes' of criminals and dispossessed. The majority of those arrested or convicted did not have previous criminal records. The only defendant in the 1866 trials with a clearly identifiable criminal past was a soldier, Luciano Coniglio, who had deserted his regiment in 1863 and become a bandit. He was also the only bandit or 'outlaw' who came before the courts.[63]

The path-breaking work of Rudé and Thompson on the composition of the revolutionary crowd shows that most riots and rebellions in

---

[59]   19 Nov. 1866, MSAC, cartella 49.

[60]   F. Brancato, 'Origini e carattere della rivolta palermitana', 187.

[61]   For a more detailed discussion of the nature of the 'crowd' in 1866, see L. Riall, 'Legge marziale a Palermo: protesta popolare e rivolta nel 1866', *Meridiana*, 24 (1995), 67–79.

[62]   ACSR, tribunali militari, b. 2 and b. 3. See also Giuffrida, 'Aspetti e problemi', 214, and Oddo, 'Le sentenze', 317–18, 324.   [63] Ibid. 299–301.

eighteenth- and nineteenth-century Europe were led by apparently
respectable artisans, rather than the 'idle' or criminal poor.[64] The
Palermo revolt of 1866 seems to have been no exception; indeed,
Palermo's artisans had been at the heart of the revolutions of 1820,
1848, and 1860 against the Bourbons. Like their counterparts in many
other European cities, the rebelliousness of Palermo's artisans seems
linked to the onset of industrialization and the erosion of guild structures, both of which threatened their livelihood.[65] In the case of
Palermo, moreover, the loss of the administrative capital in 1815 and
the subsequent crisis of the nobility had led to a rapid fall in demand for
luxury goods, which Palermo's artisans had hitherto produced in abun-
dant quantities. Government policy since unification also appeared to
have made the economic position of artisans dramatically worse. Unification had brought free trade to damage Palermo's economy, along
with administrative centralization to deprive the city of more of its
administrative functions (a large number of government employees
were dismissed in 1866).[66] Since 1863, furthermore, the lives of Palermo's poor had been disrupted by military conscription and the campaigns to enforce it and, worst of all, by the frightening levels of
mortality during the severe cholera epidemic of 1865. There was a
widespread feeling that Sicily had been discriminated against in terms
of taxation and public expenditure. For instance, the decision to levy
taxes on new buildings had led to a crisis in Palermo's construction
industry.[67] A colleague of Crispi, Michele Russo, told him that the
population in Palermo had rebelled against intolerable conditions:

> there is no trade, no public expenditure, no roads, no communication with the
> rest of Sicily . . . taxes on tobacco, taxes on salt, taxes on personal property,
> stamp duties . . . provincial and communal taxes use up all of Sicily's produc-
> tive forces. For the unfortunate Sicilians there is only hunger and poverty.[68]

---

[64] G. Rudé, *The Crowd in the French Revolution* (Oxford, 1959) and *The Crowd in
History: A Study of Popular Disturbances in France and England 1730–1848* (London, 1964;
2nd edn., 1981), E. P. Thompson, 'The Moral Economy of the English Crowd in the
Eighteenth Century' and 'The Moral Economy Reviewed', both in *Customs in Common*
(London, 1991).

[65] For a useful comparison, see T. S. Hamerow, *Restoration, Revolution, Reaction:
Economics and Politics in Germany, 1815–1871* (Princeton, 1958); also Riall, 'Legge marziale a Palermo', 71–5.

[66] Emerico Amari to the parliamentary commission of inquiry, *I moti di Palermo*, 8 May
1867, 49.

[67] Statement by Antonio Emanuele to the parliamentary commission of inquiry, ibid.
30 May 1867, 340–1.   [68] 21 Oct. 1866, in Giuffrida, 'Aspetti e problemi', 198–201.

The poor harvest of 1866 and a sharp increase in grain prices between 1865 and 1866 also did little to calm popular agitation.[69]

The impact of this economic crisis was still further increased by the government's suppression of religious orders, a measure which became law in July 1866. The law destroyed a vital source of charitable relief and employment for the poor. According to one estimate, over 2,000 families in Palermo lived off Church charity; large numbers of workmen were also employed to look after Church property.[70] Vito d'Ondes Reggio told the parliamentary commission that the abolition of religious orders was one of the major causes of unrest throughout Sicily; hitherto, religious orders had offered work and were 'a source of gain for a vast proportion of citizens, particularly artisans'.[71] The prevailing view was summed up by Crispi when questioned by the parliamentary commission of inquiry: 'A way must be found,' he told the commission, 'to improve the economy of Palermo. Otherwise every other effort will be in vain.'[72]

There was a general feeling that, in the six years since unification, the government had failed to revitalize the economy, enforce the law, or uphold its own authority. Its low prestige and isolation were noticed even by the normally insensitive Cadorna, who wrote to Prime Minister Ricasoli that it had been a mistake deliberately to distance the autonomist party from government.[73] The government's handling of law and order had caused particular resentment. Di Rudinì told Ricasoli that, in despair, property owners had taken to hiring bandits so as to guarantee themselves a measure of security.[74] At the same time, the government itself was perceived to have little respect for the law. Emerico Amari told the parliamentary commission of inquiry that 'towards Sicily the government uses only those methods which are more or less arbitrary, illegal and invariably exceptional'.[75] For the deputy d'Ondes Reggio, the government's policing methods, in particular political interference in judicial matters, gave 'perhaps more offence than anything else'.[76] A sense of general alienation was summed up by the prefect of Trapani, who wrote to Ricasoli that 'the authorities for the most part have either been completely ignorant of or poorly versed in our customs, prejudices and local traditions, they have been easily led into error and, unwit-

---

[69] See the figures in R. Romanelli, *L'Italia liberale* (Bologna, 1979), 450–1.

[70] These figures were given by Emerico Amari to the parliamentary commission of inquiry on 8 May 1867, *I moti di Palermo*, 49.   [71] Ibid. 7 May 1867, 41–2.

[72] Ibid. 14 May 1867, 107.   [73] 30 Oct. 1866, in Scichilone, *Documenti*, 205.

[74] 11 Oct. 1866, in Pagano, *Avvenimenti del 1866*, 248–9.

[75] *I moti di Palermo*, 8 May 1867, 49.   [76] Ibid. 7 May 1867, 42.

tingly, increase disorder and general unrest'.[77] The noted autonomist, Tommaso Crudeli-Corrado, was even more explicit, speaking of 'a deep hatred against this foreign government and, what is worse, a disrespect even deeper than hatred'. The government, he went on, was described as 'a government of thieves, without force and without energy'.[78]

For an administration which, from the time of its organization in 1860–1, had conducted its policy towards Sicily on the basis of good and strong government, the accusation of bad government was a supreme irony.[79] Unfortunately, in the political backlash following the revolt, neither the military nor the civilian administration seemed prepared to face up to the implications of this judgement. Both Cadorna's insistence that Rome was behind the revolt and di Rudinì's blaming the Palermo 'mob' for its innate violence can be seen as ways of avoiding this accusation. Even in the short term, however, the failure to address the political and popular discontent underlying the Palermo revolt virtually guaranteed that repression in its aftermath would be a failure.

II

During 1866, long before the Palermo revolt, the Italian government had suffered a series of setbacks. In the spring, a currency crisis had contributed to a sharp economic downturn which affected the whole of Italy. The war against Austria for control of the Veneto was a disaster; both the Italian army and (particularly) the navy suffered humiliating defeats. Thus, the acquisition of Venetia from Austria, envisaged as a moment of national unity and celebration, was marred by bitter recriminations. Finally, the 1865 law on religious property which caused such problems in Palermo was also unpopular elsewhere, badly damaging the internal unity of the Right.[80] Moreover, that the events of September 1866 happened at all showed the extent of policy 'drift'. Although there were plenty of warning signs during 1866 of the gathering storm, central government in Florence had persistently ignored the reports from Palermo.[81] Needing reinforcements for the war in

---

[77] ACSR, Ricasoli-Bianchi, b. 2B, f. 17(5), 1.

[78] 14–19 Nov. 1866, published in *Il Giornale di Sicilia*, 17 July 1910.

[79] Riall, 'Legge marziale a Palermo', 78–9.

[80] G. Candeloro, *Storia dell'Italia moderna*, v: *la costruzione dello stato unitario* (Milan, 1968), 287–319, 324–9.

[81] In a series of letters between 17 Apr. and 31 Aug. 1866 to the Minister of the Interior, the prefect of Palermo had alerted the central government to the activities of bandits. During the summer he had sought to control the disturbances through a system of what he called 'flying columns'. Scichilone, *Documenti*, 170–84.

Northern Italy against Austria, the Ministry of War had actually withdrawn almost all its troops from the province. By the time of the revolt
in September, there were only around 900 soldiers stationed in Palermo.

When he declared a state of siege in Palermo in September 1866,
Cadorna would have been all too aware of the prevailing atmosphere of
crisis. In some respects, his decision to declare a state of siege and, in
particular, the use of military courts to try the insurgents reflected
established government policy in moments of crisis. Since at least as
early as 1862, members of the government had been prepared to ignore
both the constitutional independence of the judiciary and the constitutional rights of Italian citizens when its authority was challenged. In one
important respect the repression of the Palermo revolt also marked a
new, and harsher, departure in government policy towards Sicily. The
state of siege was declared after the revolt had been defeated. Moreover,
it was given retroactive powers stretching back to 1865 so as to enable
the government to try Badia under martial law.

Yet if the imposition of a state of siege in 1866 was a declaration of
the government's determination to enforce its authority in defiance of
the constitution, it was also an indication of its inability to do so. For
instance, the initiative behind the declaration of the siege in 1866 did
not come from central government at all: it was, in fact, the procurator
general Giovanni Interdonato and the local judicial administrators who
encouraged the military and, specifically, Cadorna to make use of
military courts. On 26 September Interdonato's office wrote to Cadorna
that the use of ordinary judicial procedures against the insurgents
would be inefficient and prone to delays, and would therefore lack
the 'moral force' necessary to re-establish government authority.[82]
The procurator general was also involved in the decision to try Badia
using martial law.[83] In a separate letter to the Minister of Justice,
Interdonato emphasized the importance of harsh measures. The need
to make an example of the rebels—'so as to create a healthy terror
among the masses'—as well as the sheer number of defendants pre-
cluded, in his view, the use of ordinary courts.[84]

The declaration of a state of siege also reflected a more widespread
concern about the reliability and loyalty of judicial personnel and of
government personnel more generally. In the course of inquiries

---

[82] From the *avvocato generale* to the procurator general, ASP, pref. gab., b. 8, f. 4, cat. 2
bis.
[83] In the same letter of 26 Sept. See also his letter of 15 Oct. to Cadorna, ibid. prat. v.
[84] 3 Oct. 1866, ACSR, grazia e giustizia, b. 8, f. 8, sf. 1.

following the revolt, the judicial personnel were found to be indolent, prone to absenteeism, and frequently corrupt.[85] The prefect of Trapani later wrote to Ricasoli detailing the delays and unreliability which had always undermined the trial process in his province.[86] More general problems with the whole of the local administration affected the decision to rely on the military. Ricasoli himself accused the administration in Palermo of incompetence, asking 'how it could be possible . . . that such and so many elements of disorder should be found in the island without provoking the slightest concern on the part of the authorities'.[87] Damaging rumours circulated in governing circles that Palermo's chief of police, the *questore* Felice Pinna, had known that bandits were about to invade the city and had done nothing to stop them. According to di Rudinì, neither Pinna nor the commander of the *carabinieri* in Palermo had notified the proper authorities about the obvious danger from armed gangs in the area. By letting the rebellion come out into the open, it was said that Pinna hoped to force a final 'showdown' against the government's opponents, and capture all those who had managed to evade arrest.[88]

Cadorna also wrote a series of letters to Ricasoli which expressed his conviction that local personnel could not be relied upon to restore order. The employees who had fled their posts during the disturbances gave, in his view, 'a rather unedifying example of disloyalty to the government' and should be dismissed.[89] Public security, he later wrote, could only be improved if diligent and loyal personnel could be found. Current high-ranking officials, including some prefects, were not, according to Cadorna, capable of fulfilling their duties to the government.[90] In other words, in declaring a state of siege Cadorna was seeking to exclude an unreliable local government from the task of restoring order in Palermo. Despite Cadorna's official worries about the 'shady' activities of priests in the province, it was the government's ability to deal adequately with them which seems to have caused him most concern.

The same correspondence between Cadorna and Ricasoli also

[85] See the report from the procurator general to officials on 15 Nov. 1866 and the report of 22 Jan. 1867, both in ACSR, grazia e giustizia, b. 7 (moved to b. 96), f. 525.

[86] Dec. 1866, ACSR, Ricasoli-Bianchi, b. 2B, f. 17(5), 1.

[87] 27 Sept. 1866, Scichilone, *Documenti*, 194–5.

[88] To Ricasoli, 22 Sept. 1866, in Brancato, 'Il Marchese di Rudinì, Francesco Bonafede', 481. These rumours were also used by members of the opposition. See Rosario Bagnasco's letter to Crispi, 30 Oct. 1866, in Giuffrida, 'Aspetti e problemi', 207.

[89] 2 Oct. 1866, in Scichilone, *Documenti*, 197.   [90] 30 Oct. 1866, ibid.

indicates that the direction of policy between September and November was largely decided by the military, in co-operation with the local judicial authorities. In his preliminary instructions to Cadorna on 18 September, Ricasoli had specifically advised against the declaration of a state of siege.[91] On 3 October he rebuked Cadorna for having disobeyed his instructions and, the next day, he ordered Cadorna to lift the siege. Ricasoli only revoked this order when Cadorna threatened to resign.[92] Thus, the decision to declare a state of siege in the city and province of Palermo was not taken by Ricasoli at all, but by Cadorna; and, in so doing, Cadorna chose to disregard central government instructions. Far from being a simple attempt by the central government to subjugate independent institutions to its will, the state of siege was implemented against the Prime Minister's wishes, and its use led to conflict between central government and the military administration, a conflict which the military administration won.

Cadorna had been to Sicily before, in 1861, and had formed strong opinions about the importance of using military force to quell unrest in the island. His experiences fighting brigandage in the Abruzzi seemed to have hardened his attitudes still further. Ricasoli, by contrast, was concerned to avoid too much drastic action which might lead to political controversy. He told Cadorna that he already had adequate powers to deal with the disturbances, and that the use of the siege was possibly illegal and definitely controversial. It was, in Ricasoli's view, 'contrary to the dignity of the Italian government' and 'not permitted by the law' to declare a state of siege against a band of criminals who had already been defeated.[93] Ricasoli was also apparently under pressure from parliament to lift the siege; when he finally did so in November it was without consulting Cadorna.[94]

Ricasoli also expressed a series of other reservations about the state of siege. He was clearly disturbed by the constitutional implications of using military courts to try civilians. On 30 September he wrote to Borgatti, the Minister of Justice, regarding the upcoming trials, and

---

[91] ACSR, interno, b. 8, f. 1, n. 2.

[92] Ricasoli's letters of 3 and 4 Oct., Cadorna's telegram of 4 Oct., and Ricasoli's replies of 5 and 6 Oct. are in R. Cadorna, *Il generale Raffaele Cadorna nel Risorgimento italiano*, ed. L. Cadorna (Rome, 1922), 283–6.

[93] Ricasoli to Cadorna, 18 Sept. 1866, ACSR, interno, b. 8, f. 1, n. 2, and 3 Oct., *il generale Raffaele Cadorna*, 283–4.

[94] Cadorna expressed his fury to Ricasoli in a letter of 13 Nov. 1866: ibid. 301–3. On parliament's concern about the state of siege, see the letter of 18 Nov. from the Minister of Justice, Borgatti, to the procurator general in Palermo, ISR, b. 552, n. 4 (9).

stressed that no special consideration should be shown to members of the nobility. The government, he told Borgatti, expected the authorities in Palermo to show that 'everybody is equal under the law, and nobody is entitled to special consideration'. Interestingly, Borgatti agreed, and sent instructions to this effect off to Palermo on the following day.[95] Ricasoli also instructed Cadorna that no political pressure was to be put on the courts. Ricasoli was particularly anxious that no move be made to anticipate the convictions of the leaders of the insurgency. He also believed that only those accused of serious crimes should be tried by the military courts.[96]

It was also Ricasoli who insisted that the military administration in Palermo be prepared to exercise clemency in the trial of the insurgents. He strongly resisted Cadorna's suggestion that the death penalty be used more frequently. Despite Cadorna's remonstrances, he was adamant that central government be consulted before a death sentence against any civilian was carried out.[97] 'I have no faith in bloodshed,' Ricasoli wrote in response to private demands for firmer action and a greater use of capital punishment, 'and I have even less faith that bloodshed will reassure those in Palermo who demand bloodshed.'[98] It is striking that, of the ten death sentences pronounced by the military courts, only those of the three soldiers (who could be executed by the military without consulting the government) were carried out. The seven civilians condemned to death all had their sentences suspended by the government and, later, commuted to hard labour.[99]

Unfortunately, this conflict between Ricasoli and Cadorna over the handling of the siege had mostly negative consequences. The government appeared to many influential citizens as indecisive and reluctant to assist a return to order. Cadorna wrote to Ricasoli on 27 October that public opinion was so disturbed by the failure to pass capital sentences on the insurgents that people had begun to flee the city, fearing renewed disturbances.[100] Although Cadorna, for obvious reasons, may have been exaggerating, his views were broadly confirmed by a more respected commentator, Tommaso Crudeli-Corrado. Crudeli-Corrado argued that

[95] Both letters are in ACSR, grazia e giustizia, b.7 (b.96), f. 525.

[96] 23 Oct. 1866, *Carteggi di Bettino Ricasoli*, eds. S. Camerani and G. Arfé (24 vols.; Bologna and Rome, 1939–92), xxiv. 165–6.

[97] See Ricasoli's letters of 8 Oct. (*Il generale Raffaele Cadorna*, 288), 28 Oct. (ASP, pref. gab., b.9, cat. 2), and 3 Nov. (ibid. b.8, cat. 2 bis).

[98] 24 Nov. 1866, in *Il Giornale di Sicilia*, 16–17 July 1910.

[99] See Ricasoli letters to Cadorna, 6 and 23 Oct. 1866, *Carteggi di Bettino Ricasoli*, xxiv. 56, 166.   [100] *Il generale Raffaele Cadorna*, 291.

Ricasoli's attempts to restrain the use of emergency powers were being taken as evidence of undue concern with his own popularity and of a lack of commitment to upholding law and order in Sicily.[101]

The inability of Ricasoli either to control the military administration in Palermo or to unite public opinion behind the government indicates what little control central government had over local affairs. Furthermore, a closer look at the state of siege reveals that it, too, was less than entirely successful. If the relatively small number of convictions (42 per cent) is anything to go by, those in charge of the military courts were equally unconvinced by the use of martial law against civilians. On a number of occasions the courts adopted a very flexible attitude towards defendants. Quite a large number were released on the basis that 'public rumours' were not sufficient proof to obtain a conviction. In the cases of Mario Barcellona and Augusto Lazzaro,[102] tried by the first military court, and of Augusto Lauriano,[103] tried by the second, such 'rumours' were discounted despite statements by the *carabinieri* that they had been shot at by the defendants. Nor was possession of objects looted during the revolt always taken as sufficient proof of guilt.[104] A large number of those found with property stolen during the murderous assault on the *carabinieri* barracks in Misilmeri were also let off.[105]

None of the defendants arrested for incitement to riot (other than the Lo Bue brothers, responsible for the atrocities in Misilmeri), or for what were termed 'insidious proclamations', were convicted. Don Giulio Castiglia had announced the revolt a week before it took place, and had told assembled friends that such an attack against an 'intolerable government' was bound to succeed; he was found not guilty, however, by the second military court, which concluded that his behaviour, though reprehensible, did not constitute a criminal act. Vito Mattaliano, who was arrested when found in possession of 'writings offensive to the sacred person of the king', was released by the third military court, which could find no evidence that he intended to circulate these writings.[106]

On the whole the military courts seemed surprisingly willing to give defendants the benefit of the doubt. In the absence of evidence to the

---

[101] In a letter to a friend, Teresa Bartolomei, 14–19 Nov. 1866, in *Il Giornale di Sicilia*, 17–18 July 1910.   [102] Oddo, 'Le sentenze', 303–4; ACSR, tribunali militari, b. 2.   [103] Ibid.

[104] See the case of Pietro Torod in Oddo, 'Le sentenze', 307–8, and ACSR, tribunali militari, b. 4.   [105] Oddo, 'Le sentenze', 316–17; ACSR, tribunali militari, b. 3.   [106] Both cases ibid. b. 2.

contrary, those who claimed they had been forced to take part were usually released. Rosario Nuccio told the second military court that he had been obliged to join an armed gang 'in order to avoid harm to himself and to his family', and the court released him. Francesco Castellana, a butcher of 'corrupt reputation' who had been seen on 17 September armed with a field gun, and who was arrested for involvement with an armed gang, was found not guilty of this offence. The court believed his claim that he had armed himself in order to protect his cattle, and that his only involvement with an armed gang was through his father. The same court also believed Agostino Rotolo's claim that he had armed himself with a revolver solely for the purpose of self-defence.[107] Many others were let off on the basis of their youth, gender, or lack of a criminal past.

For all the powers at their disposal, in other words, the military courts seem to have been more concerned to exercise clemency and uphold justice than to secure convictions. Perhaps unsurprisingly, and despite Ricasoli's instructions, there is evidence that educated and/or influential figures tended to benefit most from the flexible approach of the courts. What is even more striking is that, on the whole, the trial and sentencing of the insurgents by the military courts lacked a precise political direction. It is also obvious that the idea hatched by Interdonato of restoring public order through exemplary trials was not a great success. Courts which acquitted over 50 per cent of defendants— even if they did so quickly—were hardly likely to create a 'healthy terror among the masses', as Interdonato had hoped.

Problems with the trials also reflected problems with Cadorna's public-order operations in the Palermo interior. Like his predecessors in 1862–3 and 1865, Cadorna never managed to win the support of the local population for his campaign. Large numbers of soldiers were required to disband and disarm the National Guards, which had been disloyal during the revolt.[108] A system of offering rewards in return for information came to nothing, since most people lacked confidence in the government's ability to make arrests. Even those who did come forward were sometimes too frightened to sign their names for receipt of the money.[109] The sub-prefect of Cefalù and the mayor of Partinico both wrote to Palermo to protest at the general order to disarm. In

---

[107] Ibid. b. 4.   [108] See the reports in ASP, pref. archivio, b. 385.
[109] Commander Longoni to Cadorna, 13 Nov. 1866, ASP, pref. gab., b. 8, cat. 2, n. 55; Cadorna to the prefecture of Palermo, 15 Nov., ibid. b. 9, cat. 9, f. 7.

present conditions, the sub-prefect of Cefalù wrote, nobody could be expected to go into the countryside unarmed.[110] Only 'honest citizens', according to the mayor of Partinico, would come forward to consign their firearms; criminals had long since concealed all of theirs.[111]

The military operations did little to restore the government's tarnished public image. There were numerous complaints about the conduct of the troops. They behaved, according to one observer, 'like wild animals' in their pursuit of reactionary priests.[112] According to another, the divisional commander Longoni was 'a cretin dressed up as a general'.[113] Cadorna's public accusations against the Church offended many; Archbishop Naselli's scathing public rebuttal of Cadorna also undermined the government's prestige. Finally, and perhaps most disastrously, Cadorna's soldiers brought another cholera epidemic into the countryside. Referring to the 'foolish superstition' that the epidemic was deliberate government policy, Cadorna noted as early as 2 October that it was assisting the government's enemies.[114] The rapid spread of cholera (its most famous victim was Giovanni Interdonato) turned to fear and hostility any welcome which the population as a whole might otherwise have given to the troops. Moreover, recent estimates put the numbers who died from cholera in 1866 and in further epidemics in 1867 at 61,380, a far higher percentage of the population than elsewhere in Italy.[115]

The failure of Cadorna's operations was noted even by Ricasoli, who wrote to Cadorna at the beginning of November asking how it was that so many fugitives continued to evade arrest.[116] The inability of the military to restore order caused considerable public concern. As early as mid-October, a colleague of Crispi's complained that 'we are back exactly where we started; notwithstanding all the effects of the siege, the bands are in control of the countryside'.[117] At around the same time the *carabinieri* in Partinico increased the size of their patrols to avoid being outnumbered by bandits.[118] Towards the end of October renewed disturbances were reported in Palermo, Cefalù, and Monreale.[119] In November the French vice-consul in Licata

---

[110] 5 Oct. 1865, ASP, pref. gab., b.9, cat. 10, f. 15 bis.   [111] 7 Oct. 1866, ibid.

[112] Domenico Peranni to Crispi, in Giuffrida, 'Aspetti e problemi', 191–8.

[113] 16 Oct. 1866, in *Il Giornale di Sicilia*, 16–17 July 1910.

[114] Scichilone, *Documenti*, 197.

[115] A. L. Forti Messina, 'L'Italia dell'Ottocento di fronte al colera', *Storia d'Italia, annali*, vii: *malattie e medicina* (Turin, 1984), 461.

[116] 3 Nov. 1866, ASP, pref. gab., b.8, cat. 2 bis.

[117] Giuffrida, 'Aspetti e problemi', 187–8.   [118] 22 Oct. 1866, MSAC, cartella 49.

[119] 25, 26, and 27 Oct. 1866, ibid.

(Girgenti) wrote that 'brigandage, far from declining since the arrival of General Cadorna and his troops, becomes bolder and more daring every day'.[120] According to the sub-prefect of Termini, no government official could leave the town without an escort, and landowners were powerless to prevent substantial robberies from taking place on their estates. He lamented that 'the hopes which were raised were as usual all in vain and also demonstrate that all the measures adopted up until now were useless'.[121]

A major source of discontent was the arrest *en masse* of those who had simply joined the revolt, while its leaders disappeared into thin air. According to *carabinieri* records, the military made some 800 arrests in October and a further 150 in November.[122] Yet a letter to Crispi complained that while hundreds of people 'of no importance whatsoever' were being arrested, 'the real murderous leaders' of the revolt were going free.[123] Furthermore, the military administration in Palermo failed to proceed rapidly with the trial of the leaders already in custody, most notably Giuseppe Badia and his associates. Although Cadorna had taken the controversial decision to try Badia under martial law, preparations for his trial did not even start until January 1867, long after the state of siege had ended. The trial itself was a huge affair, involving some seventy-eight defendants, of whom only forty-four were in custody, and with charges dating back to 1865.[124] Perhaps as a result of the scale of the trial, the investigating magistrates encountered endless difficulties in collecting evidence and organizing witnesses. It was eventually decided to move the proceedings away from Palermo to Messina, and to transfer the defendants to a more secure prison on the island of Lipari.[125] Badia was found guilty on 28 March 1867, but was given leave to appeal against his sentence.[126] Preparations for the trials of professional criminals involved in the revolt—the gang of Lorenzo Mineci and the gang of Corretta—were similarly delayed. A sentence against the Mineci band was not pronounced until September

---

[120] 20 Nov. 1866, in Brancato, 'Origini e carattere', 204–5.
[121] This report is included in Cadorna's of 13 Nov. 1866, ASP, pref. gab., b. 8, cat. 2, f. 20.   [122] MSAC, cartella 49.
[123] In Giuffrida, 'Aspetti e problemi', 191–8.
[124] See the 'allegato' to a letter of 30 Jan. 1867 from the procurator general to the Minister of Justice, ACSR, grazia e giustizia, b. 8, f. 2.
[125] The procurator general (?) to the Minister of Justice, 23 March 1867, ACSR, interno, b. 8, f. 1, n. 245 and 25 March, ibid. n. 190.
[126] The procurator general to the Minister of Justice, 11 Apr. 1867, ibid. grazia e giustizia, b. 8, f. 2.

1867;[127] in the same month Badia's deputy in September 1866, Francesco Bonafede, was condemned in his absence for his part in the revolt, as the authorities had been unable to arrest him.[128]

Thus, one of the principal justifications for the declaration of a state of siege in 1866—to speed up and control the trials of the insurgents—was completely ineffective in the trials and sentencing of the leaders of the revolt. The use of military courts also failed to remove other delays in the judicial system. After the end of the siege, the numbers in prison awaiting trial remained at alarmingly high levels. In May 1867, the total number in prison was put at 2,467, of whom only 221 were convicted men and 212 of whom were in the process of being tried. All of the rest were still awaiting trial.[129] Members of the parliamentary commission of inquiry found that the prisons in Palermo were filled with 'hundreds of detainees who had no idea why they had been imprisoned, [and] who had no idea under whose authority they had been imprisoned'.[130] The use of military courts, in other words, failed to offer any solution to the inability of either the judicial or the penal system to deal with large numbers of arrests.

III

The Palermo revolt was an anti-government insurgency led by republicans in alliance with Bourbon supporters and professional criminals. It saw the complete collapse of government authority and, to an almost equal extent, of the entire machinery of government. In Palermo and other towns in the province, local officials abandoned their posts together with any semblance of loyalty to the government. In extreme cases, for instance in Lercara, officials themselves joined in and sometimes led the disturbances. The National Guard often switched their allegiance to the side of the rebels. Moreover, the welcome given by the Palermo masses to the invading gangs, and the attacks on government offices and representatives, provided an overwhelming indication of the government's unpopularity.

If anything, Cadorna's repression of the revolt, like Govone's and

---

[127] The procurator general to the procurator general of the court of cassation, 12 May 1868, ibid.

[128] Bonafede fled to Trieste in 1868, returned to Sicily in 1872, and lived there until his death in 1905. Brancato, 'Il Marchese di Rudinì, Francesco Bonafede', 472–3.

[129] *I moti di Palermo*, 344.

[130] The procurator general to the Minister of Justice, 1 June 1867, ACSR, grazia e giustizia, b. 8, f. 8, sf. 1.

Medici's campaigns before him, did further damage to the government's prestige and moral standing. Cadorna's policy in 1866 relied on a military solution to what was essentially a political problem. Distrusting those around him in Palermo, and correctly identifying the lack of support for the government in governing circles, he excluded local officials from any part in the formulation of policy. He deployed troops to reinforce and replace the local police and attempted to use swift and retributive justice against the rebels. However, his manner of proceeding was such that he increased the Palermo's administration's isolation and reinforced opposition to its policies.

The use of military operations to capture insurgents and the use of military courts to try them was ineffective. The military was unable to capture the insurgents, and the military courts failed to proceed rapidly and decisively against those already in custody. The penal system proved inadequate in the face of the demands placed upon it. Furthermore, the combination of Cadorna's callous disregard of Sicilian sensibilities and Ricasoli's fumbling attempts to respect the constitutional rights of the insurgents impressed nobody. Central government policy was not implemented by Cadorna, who disobeyed instructions in declaring a state of siege; while Ricasoli's commitment to liberal 'self-government' merely hindered the military as it attempted to establish public order in Palermo.

Both the Palermo revolt and the repression in its aftermath indicated that the policy of good government had been a failure. The implications of the revolt were, in reality, deeply embarrassing to the government. According to the official explanation of the revolt, an imprisoned republican, together with a few retrograde aristocrats, priests, and bandits, had managed—with the help of a 'mob'—to hold a major Italian city captive for an entire week in defiance of government authority. Within governing circles, there was little agreement about how to respond to this crisis. The policy pursued by Cadorna failed to achieve any of its aims, and Ricasoli was unable to enforce his more conciliatory objectives. The conduct of the state of siege in 1866, so notorious, in retrospect, for the use of martial law against civilians, in reality exemplified the inability of the centre to direct local affairs.

Conclusion

In January 1867 an amnesty was offered to political prisoners from the Palermo revolt. Yet the government's long-standing decision to deny political legitimacy to its opponents in Sicily undermined the effect of the amnesty. Since almost everyone involved in the insurrection had been treated as a criminal, few convicted men or detainees were released from prison. The only immediate beneficiaries were the members of the revolutionary committee formed in the first days of the revolt; prominent Bourbons who had all already been provisionally released by the authorities.[1] Thus the amnesty, which was introduced at the insistence of di Rudinì (prefect of Palermo since December 1866) in order to speed up the judicial process and to gain moral support for the government, had very little positive impact.[2] It could not relieve pressure on either the judicial or the penal system; nor could it give any impression of impartiality, clemency, or a desire to conciliate. It also failed to reassure those already concerned about the government's apparent inconsistency and its lack of commitment to maintaining law and order in the Palermo area. Even the procurator general questioned di Rudinì's motives, arguing that the amnesty would encourage honest citizens to make private deals with criminals.[3]

The appointment of di Rudinì, a Sicilian and prominent member of the Palermo nobility, seemed to indicate some official recognition that the government's problems were being caused by the lack of support for its policies. A parliamentary inquiry, set up to investigate the 'moral and economic' causes of the revolt, also reflected a willingness to consult local opinion and reach an agreement with the Palermo élite. However, although the interviews conducted in Palermo during 1867 were a

---

[1] A number of those arrested in connection with the disturbances in Palermo in May 1865 were also released. See the letter from the procurator general to the Minister of Justice, 9 Feb. 1867, ACSR, grazia e giustizia, b. 8, f. 8, sf. 1.

[2] On di Rudinì's 'conditions' upon becoming prefect, see Cadorna to Ricasoli, 24 Nov. 1866, G. Scichilone, *Documenti sulle condizione della Sicilia dal 1860 al 1870* (Rome, 1952), 206–7.

[3] 13 Dec. 1866, Jan. 1867, ACSR, grazia e giustizia, b. 7 (b. 96), f. 525 and b. 8, f. 2.

remarkable record of the state of anti-government sentiment at this time, the government did little to act upon its findings. The final report of the commission, presented to parliament in April 1867, glossed over many of the grievances and only stressed the city's economic problems. Although the report made a number of important proposals for improving the economy, proposals which were enthusiastically endorsed by many members of the Right, it failed to address or offer any solution to the chronic difficulties of implementing them.

Di Rudinì went on to enjoy an immensely successful career as a national politician, becoming Prime Minister in 1891–2 and again between 1896 and 1898. His brief period as prefect of Palermo was less glorious. He ordered further military operations in early 1867. Led this time by General Medici, their aim was to arrest large numbers of wanted men, including draft-evaders, military deserters, those who had contravened their 'admonishment', and anyone who 'gave the appearance' of being part of an armed gang.[4] In practice, these measures—which continued off and on throughout 1867—met with little success. Many famous bandits, targeted for their involvement in the disturbances, continued to evade arrest. The conduct of the military was once again the subject of discussion in newspapers and among members of the civilian administration; there were frequent allegations of brutality and illegality on the part of government forces.[5] Renewed disturbances in Palermo during April 1867 indicated that the government's control of the city and province remained fragile.

When, in early 1868, General Medici took over as prefect of Palermo while still the military commander of Sicily, the contradictions of a policy which criminalized opposition to the government and enforced liberal government through military repression became even more apparent. Medici continued using the military against the renewed threat from republicans and (increasingly) anarchists. At the same time, Medici's chief of police, Giuseppe Albanese, resumed the Bourbon practice of colluding with criminals as a means of maintaining public order. Thus, the Sicilian mafia emerged in the 1870s as political 'middlemen', and as a permanent shadow over Sicilian public life; without a legitimate basis for political consensus in Sicily, the mafia assumed responsibility for negotiating the acceptance of government

---

[4] See Medici's report in Scichilone, *Documenti*, 207. Medici's instructions to troops are in ASP, pref. gab., b. 12, n. 200, cat. 20.

[5] The correspondence relating to a series of illegal shootings by troops in Jan. 1867 is in ACSR, grazia e giustizia, b. 8, f. 16.

policy and ensuring the success of government candidates in elections through illicit and violent means. The mafia's growing political role in the 1870s had its origins in the failure of liberal government in the 1860s. In 1871 the intricate web of complicity between local government and the mafia first became visible when the new procurator general, Diego Tajani, issued a warrant for Albanese's arrest. Even more revealing was the ultimate fate of Tajani's initiative. The government ordered the case closed due to lack of evidence, and Tajani's five key witnesses were murdered.[6] By the time Giaocchino Rasponi took over as prefect of Palermo in 1873, the unofficial link between the mafia and political corruption had become entrenched and institutionalized. Yet a solution to the Right's difficulties in Sicily—to the lack of a stable basis of political consent—seemed further away than ever.

The Sicilian Left triumphed in the national elections of 1874. The electoral campaign was marked by open hostility to the central government and, in particular, to Prime Minister Minghetti's proposals for emergency legislation to restore order in Sicily. The crisis of the Historic Right and the so-called 'parliamentary revolution' of 1874–6 which brought the Left to power in Italy also gave the Southern élites a place in the national government for the first time since national unification.[7] Minghetti had ordered a parliamentary inquiry on Sicily in 1875, hoping that by revealing the crisis of public order Sicilian demands for autonomy and decentralization would be deflected. His plan backfired when the inquiry, which submitted its report after the Left came to power, underplayed the evidence of criminal conspiracy and official corruption and denied the need for reform.[8] In one sense, the government of the Left succeeded after 1876 where previously the Right had failed: they managed to establish a viable working relationship with the élites in Sicily. Indeed, the new Prime Minister (and former prodictator of Sicily), Agostino Depretis, made the compromise with Southern élites a cornerstone of the Left's parliamentary majority. He did so, however, on the basis of a policy which accepted the political status quo in the South, which seemed to endorse the growing violence

---

[6] P. Alatri, *Lotte politiche in Sicilia sotto il governo della Destra, 1866–1874* (Turin, 1954), 346–417.

[7] G. Procacci, *Le elezioni del 1874 e l'opposizione meridionale* (Milan, 1956), and F. Renda, 'La "questione sociale" e i Fasci, 1874–1894', in M. Aymard and G. Giarrizzo (eds.), *La Sicilia* (Turin, 1987), 159–76.

[8] G. C. Marino, *L'opposizione mafiosa: mafia e politica, baroni e stato* (Palermo, 1964; 3rd edn., 1996), esp. 110–69.

and corruption of public life, and which, effectively, abandoned the attempt at reform.

In the year after the Right's fall from power and the official parlimentary inquiry on Sicily, a private inquiry on Sicily by two prominent Right reformers—Leopoldo Franchetti and Sidney Sonnino—was published. Ironically, their two-volume report, *La Sicilia nel 1876*, reflected the most forward-looking and the more reforming aspects of the Right's period in government. Sonnino analysed in careful and meticulous detail the social and economic conditions prevailing in Sicily; he focused in particular on the contractual relationships between landowner and peasant as a means of explaining the poverty of the peasantry.[9] Franchetti explored and illuminated the links between poverty, crime, and political corruption. Both men called for urgent and far-reaching reform in order to bring about a successful process of modernization in Sicily. Yet Franchetti also recommended that the entire system of government administration should be restructured to give more control from the centre, that the bureaucracy and police should be 'purged' of Sicilians and replaced by an educated élite from outside the island, and that massive police operations should be organized to bring criminals to justice. In this way, Franchetti's inquiry not only represented the best traditions of the Right's *buongoverno*, he also epitomized the authoritarian response of a paternalistic authority when faced with an 'ungrateful' population.[10]

Why did the Right fail to establish support for its policies in Sicily? We have seen that, contrary to the Marxist interpretation which stresses the basic illiberalism of the Right, the government made genuine, if sporadic and unsuccessful, attempts at reform after 1860. The Right also had proven skills in the business of government and administration; in Piedmont, the success at 'state-making' stood in striking contrast to the failures of the Bourbon monarchy in the Two Sicilies. Yet, in the event, the Right suffered just as many setbacks in Sicily as the Bourbons. Attempts to establish a liberal government, an effective system of administration, and a measure of economic and social stability

[9] S. Sonnino, 'I contadini in Sicilia', in L. Franchetti and S. Sonnino, *Inchiesta in Sicilia* (1876; Florence, 1974 edn.).

[10] L. Franchetti, *Condizione politiche e amministrative della Sicilia* (1876; Rome, 1993 edn.), 142–94, 229–46. For an analysis of the intellectual and cultural concerns underpinning Franchetti's inquiry, see J. Dickie, *Darkest Italy: The Nation and Stereotypes of the Mezzogiorno, 1860–1900* (forthcoming). See also R. de Mattei, 'L'inchiesta siciliana di Franchetti e Sonnino', *Annali del Mezzogiorno*, 3 (1963), 113–47, and Z. Ciuffoletti, 'Nota storica', in L. Franchetti and S. Sonnino, *Inchiesta in Sicilia* (Florence, 1974).

in Sicily did not work. Attempts to restore political order via a series of military campaigns were equally unsuccessful. Indeed, the recourse to the military and the abuses of power which marked the campaigns were, as John Davis has commented, indications of the 'administrative and political weaknesses' of the state, not of its strength.[11]

The failure of liberal policy in Sicily was all the more startling because there was nothing apparently unique about the problems of government there. Peasant unrest over land-usage and landownership was widespread, from Ireland to the Russian Empire, in this period; there was also nothing particularly unusual about the hostile attitudes of Sicilian élites to the central government. What was mystifying, however, was the liberal government's apparent inability to resolve these problems, either through coercion or by creating some basis for consent. It was, in other words, the remarkable persistence of Sicily's problems which made them distinctive, together with the persistent failure of liberal policy.

The confrontational nature of the Southern Question and its political significance in modern Italian history has meant that historians have never been able to agree on the sources of Sicily's 'ungovernability'. As I argued in the Introduction to this book, the problem of the South has produced more than its share of controversy among historians of modern Italy. The deep divide between liberal and Marxist historians in Italy and the tendency, in turn, for revisionist historians to reject both interpretations as inadequate, has produced a kind of 'dialogue of the deaf', where each side talks past the others. This is a pity, because, for Sicily at least, the explanation for its political instability seems to lie in something of a synthesis of the various conflicting accounts.

There were, as Romeo reminds us, specific policy constraints which can explain some aspects of the Right's failure in Sicily. Specifically, there were obvious physical features of the Sicilian countryside—the pattern of settlement in the interior which left the countryside largely uninhabited, the lack of adequate communications—which undermined policing and military operations. The immense geographical distance between the Sicilian countryside and the political capital (even further apart after national unification than before), coupled with the lack of financial resources, also frustrated attempts to establish an efficient bureaucracy. All this made the problems of state formation much

[11] J. A. Davis, *Conflict and Control: Law and Order in Nineteenth-Century Italy* (London, 1988), 5.

greater in Sicily than in Piedmont. It is clear, moreover, that in 1860 the vast majority of Piedmontese moderate liberals had little or no idea about the real conditions prevailing in Sicily. Their intentions were liberal, but they were too preoccupied by other problems to deal adequately with the chaotic aftermath of revolution in 1860.

However, problems of this nature do not, by themselves, explain the failure of liberal policy in Sicily. The existence of such practical problems merely increased the government's dependence on the support of local élites. Why was this support not forthcoming? Whereas both liberal and Marxist historians pointed to the atavistic attitudes and economic backwardness of Sicilian élites to explain their failure to support liberal government, revisionist research points in another direction entirely. Indeed, recent research suggests that, the political behaviour of these élites, and particularly the self-serving attitude which they adopted towards central government, can best be explained by reference to their personal experience of rapid economic and political change. Moreover, the 'peculiarities' of this modernizing process can be traced to political rather than economic causes. Government reforms to the structure of local administrations and to landownership were responsible for much of the social and political mobility which took place in the rural communities of nineteenth-century Sicily. Consequently, for the new élites created by these reforms, control and manipulation of local government became central to their power within the community as a whole. Thus the relationship between central government and local élites tended to be based more on short-term, private gain than on any principle of public service or bureaucratic rationality. This situation undermined in obvious ways central government's attempts to control local administrations. Paradoxically (and crucially), this same situation also greatly increased the dependence of local élites on central government.

This was all the more true because the rapid social and political transformation which took place in Sicily brought little security to the newly established élites, and significantly increased the conflicts within communities. By opening up local government to new élites, government intervention also increased the factional struggles between them; factional rivalry meant that what control any group possessed over a community was precarious and subject to frequent challenges. Notwithstanding their 'strong-arm' appearance, rural élites lacked solidarity and had to rely on short-term impromptu deals to protect their property and position. Furthermore, travel outside the community was hazardous, and any property-owner was at risk from robbers, kidnappers, or worse. Above all, violent peasant unrest over land, which increased steadily during this period, posed a huge threat to the immediate security and the longer-term economic position of rural élites. Thus, the unstable conditions produced by modernization in Sicilian rural communities increased the need for the kind of fiscal and coercive strength which only a modern state could offer. Élite resistance to central government interference in Sicily, in other words, coexisted with a need for the state's presence.

It was, in short, not backwardness which caused the problems of government in post-unification Sicily, but a 'peculiar' experience of modernization. What made Sicily different from Piedmont was a profoundly different relationship between state and society, which had developed largely as a result of Bourbon reforms in the late eighteenth and early nineteenth centuries. It is therefore ironic that while both the Bourbons and the Right realized that effective reform was the key to governing Sicily, their attempts to implement reform actually made the problem worse. By increasing the power of the state in rural areas they simultaneously introduced new elements of conflict into the communities and reinforced the position of those groups who had most at stake in maintaining the status quo. Administrative centralization added another layer of corruption to local government and made Sicily more, not less, ungovernable than before.

Moreover, the key to explaining the failure of liberal policy in Sicily lies not just in the relationship between local élites and the state, but also in that between rival factions of the élite, and between the local élites and the peasantry. In fact, political conflict in Sicily produced a kind of mutual insecurity, or 'interdependence', which determined the nature of the relationship between central government (whether Bourbon or liberal) and the élites.[12] This 'interdependence' accounts for the curious sense of continuity which seems such a striking, if deceptive, feature of Sicilian politics at this time. Similarly, the disunity of the Sicilian democratic movement helps to explain the clear absence of viable political alternatives, at least between 1860 and 1866. Thus, only a study of the whole complex of political and social relationships

[12] J. A. Davis, 'Changing Perspectives on Italy's "Southern Problem"' in C. Levy (ed.), *Italian Regionalism: History, Identity, Politics* (Oxford, 1996), 63–4. See also A. de Francesco's remarks in 'Cultura costituzionale e potere politico nell'età della restaurazione', in F. Benigno and C. Torrisi (eds.), *Élites e potere in Sicilia dal medioevo ad oggi* (Rome, 1995), 127.

prevailing in Sicily at the time of unification can make sense of the fact that, despite the enduring and widespread opposition to central government, Sicilian élites never entirely rejected its authority to establish local autonomy for themselves.

In this respect, Gramsci was not wrong to argue that the origins of the Southern Question lay in the failure of democratic revolution. The failure to 'liberate' the Sicilian peasantry—on a practical level, to introduce effective land reform—meant that it was impossible to suppress the violent conflict over land-usage and landownership which in the latifundist interior was the major cause of popular unrest. Without land reform, the mutually corrupting relationship between local élites and central government would endure. Furthermore, since one of the main reasons for the factional struggle over local government was that it gave control over a great deal of land, the failure to resolve the land question also made it difficult to stabilize the tensions between the élites and the crime connected to them. Without a resolution of these conflicts it was, in turn, impossible to set up an effective system of local government. And without an effective system of local government, coercion and military solutions were equally hard to enforce.

In conclusion, it is clearly misleading to suggest, as Romeo seems to, that the failure of liberal policy in Sicily was not the government's fault. The desire of Cavour and his successors to outwit their political opponents, and their fear of social and political unrest, committed them to preserving the status quo in Sicily. In practice, this committed the liberals to supporting those groups who had the least to gain from liberal government, and to propping up an unstable and violent social order in the Sicilian countryside. As Gramsci suggests, it tied the new government to a political alliance from which it could draw little benefit.

As a result, the Piedmontese bureaucractic system which had, before 1860, drawn it's legitimacy from an ability to guarantee social order, was undermined, in Sicily after unification, by the resistance of a resentful population. The Piedmontese ruling élite which had, hitherto, prided itself on its capacity for good government acquired, after 1860, a reputation for incompetence and corruption. And a political leadership which, alone in Italy before 1860, had established a genuine (if limited) consensus in favour of reform became subsequently entangled in a tawdry marriage of convenience where the protagonists soon learnt to loathe each other. Thus, in Sicily, moderate liberals were forced to confront the limitations of the Piedmontese 'solution': the restricted choices which the compromise between absolutism and liberalism imposed on them and which had hitherto brought them great success. In itself, the liberal government's attempt to coerce the Sicilian countryside into submission is neither unusual nor surprising. Of much greater significance is the fact that they had little choice but to do so, and had even less chance of succeeding. The manner in which the liberals came to power in Sicily offered them no basis whatever for establishing stability there. For Sicily, and for Italy, the consequences of Cavour's determination to defeat the democrats in 1860 was chronic political turmoil.

Bibliography

Archives

Archivio Centrale dello Stato, Rome
Carte Crispi (Archivio di Stato di Palermo).
Carte Depretis.
Carte Ricasoli-Bianchi.
Gabinetto Ministero Interno, atti diversi (1849–95).
Ministero di Grazia e Giustizia, direzione generale affari penali, miscellanea.
Tribunali Militari di Guerra di Palermo, Messina, Catania, e Catanzaro (1862).
Tribunali Militari di Guerra di Palermo (1860–6).

Archivio dello Stato, Agrigento
Carte di Pubblica Sicurezza (1862–1932).

Archivio dello Stato, Palermo
Ministero e Real Segretaria di Stato per gli Affari di Sicilia, polizia.
Ministero e Real Segretaria di Stato presso il Luogotenente Generale, interno.
Ministero e Real Segretaria di Stato presso il Luogotenente Generale, polizia.
Miscellanea.
Prefettura di Palermo, serie gabinetto (1860–1905).
Prefettura di Palermo, archivio generale (1860–7).
Prefettura di Palermo, ufficio provinciale di pubblica sicurezza (1862–79).
Questura di Palermo, 1 divisione, gabinetto (1860–80).
Sentenza del Tribunale Militare di Guerra di Palermo (1866), n. 2901.

Archivio Mordini, Barga
Biblioteca Communale di Palermo
Biblioteca Nazionale di Florence
Carte Peruzzi.

Istituto per la Storia del Risorgimento, Milan
Istituto per la Storia del Risorgimento, Rome
Museo Storico dell'Arma dei Carabinieri, Archivio Storico, Rome
Public Record Office, London
Foreign Office papers.

Newspapers

Il Corriere Siciliano.
Il Giornale della Sicilia.
Il Precursore.
L'Arlecchino.

Other Primary and Unpublished Sources

Atti Parlamentari, Camera dei deputati, discussioni, 1860–1867.
'Changes in Rural Society: Piedmont and Sicily', *BBC Open University* (1996).
EMSLEY, C., 'The Nineteenth-century Gendarme: Attitudes and Mentalities', unpubl. MS.
DICKIE, J., *Darkest Italy: The Nation and Stereotypes of the Mezzogiorno, 1860–1900*, unpubl. MS.

Published Primary and Secondary Sources

ACTON, H., *The Last Bourbons of Naples, 1825–1861* (London, 1961).
ALATRI, P., *Lotte politiche in Sicilia sotto il governo della Destra, 1866–1874* (Turin, 1954).
ALBANESE, A., 'Premessa per uno studio storico-giuridico sulla legislatura della dittatura e della prodittatura in Sicilia', in *Atti del xxxix congresso di storia del Risorgimento in Italia: la Sicilia e l'unità d'Italia* (Milan, 1962).
AMARI, M., *Carteggio di Michele Amari*, ed. A. d'Ancona (3 vols.; Turin, 1896).
ANDERSON, P., 'Origins of the Present Crisis', *New Left Review*, 23 (1964), 26–53.
—— 'The Antinomies of Antonio Gramsci', *New Left Review*, 100 (1976), 1–78.
AQUARONE, A., *L'unificazione legislativa e i codici del 1865* (Milan, 1960).
ARTOM, E., 'Il conte di Cavour e la questione napoletana', *Nuova Antologia*, 180 (1901), 144–52.
ASPRONI, G., *Diario politico, 1855–1876* (7 vols.; Milan, 1974–91).
ASSANTE, F., 'Le trasformazioni del paesaggio agrario', in A. Massafra (ed.), *Il Mezzogiorno preunitario: economia, società, istituzioni* (Bari, 1988).
AYMARD, M., and GIARRIZZO, G. (eds.), *La Sicilia* (Turin, 1987).
BACH JENSEN, R., *Liberty and Order: The Theory and Practice of Italian Public Security Policy. 1848 to the Crisis of the 1890s* (New York, 1991).
BALLINI, P. L., *Le elezioni nella storia d'Italia dall'unità al fascismo* (Bologna, 1988).
BALSAMO, P., *Memorie inedite di pubblica economia e agricoltura* (Palermo, 1845).
BANTI, A. M., 'Il Sud come problema della storia italiana', *Società e Storia*, 68 (1995), 341–52.

BARGONI, A., *Memorie di Angelo Bargoni, 1829–1901*, ed. A. Bargoni (Milan, 1911).

BARONE, G., 'Dai nobili ai notabili: note sul sistema politico in Sicilia in età contemporanea', in F. Benigno and C. Torrisi (eds.), *Élites e potere in Sicilia dal medioevo ad oggi* (Rome, 1995).

—— and TORRISI, C. (eds.), *Economia e società nell'area dello zolfo* (Caltanissetta and Rome, 1989).

BATTAGLIA, R., 'Qualità e trasformazione del ceto mercantile siciliano a metà dell'Ottocento', in A. Massafra (ed.), *Il Mezzogiorno preunitario: economia, società, istituzioni* (Bari, 1988).

—— *Mercanti e imprenditori in una città maritima: il caso di Messina (1850–1900)* (Milan, 1992).

BEALES, D., *England and Italy, 1859–1860* (Edinburgh, 1961).

BENIGNO, F., 'Fra mare e terra: orizzonte economico e mutamento sociale in una città meridionale: Trapani nella prima metà dell'Ottocento', in A. Massafra (ed.), *Il Mezzogiorno preunitario: economia, società, istituzioni* (Bari, 1988).

—— 'Aspetti territoriali e ruralizzazione nella Sicilia del Seicento: note per una discussione', in *La popolazione della campagne italiane in età moderna* (Bologna, 1993).

—— 'Introduzione', in F. Benigno and C. Torrisi (eds.), *Élites e potere in Sicilia dal medioevo ad oggi* (Rome, 1995).

BERSELLI, A., 'Amministrazione e ordine pubblico dopo l'unità', in *Amministrazione della giustizia e poteri di polizia dagli stati preunitari alla caduta della Destra: atti del lii congresso di storia del Risorgimento italiano* (Rome, 1986).

BERTI, G., *I democratici e l'iniziativa meridionale nel Risorgimento* (Milan, 1962).

BERTINI, E., *Rapporto sui fatti di Bronte del 1860* (Palermo, 1985).

BERTONI JOVINE, D., 'La legge Casati', in *Problemi dell'unità d'Italia: atti del ii convegno di studi gramsciani* (Rome, 1962).

BEVILACQUA, P., *Breve storia dell'Italia meridionale* (Rome, 1992).

BLACKBOURN, D., and ELEY, G., *The Peculiarities of German History* (Oxford, 1984).

BLACKBOURN, D., and EVANS, R. J. (eds.), *The German Bourgeoisie* (London, 1991).

BLANCH, L., 'Luigi de' Medici come uomo di stato e amministratore', *Scritti storici*, vol. ii: *il regno di Napoli dalla restaurazione borbonica all'avvento di Re Ferdinando II (1815–1830)* (Bari, 1945).

BLOK, A., 'South Italian Agro-Towns', *Comparative Studies in Society and History*, 11 (1969), 121–35.

—— *The Mafia of a Sicilian Village: A Study of Violent Peasant Entrepreneurs* (Oxford, 1974).

BONETTA, G., *Istruzione e società nella Sicilia dell'Ottocento* (Palermo, 1981).

BRANCATO, F., 'Origini e carattere della rivolta palermitana del 1866', *Archivio Storico Siciliano*, serie iii, 5 (1952–3), 139–205.

BRANCATO, F., *La Sicilia nel primo ventennio del regno d'Italia* (Bologna, 1956).

—— 'La partecipazione del clero alla rivoluzione siciliana del 1860', in *La Sicilia e l'unità d'Italia* (Palermo, 1960).

—— 'L'amministrazione garibaldina e il plebiscito in Sicilia', in *Atti del xxxix congresso di storia del Risorgimento in Italia: la Sicilia e l'unità d'Italia* (Milan, 1962).

—— *Francesco Perroni Paladini* (Palermo, 1962).

—— *La dittatura garibaldina nel Mezzogiorno e in Sicilia* (Trapani, 1965).

—— 'Il Marchese di Rudinì, Francesco Bonafede e la rivolta del 1866', *Nuovi Quaderni del Meridione*, 16 (1966), 460–91.

BROERS, M., 'Policing Piedmont: The "well-ordered police state" in the Age of Revolution 1789–1821', *Criminal Justice History*, 15 (1994), 39–57.

—— *Europe after Napoleon: Revolution, Reaction and Romanticism, 1814–1848* (Manchester, 1996).

CADORNA, R., *Il generale Raffaele Cadorna nel Risorgimento italiano*, ed. L. Cadorna (Milan, 1922).

CAFAGNA, L., 'La questione delle origini del dualismo economico italiano', in *Dualismo e sviluppo nella storia d'Italia* (Venice, 1989).

—— *Nord e Sud: non fare a pezzi l'unità d'Italia* (Venice, 1994).

CAFFIERO, M., 'Usi e abusi: comunità rurale e difesa dell'economia tradizionale nello stato pontificio', *Passato e Presente*, 24 (1990), 73–93.

CAIN, P. J., and HOPKINS, A. G., *British Imperialism: Innovation and Expansion 1688–1914* (London, 1993).

CAMAIANI, P. G., *La rivoluzione e conservazione nell'unità d'Italia* (Turin, 1978).

CAMMARANO, F., 'La costruzione dello stato e la classe dirigente', in G. Sabatucci and V. Vidotto (eds.), *Storia d'Italia*, ii: *il nuovo stato e la società civile* (Bari and Rome, 1995).

CANCILA, O., *Barone e popolo nella Sicilia del grano* (Palermo, 1983).

—— *Palermo* (Rome and Bari, 1988).

—— 'Dal feudo alla proprietà borghese: la distribuzione della terra', in *L'economia della Sicilia: aspetti storici* (Palermo, 1992).

—— *Storia dell'industria in Sicilia* (Rome and Bari, 1995).

CANCIULLO, G., 'Ferrovie e commercio zolfifero', in G. Barone and C. Torrisi (eds.), *Economia e società nell'area dello zolfo* (Caltanissetta and Rome, 1989).

CANDELA, S., *I Florio* (Palermo, 1986).

CANDELORO, G., *Storia dell'Italia moderna* (vols. ii–v; Milan, 1958–68).

CARACCIOLO, A., *Stato e società civile: problemi dell'unificazione italiana* (Turin, 1959).

—— (ed.), *La formazione dell'Italia industriale* (Bari, 1973).

CARDOZA, A., 'Tra casta e classe: clubs maschili dell'élite torinese, 1840–1914', *Quaderni Storici*, 77 (1991), 363–88.

CASSESE, S. (ed.), *Storia della società italiana dall'unità ad oggi: l'amministrazione centrale* (Turin, 1984).

CAVOUR, C., *Lettere edite ed inedite di Camillo di Cavour* (Turin, 1885).

—— *Diario inedito con note autobiografiche*, ed. D. Berti (Rome, 1888).

—— *Il carteggio Cavour-Nigra dal 1858 al 1861* (4 vols.; Bologna, 1926–9).

—— *La liberazione del Mezzogiorno e la formazione del regno d'Italia: carteggi di Camillo Cavour con Villamarina, Scialoja, Cordova, Farini ecc* (5 vols.; Bologna, 1949–54).

—— *Carteggio Cavour-Salmour* (Bologna, 1961).

—— *Epistolario* (14 vols.; Bologna, 1962–8, and Florence, 1973–94).

CERRITO, G., 'La questione della liquidazione dell'asse ecclesiastico in Sicilia', *Rassegna Storico del Risorgimento*, 43 (1956), 270–83.

CHABOD, F., 'Croce storico', *Rivista Storica Italiana*, 64 (1952), 473–530.

—— *Storia della politica estera italiana dal 1876 al 1896, vol. i: le premesse* (Bari, 1954).

CIAMPI, G., *I liberali moderati siciliani in esilio nel decennio di preparazione* (Rome, 1979).

CINGARI, G., 'Gli ultimi Borboni: dalla restaurazione all'unità', in *Storia della Sicilia*, 8 (Naples, 1977).

—— (ed.), *Garibaldi e il socialismo* (Rome and Bari, 1984).

CIOTTI, G., *Cenni storici sugli avvenimenti di settembre 1866* (Palermo, 1866).

CIUFOLETTI, Z., 'Nota storica', in L. Franchetti and S. Sonnino, *Inchiesta in Sicilia* (Florence, 1974).

—— 'Affarismo e lotta politica nell'impresa dei Mille: Garibaldi e le ferrovie meridionali', in G. Cingari (ed.), *Garibaldi e il socialismo* (Rome and Bari, 1984).

COMPOSTO, R., 'Fermenti sociali del clero minore siciliano prima dell'unificazione', *Studi Storici*, 5 (1964), 263–80.

CONTUZZI, F., 'Stato d'assedio', *Digesto Italiano*, 22/2 (Turin, 1895).

COPPA, F., *The Origins of the Italian Wars of Independence* (London, 1992).

CORLEO, S., *Storia dell'enfiteusi dei terreni ecclesiastici di Sicilia*, ed. A. li Vecchi (Caltanissetta and Rome, 1977).

COSTANZA, S., 'La rivolta contro i "cutrara" a Castellamare del Golfo (1862)', *Nuovi Quaderni del Meridione*, 16 (1966), 421–30.

CRISPI, F., *Memoirs of Francesco Crispi*, vol. i: *The Thousand*, ed. T. Palmenghi-Crispi, trans. M. Pritchard-Agnetti (3 vols.: London, 1912–14).

CROCE, B., *A History of Italy from 1871 to 1915*, trans. C. M. Ady (Oxford, 1929).

—— *Uomini e cose della vecchia Italia* (Bari, 1943).

DA PASSANO, M. (ed.), *I moti di Palermo: verbali della commissione parlamentare di inchiesta* (Rome, 1981).

D'ADDIO, M., *Politica e magistratura, 1848–1870* (Milan, 1966).

D'ALESSANDRO, V., *Brigantaggio e mafia in Sicilia* (Messina, 1950).

D'ANGELO, M., 'Vincenzo Florio, mercante-imprenditore', in A. Massafra (ed.), *Il Mezzogiorno preunitario: economia, società, istituzioni* (Bari, 1988).

DE CESARE, R., *La fine di un regno* (3 vols.; Milan, 1900; 3rd edn., 1909).

DE CLEMENTI, A., *Vivere nel latifondo: le communità della campagna laziale fra '700 e '800* (Milan, 1989).

DE FRANCESCO, A., *La guerra di Sicilia: il distretto di Caltagirone nella rivoluzione del 1820–21* (Catania, 1992).

—— 'Cultura costituzionale e potere politico nell'età della restaurazione', in F. Benigno and C. Torrisi (eds.), *Élites e potere in Sicilia dal medioevo ad oggi* (Rome, 1995).

DE MATTEI, R., 'L'inchiesta siciliana di Franchetti e Sonnino', *Annali del Mezzogiorno*, 3 (1963), 113–47.

DE STEFANO, F., and ODDO, F. L., *Storia della Sicilia dal 1860 al 1910* (Bari, 1963).

DEL CARRIA, R., *Proletari senza rivoluzione* (Milan, 1966).

DEL MONTE, A., and GIANNOLA, A., *Il Mezzogiorno nell'economia italiana* (Bologna, 1978).

DELLA PERUTA, F., 'I contadini nella rivoluzione lombarda del 1848', and 'Aspetti sociali del '48 nel Mezzogiorno', in della Peruta, *Democrazia e socialismo nel Risorgimento* (Rome, 1977).

—— 'La conoscenza dell'Italia reale alla vigilia dell'unità', in *Realtà e mito nell'Italia dell'ottocento* (Milan, 1996).

DI CIOMMO, E., 'Élites provinciali e potere borbonico: note per una ricerca comparata', in A. Massafra (ed.), *Il Mezzogiorno preunitario: economia, società, istituzioni* (Bari, 1988).

DI LAMPEDUSA, T., *The Leopard*, trans. A. Colquhoun (London, 1960).

DI SETA, C., and DI MAURO, L., *Palermo* (Bari, 1981).

DAUNTON, M., '"Gentlemanly capitalism" and British industry 1820–1914', *Past and Present*, 122 (1989), 119–58.

DAVIS, J. A., 'Introduction: Antonio Gramsci and Italy's passive revolution', in J. A. Davis (ed.), *Gramsci and Italy's Passive Revolution* (London, 1979).

—— 'The South, the Risorgimento and the origins of the "Southern problem"', in Davis (ed.), *Gramsci and Italy's Passive Revolution* (London, 1979).

—— 'Palmerston and the Sicilian sulphur crisis of 1840: an episode in the imperialism of free trade', *Risorgimento*, 1/2 (1982), 5–24.

—— *Conflict and Control: Law and Order in Nineteenth-Century Italy* (London, 1988).

—— 'Lo stato e l'ordine pubblico nel Mezzogiorno e in Sicilia nella prima metà dell xix secolo', in *Contributi per un bilancio del regno borbonico, 1815–1860*, ed. F. Pilliteri (Palermo, 1990).

—— 'The Napoleonic Era in Southern Italy: An Ambiguous Legacy?', *Proceedings of the British Academy*, 80 (1993), 133–48.

—— 'Remapping Italy's Path to the Twentieth Century', *Journal of Modern History*, 66 (1994), 291–320.

—— 'Changing perspectives on Italy's "Southern problem"', in C. Levy (ed.), *Italian Regionalism: History, Identity, Politics* (Oxford, 1996).

—— and GINSBORG, P. (eds.), *Society and Politics in the Age of the Risorgimento: Essays in Honour of Denis Mack Smith* (Cambridge, 1991).

DEMARCO, D., 'L'economia degli stati italiani prima dell'unità', *Rassegna Storica del Risorgimento*, 44 (1957), 191–258.

DICKIE, J., 'A Word at War: The Italian Army and Brigandage, 1860–1870', *History Workshop Journal*, 33 (1992), 1–24.

—— 'Una risposta sul brigantaggio', *Passato e Presente*, 28 (1993), 193–5.

DUGGAN, C., *Fascism and the Mafia* (London, 1989).

DUNNAGE, J., 'Law and Order in Giolittian Italy: A Case Study of the Province of Bologna', *European History Quarterly*, 25 (1995), 381–408.

ELEY, G., 'Liberalism, Europe and the Bourgeoisie 1860–1914', in D. Blackbourn and R. J. Evans (eds.), *The German Bourgeoisie* (London, 1991).

EPSTEIN, S. R., *An Island for Itself: Economic Development and Social Change in Late Medieval Sicily* (Cambridge, 1992).

EVANS, R. J., 'The Myth of Germany's Missing Revolution', in *Rethinking German History* (London, 1987).

—— 'Epidemics and Revolutions: Cholera in Nineteenth-Century Europe', in T. Ranger and P. Slack (eds.), *Epidemics and Ideas: Essays on the Historical Perception of Pestilence* (Cambridge, 1992).

FALCONCINI, E., *Cinque mesi di prefettura in Sicilia* (Florence, 1863).

FEMIA, J., *Gramsci's Political Thought: Hegemony, Consciousness and the Revolutionary Process* (Oxford, 1981).

FIUME, G., *La crisi sociale del 1848 in Sicilia* (Messina, 1982).

—— *Le bande armate in Sicilia, 1819–1849* (Palermo, 1984).

—— 'Introduzione', in G. Rampolla, *Suicidio per mafia* (Palermo, 1986).

—— 'Bandits, Violence and the Organization of Power in Sicily in the Early Nineteenth Century', in J. A. Davis and P. Ginsborg (eds.), *Society and Politics in the Age of the Risorgimento: Essays in Honour of Denis Mack Smith* (Cambridge, 1991).

FLORA, E., 'Lo statuto albertino: l'avvento del regime parlamentare nel regno di Sardegna', *Rassegna Storica del Risorgimento*, 45 (1958), 26–38.

FORTI MESSINA, A., 'L'Italia dell'Ottocento di fronte al colera', *Storia d'Italia, annali*, vol. vii: *malattie e medicina* (Turin, 1984).

FRANCHETTI, L., *Condizioni politiche e amministrative della Sicilia* (1876; Rome, 1993 edn.).

FRIED, R., *The Italian Prefects: A Study in Administrative Politics* (New Haven, 1963).

FULBROOK, M. (ed.), *National Histories and European History* (London, 1993).

FURET, F., *Interpreting the French Revolution* (Cambridge, 1981).

GABRIELE, M., 'La marina militare alla riconquista di Palermo (settembre 1866)', *Nuovi Quaderni del Meridione*, 16 (1966), 442–52.

GAMBETTA, D. (ed.), *Trust: Making and Breaking Co-operative Relations* (Oxford, 1988).

—— *The Sicilian Mafia: The Business of Private Protection* (Cambridge, Mass., 1994).

GATRELL, V. A. C., LENMAN, B., and PARKER, G. (eds.), *Crime and the Law: The Social History of Crime in Western Europe since 1500* (London, 1980).

GERSHENKRON, A., 'Rosario Romeo and the Original Accumulation of Capital', in *Economic Backwardness in Historical Perspective* (Cambridge, Mass., 1966).

GHERARDI, R., *L'arte del compromesso: la politica della mediazione nell'Italia liberale* (Bologna, 1993).

GHISALBERTI, C., *Storia costituzionale d'Italia, 1848–1948* (Rome and Bari, 1989).

GIARRIZZO, G., *Un comune rurale nella Sicilia etnea (Biancavilla 1810–1860)* (Catania, 1963).

—— 'Il "popolo" di Garibaldi', in G. Cingari (ed.), *Garibaldi e il socialismo* (Rome and Bari, 1984).

—— 'La Sicilia dal Cinquecento all'unità d'Italia', in V. d'Alessandro and G. Giarrizzo, *La Sicilia dal vespro all'unità d'Italia* (Turin, 1989)

—— 'Per una storia della Sicilia', 'La Sicilia e la crisi agraria', in G. Giarrizzo, *Mezzogiorno senza meridionalismo: la Sicilia, lo sviluppo, il potere* (Venice, 1992).

GINSBORG, P., *Daniele Manin and the Venetian Revolution of 1848–49* (Cambridge, 1979).

—— 'Gramsci and the Era of Bourgeois Revolution in Italy', in J. A. Davis (ed.), *Gramsci and Italy's Passive Revolution* (London, 1979).

—— 'Risorgimento rivoluzionario: mito e realtà di una guerra di popolo', *Storia e Dossier*, 47 (1991), 61–97.

GIUFFRIDA, R., 'Aspetti e problemi della rivolta palermitana del settembre 1866', *Archivio Storico Siciliano*, serie iii, 7 (1955), 157–215.

—— 'La dittatura di Garibaldi ed il problema ferroviario in Sicilia', in *La Sicilia e l'unità d'Italia* (Palermo, 1960).

—— 'La rivolta palermitana del settembre 1866 nella diagnosi del Crispino Giuseppe Maria Puglia', *Nuovi Quaderni del Meridione*, 16 (1966), 492–502.

—— *Politica ed economia nella Sicilia dell'Ottocento* (Palermo, 1980).

GOETHE, J. W., *Italian Journey*, trans. W. H. Auden and E. Mayer (London, 1962).

GOVONE, G., *Il generale Giuseppe Govone: frammenti di memorie*, ed. U. Govone (Turin, 1902).

GRAMSCI, A., *Il Risorgimento* (Turin, 1949).

—— *Selections from the Prison Notebooks of Antonio Gramsci*, Q. Hoare and G. Nowell Smith (eds. & trans.) (London, 1971).

—— 'Some Aspects of the Southern Question' in A. Gramsci, *Pre-Prison Writings*, ed. R. Bellamy, trans. V. Cox (Cambridge, 1994).

GREENFIELD, K. R., *Economics and Liberalism in the Risorgimento: A Study of Nationalism in Lombardy* (Baltimore, 1934; 2nd edn., 1965).

GREW, R., *A Sterner Plan for Italian Unity: The Italian National Society in the Risorgimento* (Princeton, 1963).

HAMEROW, T. S., *Restoration, Revolution, Reaction: Economics and Politics in Germany, 1815–1871* (Princeton, 1958).

HEARDER, H., *Italy in the Age of the Risorgimento* (London, 1983).

HOBSBAWM, E., *Primitive Rebels* (Manchester, 1959; 2nd edn. 1971).

—— *Bandits* (London, 1969; 2nd edn. 1985).

HUGHES, S. C., *Crime, Disorder and the Risorgimento: The Politics of Policing in Bologna* (Cambridge, 1994).

IACHELLO, E., 'Potere locale e mobilità delle élites a Risposto nella prima metà dell'Ottocento', in A. Massafra (ed.), *Il Mezzogiorno preunitario: economia, società, istituzioni* (Bari, 1988).

—— 'Centralisation étatique et pouvoir local en Sicile au xixe siècle', *Annales, Histoire, Sciences Sociales*, 1 (1994), 241–66.

—— 'La trasformazione degli apparati periferici dello stato nel xix secolo: la riforma amministrativa del 1817' in F. Benigno and C. Torrisi (eds.), *Élites e potere in Sicilia dal medioevo ad oggi* (Rome, 1995).

—— and SIGNORELLI, A., 'Borghesie urbane dell'Ottocento', in M. Aymard and G. Giarrizzo (eds.), *La Sicilia* (Turin, 1987).

JEMOLO, A. C., *Church and State in Italy, 1850–1950* (Oxford, 1960).

KNIGHT, A., 'Social Revolution: A Latin American Perspective', *Bulletin of Latin American Research*, 9/2 (1990), 175–202.

LAUDANI, S., *La Sicilia della seta: economia, società e politica* (Rome, 1996).

LEVY, C. (ed.), *Italian Regionalism: History, Identity, Politics* (Oxford, 1996).

LOVETT, C. M., *The Democratic Movement in Italy* (Cambridge, Mass., 1982).

LUPO, S., *Il giardino degli aranci: il mondo degli agrumi nella storia del Mezzogiorno* (Venice, 1990).

—— *Storia della mafia dalle origini ai giorni nostri* (Rome, 1993).

—— 'Usi e abusi del passato: le radici dell'Italia di Putnam', *Meridiana*, 18 (1993), 151–68.

LUZZATO, G., *L'economia italiana dal 1861 al 1914*, vol. i: *1861–1894* (Milan, 1963).

LYTTLETON, A., 'A New Past for the Mezzogiorno?', *Times Literary Supplement*, 4618 (4 October 1991), 14–15.

—— 'The Middle Classes in Liberal Italy', in J. A. Davis and P. Ginsborg (eds.), *Society and Politics in the Age of the Risorgimento: Essays in Honour of Denis Mark Smith* (Cambridge, 1991).

MACK SMITH, D., *Italy: A Modern History* (Ann Arbor, 1959).

—— 'The *Latifundia* in Modern Sicilian History', *Proceedings of the British Academy*, 51 (1965), 85–124.

MACK SMITH, D., *A History of Sicily*, vol. ii: *Modern Sicily After 1713* (London, 1968).

—— 'The Peasants' Revolt in Sicily: 1860', in *Victor Emmanuel, Cavour and the Risorgimento* (London, 1971).

—— *Cavour and Garibaldi. A Study in Political Conflict* (Cambridge, 1954; 2nd edn., 1985).

—— *Cavour* (London, 1985).

—— (ed.), *The Making of Italy, 1796–1866* (London, 1968; 2nd edn., 1988).

MACRY, P., 'Le élites urbane: stratificazione e mobilità sociale, le forme del potere locale e la cultura dei ceti emergenti', in A. Massafra (ed.), *Il Mezzogiorno preunitario: economia, società, istituzioni* (Bari, 1988).

MAGGIORANI, V., *Il sollevamento della plebe di Palermo e del circondario nel settembre 1866* (Palermo, 1867).

MAGGIORE PERNI, F., *Palermo e le sue grandi epidemie dal secolo xvi al xix* (Palermo, 1894).

MANGIAMELI, R., 'Dalle bande alle cosche: la rappresentanza della criminalità in provincia di Caltanissetta', in G. Barone and C. Torrisi (eds.), *Economia e società nell'area dello zolfo* (Caltanissetta and Rome, 1989).

—— 'Banditi e mafiosi dopo l'unità', *Meridiana*, 7–8 (1990), 73–118.

MARALDI, C., 'La rivoluzione siciliana del 1860 e l'opera politico-amministrativa di Agostino Depretis', *Rassegna Storica del Risorgimento*, 19 (1932), 434–574.

MARANINI, G., *Storia del potere in Italia dal 1848 al 1967* (Florence, 1967).

MARINO, G. C., *Saverio Friscia: socialista libertario* (Palermo, 1986).

—— *L'opposizione mafiosa: mafia e politica, baroni e stato* (Palermo, 1964; 3rd edn., 1996).

MARINO, R., 'Nuova borghesia e amministrazione locale nelle cronache giudiziarie del Principato Citra', in A. Massafra (ed.), *Il Mezzogiorno preunitario: economia, società, istituzioni* (Bari, 1988).

MARTUCCI, R., *Emergenza e tutela dell'ordine pubblico nell'Italia liberale, 1861–1865* (Bologna, 1980).

MASSAFRA, A., 'La ragioni di una proposta', in A. Massafra (ed.), *Il Mezzogiorno preunitario: economia, società, istituzioni* (Bari, 1988).

MAURICI, A., *Il regime dispotico del governo d'Italia dopo Aspromonte* (Palermo, 1915).

—— *Genesi storica della rivolta del 1866* (Palermo, 1916).

MAZZONIS, F., *Divertimento italiano: problemi di storia e questioni storiografiche dell'unificazione* (Milan, 1993).

MERIGGI, M., *Amministrazione e classi sociale nel Lombardo-Veneto* (Bologna, 1983).

—— *Il regno Lombardo-Veneto* (Turin, 1987).

—— 'La borghesia italiana', in J. Kocka (ed.), *Borghesie europee dell'Ottocento* (Venice, 1989).

MERLINO, F. S., *Politica e magistratura dal 1860 ad oggi* (Milan, 1925; 1974 edn.).

MINGHETTI, M., *I miei ricordi* (3 vols.; Turin, 1888–90).

MOE, N., '"Altro che Italia!": il Sud dei piemontesi (1860–61)', *Meridiana*, 15 (1992), 53–89.

MOLFESE, F., *Storia del brigantaggio dopo l'unità* (Milan, 1964).

MONNIER, M., *Garibaldi: histoire de la conquête des Deux-Siciles* (Paris, 1861).

MONTALE, B., *Parma nel Risorgimento: istituzione e società (1814–1859)* (Milan, 1993).

MORI, G., 'Rosario Romeo: un grande storico per una grande illusione?', *Passato e Presente*, 13 (1987), 3–14.

MOSCATI, R., *Il Mezzogiorno d'Italia ed altri saggi* (Messina, 1953).

—— *La fine del regno di Napoli: documenti borbonici del 1859–60* (Florence, 1960).

NADA, N., *Dallo stato assoluto allo stato costituzionale: storia del regno di Carlo Alberto dal 1831 al 1848* (Turin, 1980).

NASELLI, G., *Lettera dello arcivescovo di Palermo indirizzata al presidente del consiglio di ministri in difesa del clero palermitano intorno gli avvenimenti di settembre 1866* (Palermo, 1866).

ODDO, F. L., 'Le sentenze del primo tribunale di guerra di Palermo per i fatti del 1866', *Archivio Storico Siciliano*, serie iii, 31–2 (1971–2), 272–332.

ODDO, G., *Lo sviluppo incompiuto: Villafrati 1596–1960* (Palermo, 1986).

ORESTANO, F., *Processo e condanne degli imputati della pugnalazione del 1 ottobre 1862* (Palermo, 1865).

PAGANO, G., *Avvenimenti del 1866: sette giorni d'insurrezione a Palermo* (Palermo, 1867).

PAGDEN, A., 'The Destruction of Trust and its Economic Consequences in the Case of Eighteenth-Century Naples', in D. Gambetta (ed.), *Trust: Making and Breaking Co-operative Relations* (Oxford, 1988).

PASSERIN D'ENTRÈVES, E., *L'ultima battaglia politica di Cavour: i problemi dell'unificazione italiana* (Turin, 1956).

PAVONE, C., *Amministrazione centrale e amministrazione periferica da Rattazzi a Ricasoli* (Milan, 1964).

PESCOSOLIDO, G., *Rosario Romeo* (Rome and Bari, 1990).

—— 'L'economia e la vita materiale', in G. Sabatucci and V. Vidotto (eds.), *Storia d'Italia*, vol. i: *le premesse dell'unità* (Rome and Bari, 1994).

PETRUSEWICZ, M., *Latifondo: economia morale e vita materiale in una periferia dell'Ottocento* (Venice, 1989).

PEZZINO, P., 'Stato, violenza, società: nascita e sviluppo del paradigma mafioso', in *Una certa reciprocità di favori: mafia e modernizzazione nella Sicilia post-unitaria* (Milan, 1990).

—— 'Quale modernizzazione per il Mezzogiorno?', 'Monarchia amministrativa ed élites locali: Naro nella prima metà dell'Ottocento', 'Leva ed ordine pubblico in Sicilia: 1860–1863', and 'Un prefetto "esemplare": Enrico Falconcini ad Agrigento (1862–1863)', in *Il paradiso abitato dai diavoli: società, élites, istituzioni nel Mezzogiorno contemporaneo* (Milan, 1992).

Pezzino, P., *La casa dei pugnalatori: un caso politico-giudiziario alle origini della mafia* (Venice, 1992).

—— 'Risorgimento e guerra civile: alcune considerazioni preliminari', in G. Ranzato (ed.), *Guerre fratricide: le guerre civili in età contemporanea* (Turin, 1994).

—— 'L'oggetto misterioso: Mezzogiorno d'Italia e revisionismo storiografico', *Società e Storia*, 68 (1995), 373–84.

—— (ed.), *Mafia: industria della violenza* (Florence, 1995).

Pick, D., *Faces of Degeneration. A European Disorder, c.1848–c.1918* (Cambridge, 1989).

Pieri, P., *Le forze armate nella età della Destra* (Milan, 1962).

Pisacane, C., *La rivoluzione in Italia* (Rome, 1968).

Pizzini, V., 'La storia della mafia tra realtà e congetture', *Studi Storici*, 35/2 (1994), 435–46.

Pontieri, E., *Il riformismo borbonico nella Sicilia* (Rome, 1945).

Prato, G., *Fatti e dottrine economiche alla vigilia del 1848: l'associazione agraria subalpina e Camillo Cavour* (Turin, 1921).

Procacci, G., *Le elezioni del 1874 e l'opposizione meridionale* (Milan, 1956).

Putnam, R. D., *Making Democracy Work: Civic Traditions in Modern Italy* (Princeton, 1993).

Raccolti degli atti del governo dittatoriale e prodittatoriale in Sicilia (Palermo, 1861).

Radice, B., 'Nino Bixio a Bronte', *Archivio Storico per la Sicilia Orientale*, 7 (1910), 252–94.

Ragionieri, E., *Politica e amministrazione dello stato unitario* (Turin, 1967).

Ranger, T., and Slack, P. (eds.), *Epidemics and Ideas: Essays on the Historical Perception of Pestilence* (Cambridge, 1992).

Ranzato, G. (ed.), *Guerre fratricide: le guerre civili in età contemporanea* (Turin, 1994).

Recupero, A., 'La Sicilia all'opposizione, 1848–1974', in M. Aymard and G. Giarrizzo (eds.), *La Sicilia* (Turin, 1987).

Renda, F., *Baroni e riformatori sotto il ministero Caracciolo (1786–1789)* (Messina, 1974).

—— *Storia della Sicilia dal 1860 al 1970*, i (Palermo, 1984).

—— 'Garibaldi e la questione contadina in Sicilia nel 1860', in G. Cingari (ed.), *Garibaldi e il socialismo* (Rome and Bari, 1984).

—— 'La "questione sociale" e i Fasci, 1874–94', in M. Aymard and G. Giarrizzo (eds.), *La Sicilia* (Turin, 1987).

Riall, L., 'A proposito di John Dickie, "Una parola in guerra: l'esercito italiano e il brigantaggio 1860–1870"', *Passato e Presente*, 27 (1991), 195–8.

—— 'Elite Resistance to State Formation: The Case of Italy', in M. Fulbrook (ed.), *National Histories and European History* (London, 1993).

—— *The Italian Risorgimento: State, Society and National Unification* (London, 1994).

—— 'Progress and Compromise in Liberal Italy', *Historical Journal*, 38 (1995), 205–13.

—— 'Legge marziale a Palermo: protesta popolare e rivolta nel 1866', *Meridiana*, 24 (1995), 67–79.

RICASOLI, B., *Carteggi di Bettino Ricasoli*, eds. S. Camerani and G. Arfé (29 vols.; Bologna and Rome, 1939–92).

RIZZI, F., 'Pourquoi obéir a l'état? Une communauté rurale du Latium aux xviiie et xixe siècles', *Études Rurales*, 101–2 (1986), 271–87.

ROMANELLI, R., *L'Italia liberale* (Bologna, 1979).

—— 'Il comando impossibile: la natura del progetto liberale del governo', and 'Tra autonomia e ingerenza: un'indagine de 1869', in *Il comando impossibile: stato e società nell'Italia liberale* (Bologna, 1988).

—— 'Political Debate, Social History and the Italian *borghesia*: Changing Perspectives in Historical Research', *Journal of Modern History*, 63 (1991), 717–39.

ROMANO, S. F., *Momenti del Risorgimento in Sicilia* (Messina, 1952).

ROMEO, R., *Il Risorgimento in Sicilia* (Bari, 1950).

—— *Risorgimento e capitalismo* (Bari, 1959).

—— *Dal Piemonte sabaudo all'Italia liberale* (Turin, 1963).

—— 'Momenti e problemi della restaurazione in Sicilia', in *Mezzogiorno e Sicilia nel Risorgimento* (Naples, 1963).

—— *Cavour e il suo tempo* (3 vols.; Bari, 1969–84).

ROSI, M., *Il Risorgimento italiano e l'azione d'un patriota cospiratore e soldato* (Rome, 1906).

ROSSELLI, J., *Lord William Bentinck and the British Occupation of Sicily* (Cambridge, 1956).

RUBINSTEIN, W. D., 'New Men of Wealth and the Purchase of Land in Nineteenth-Century England', in *Elites and the Wealthy in Modern British History: Essays in Social and Economic History* (Brighton, 1987).

RUDÉ, G., *The Crowd in the French Revolution* (Oxford, 1959).

—— *The Crowd in History: A Study of Popular Disturbances in France and England, 1730–1848* (London, 1964; 2nd edn., 1981).

RUFFILLI, R., *Istituzioni, società, stato*, i: *il ruolo delle istituzione amministrative nella formazione dell'Italia unita* (Bari, 1967).

SABATUCCI, G., and VIDOTTO, V. (eds.), *Storia d'Italia*, i–ii (Bari and Rome, 1994–5).

SALVADORI, M., *Il mito del buongoverno: la questione meridionale da Cavour a Gramsci* (Turin, 1960).

SALVEMINI, B., 'Sulla nobile arte di cercare le peculiarità del Mezzogiorno', *Società e Storia*, 68 (1995), 353–72.

SCHNEEGANS, A., *La Sicilia nella natura, nella storia e nella vita* (Florence, 1890).

SCHNEIDER, J., and SCHNEIDER, P., *Culture and Political Economy in Western Sicily* (New York, 1976).

SCIASCIA, L., 'Verga e la libertà', in *La corda pazza* (Turin, 1970).

—— *I pugnalatori* (Turin, 1976).

SCICHILONE, G., *Documenti sulle condizione della Sicilia dal 1860 al 1870* (Rome, 1952).

SCIROCCO, A., *I democratici italiani da Sapri a Porta Pia* (Naples, 1969).

—— *L'Italia del Risorgimento* (Bologna, 1990).

SERENI, E., *Il capitalismo nella campagne (1860–1900)* (Turin, 1947; 1968 edn.).

SERENI-PIRETTI, M., and GUIDI, G., *Emilia Romagna in parlamento (1861–1919)* (Bologna, 1992).

SETON-WATSON, C., *Italy from Liberalism to Fascism, 1870–1925* (London, 1968).

SFORZA, C., *Contemporary Italy* (New York, 1944).

SHUBERT, A., *A Social History of Modern Spain* (London, 1990).

SNOWDEN, F. M., *Naples in the Time of Cholera, 1884–1911* (Cambridge, 1995).

SONNINO, S., 'I contadini in Sicilia', in L. Franchetti and S. Sonnino, *Inchiesta in Sicilia* (1876; Florence, 1974 edn.).

SPAGNOLETTI, A., 'Centri e periferie nello stato napoletano del primo Ottocento', in A. Massafra (ed.), *Il Mezzogiorno preunitario: economia, società, istituzioni* (Bari, 1988).

THOMPSON, E. P., 'The Peculiarities of the English', in *The Poverty of Theory and Other Essays* (London, 1987).

—— 'The Moral Economy of the English Crowd in the Eighteenth Century', and 'The Moral Economy Reviewed', in *Customs in Common* (London, 1991).

THOMSON, D. W., 'Prelude to the Sulphur War of 1840: The Neapolitan Perspective', *European History Quarterly*, 25 (1995), 163–80.

TOMBS, R., 'Crime and the Security of the State: The "Dangerous Classes" and Insurrection in Nineteenth-Century Paris', in V. A. C. Gatrell, B. Lenman, and G. Parker (eds.), *Crime and the Law: The Social History of Crime in Western Europe since 1500* (London, 1980).

TRANFAGLIA, N. (ed.), *L'Italia unita nella storiografia della seconda guerra* (Milan, 1980).

TREVELYAN, R., *Princes under the Volcano* (London, 1972).

URBAN, M., *British Opinion and Policy on the Unification of Italy, 1856–1861* (Scottsdale, Pa., 1938).

VERGA, G., 'Libertà', in *Tutte le novelle*, i (Milan, 1942; 1983 edn.).

VERGA, M., 'Il "Settecento del baronaggio": l'aristocrazia siciliana tra politica e cultura', in F. Benigno and C. Torrisi (eds.), *Élites e potere in Sicilia dal medioevo ad oggi* (Rome, 1995).

VILLANI, P., 'Il decennio francese', *Storia del Mezzogiorno*, iv (Rome, 1986).

VILLARI, R. (ed.), *Il Sud nella storia d'Italia* (Rome and Bari, 1961; 3rd edn., 1988).

VIOLANTE, L., 'La repressione del dissenso politico nell'Italia: stato d'assedio e giustizia militare', *Rivista di Storia Contemporanea*, 5 (1976), 481–524.

WALKER, M., *Plombières: Secret Diplomacy and the Rebirth of Italy* (Oxford, 1968).

WEINER, M. J., *English Culture and the Decline of the Industrial Spirit, 1850–1980* (Cambridge, 1981).

WILSON, S., *Feuding, Conflict and Banditry in Nineteenth-Century Corsica* (Cambridge, 1988).

WOOLF, S. J., *A History of Italy, 1700–1860: The Social Constraints of Political Change* (London, 1979).

Index